THE FAITH
of a
RELIGIONIST

THE FAITH
of a
RELIGIONIST

Reflections Mundane and Sublime

HERB GRUNING

WIPF & STOCK · Eugene, Oregon

THE FAITH OF A RELIGIONIST
Reflections Mundane and Sublime

Copyright © 2024 Herb Gruning. All rights reserved. Except for brief quotations in critical publications or reviews, no part of this book may be reproduced in any manner without prior written permission from the publisher. Write: Permissions, Wipf and Stock Publishers, 199 W. 8th Ave., Suite 3, Eugene, OR 97401.

Wipf & Stock
An Imprint of Wipf and Stock Publishers
199 W. 8th Ave., Suite 3
Eugene, OR 97401

www.wipfandstock.com

PAPERBACK ISBN: 979-8-3852-2824-9
HARDCOVER ISBN: 979-8-3852-2825-6
EBOOK ISBN: 979-8-3852-2826-3

VERSION NUMBER 101424

All Scripture quotations, unless otherwise indicated, are taken from the Holy Bible, New International Version™, NIV™, Copyright © 1973, 1978, 1984, 2011 by Biblica, Inc.™ Used by permission of Zondervan. All rights reserved worldwide. www.zondervan.com The "NIV" and "New International Version" are trademarks registered in the United States Patent and Trademark Office by Biblica, Inc.™

Scripture quotations marked (NRSV) are from the New Revised Standard Version Bible, copyright © 1989 National Council of the Churches of Christ in the United States of America. Used by permission. All rights reserved worldwide.

For Alice, my wife
and best friend

Contents

Introduction | ix

A Fine Mess | 1

A Time to Speak and a Time to Sh . . . Refrain (Based on Ecclesiastes 3:7b) | 6

Poor Richard's Almanac | 20

That's Using Your Head | 31

By Way of Comparison | 40

That Makes Two of Us | 51

The Plain (or Plane) Truth | 61

What I (Tentatively) Believe | 66

Old Souls | 98

The Way Things Thankfully Aren't | 100

What Do We Expect? | 102

Efficacy and Proportionality | 112

Letters from Home | 117

What or Who Would You Rather Do Without? | 122

Climate Control | 125

Condemned to Evolve | 129

Mixing Promotes Health (The Headline Reads) | 131

I Have a Mind to Object to This | 136

Plant One on Me | 142

Made-to-Order Hypothetical Entities | 144

The Day before Tomorrow | 147

The Decline and Fall of Materialism? | 152
The Rules of the Game | 159
The Its Have It | 172
The Limit Is the Sky with AI | 183
Futures—Concerning the End | 185
Conclusion | 188

Appendix | 193
Bibliography | 197

Introduction

SOME ADDITIONAL THOUGHTS HAVE been percolating in me for a protracted period (as have alliterative combinations), so I thought I would jot them down on paper for posterity (should there be any—you will see what I mean in a later story). The title is a deliberate play on John Polkinghorne's volume *The Faith of a Physicist*, he having a greater background in science than do I, though a roughly equivalent amount in philosophy-theology.

But first a message from our sponsor—the English language. Here are some of its quirks. Curious that there is no other word beginning with the letter *o* that operates like the term "one." All other terms are enunciated with either a long or short *o*, or in the instances of the double *oo* as in "food," though not in "blood." But this word phonetically sounds as though it should be spelled "wun." "Who" does not require a *w*, but "one" could benefit from "one." And while we are on the topic, why are the words "to" and "do" pronounced as though the *o* were doubled, when the word "so" is pronounced with a long *o*? Furthermore, this is the language in which "wave" is pronounced the same as "waive," "berth" the same as "birth," "higher" the same as "hire," "straight" the same as "strait," and given that "supple" is spelled as it is, one wonders why "subtle" is not spelled "suttle," plus why "cough" is not spelled "koff." And if the term "extradite" can manage quite nicely without a *c*, why then does "indict" require one?

Moreover, "honesty" and "honor" could do without *h*s, but not "hone," and the term "refuse" when used as a verb is pronounced differently than when used as a noun. Plus, to have a fullness of awe as in "awful" is a negative thing, but to experience only some of it as in "awesome" is positive. Taking state names as another example, a Tennessee is the holder of a Tenness, presumably from a Tennesser, who is a purveyor of Tennesses. Or from a wider geographical vantage point, if there is a Brittany in France, can there also be a Francey in Britain? In comparing languages, "gift" in English means "something apportioned," while in German it means "poison." Among the greatest offenders in English is the term "yacht," which sounds like it should be spelled "yot." There are many such oddities, including if we can mishear, can we also mislisten? if we can misread, can we also missee, barring hallucinations? and most importantly, we can make a mistake, but can we also make a misgive? Granted, the British might have a different perspective on this exercise.[1]

We need look no further for an example of perspective than, speaking of the United Kingdom, a British official whose duties involved traveling to North American shores on, what else? an official visit. When he was about to depart on the return trip home he was asked what he thought was one of the main differences between England and North America. His response was "in Britain, one hundred miles is a long way; in North America, one hundred years is a long time." To a North American, something one hundred miles distant is but a drop in the bucket; so too is time for someone from "the old country."

German was my first language and English my second. When I was learning the latter, I thought it was daft owing to its imprecision. I now see it as a resource that can communicate shades of meaning more so than many others. In its favor, English has the most entries in its dictionaries with over 170,000,[2] and there are virtually no other languages for which thesauruses are compiled. English can, but the terms contained therein are not so much "other words for" as opposed to having subtleties and nuances that related listed terms do not. English, then, affords greater descriptive power than others, and, difficult for a German to admit, despite its quirkiness, I am glad I write in it. Hail English!

Having "written" this (what is written is not thereby also "said"), there are most definitely quirks on display in English as evidenced in most dictionaries; and while not unproudly exhibited therein, some entities betray uncomfortable interconnections, as with estranged relatives, when cross-referenced, at least at first "blush." Here is what I mean, using key examples. What, for instance, is the pragmatic advantage in having a term such as "tidbit" in addition to that of "snippet"? Certainly, as mentioned, the glory of English is its arrays of multiple related terms, containing as they do differences enabling turns of phrase not duplicated by all others. In the former, a small portion of food can be intended, another word for which is "morsel"; in the latter, such a small portion is not food and can be snipped off something. Therefore are we better off for having this distinction? We rarely come

---

1. Just checking to determine that these footnotes work. It is now confirmed.

2. The *Oxford English Dictionary* contains over 170,000 entries of terms in current usage as well as over 47,000 of obsolete items. Dexter, "How Many Words."

to blows when one of those terms has been employed when the other may be more appropriate. So is it better to have a tidbit or a snippet? It depends on what the substance in question is. Unlikely to cause an international incident in any event.

Similarly, is it better to have "flotsam" as opposed to "jetsam"? The latter is thought to be an abbreviation of "jettison." Does this imply the longer version of the former, then, is "flottison"? Hardly. Jetsam refers to what is jettisoned overboard a ship or boat so as to lighten the load when warranted for stability purposes—a ballast issue; whereas flotsam are those very items themselves, some of which float, hence the term. Thus jetsam occurs prior in time to flotsam, for tossing occurs before floating, should the latter also be within the capacity of the former. Flotsam would be entirely ineffectual were it to lack a buoyant quality, intending by this no disrespect to submarines, which, as is well known, can still float. Yet not everything that is jettisoned and becomes flotsam floats, especially if it happens to be something like sand or water-logged materials. Thus are we any further ahead in having a multitude of terms with all their subtleties? Well if we hadn't, I would have at least one fewer theme to write about. Perhaps by this I have "said" too much.

But before we set sail (apt terminology given the above), I wanted to regale you with this tale. I was born in Toronto in the Great Lakes area of Canada. Summers were hot and winters cold. The features of summers included high humidity, which became oppressive to the point where I had had enough and sought refuge in Canada's prairies (plains). Well that was worse. The dryness there confirmed to me that I am a moisture guy and I returned to the humidity of the Great Lakes. The point to be made is that we are not always slaves of our early upbringing, which would be forever indelibly imprinted into our constitutions. We can come to see and perhaps even decide that we actually prefer something that we initially either disliked or never experienced. I no longer disparage heat and humidity but purposefully seek it out. Evidence that we and lizards had a common ancestor. Quite a turnaround. I came to appreciate what I failed to early on.

For those unfamiliar with my method of operation, I begin with segments on religion and end with sections on science, but since the previous two works began with a story, this volume will not only do the same but contain several. So with that, we turn to fiction.

A Fine Mess

GOD WAS DEEP IN thought and assumed the posture of the sculpture known as "The Thinker." This is how God marshalled the creativity to do God's best work. At one point there was a lull in the action, the action being the longstanding war in heaven (Rev 12:7), and the lull because both sides were seeking to reload. One of the combatants on God's side approaches God; his name is Bartholomew.

B: Reporting for duty sir.
G: Fine, fine. But I have had a different sort of idea today than battle.
B: What else is there?
G: Well, I have had the notion to create some more.
B: You have already done so, sir.
G: No, no, I mean a different quality of creation.
B: In terms of what, sir?
G: Well, in terms of mortality. I wish to create mortals.
B: Would that not be a step down, sir?
G: From a longevity standpoint, yes. But there is more to it. I would create them from material and have them take over the reins from there to bring about more creativity on their own.
B: You lost me, sir, what is material?
G: You are material in one sense, just not the mortal kind. You possess a spiritual body; theirs would be more fully material, the kind that can grow and develop.
B: Into what?
G: To full maturity, starting with the simple and leading to the more complex.
B: I hate to be a negative Nelly, but why not just start with the complex?
G: Because part of the beauty will be in the development.
B: There is a much faster way.

G: But not one with the brilliance of the formation of the already toward the fruition of the not yet.

B: Why bother with the before picture if you can simply jump right ahead to the after?

G: Think of it as the thrill of the chase, the adventure of the hunt. We will give them the ability to carve and sculpt and forge out their own visions of beauty. (Much later this would be termed humanity's "first rodeo.")

B: I thought that was your department.

G: I wish to confer this onto others.

B: Well, I am standing right here.

G: No, you and those like you will have the important task of delivering messages to them from our court when the need arises.

B: I am no one's mule.

G: What was that?

B: Nothing. That sounds swell.

G: I knew you would be on board. One knows these things.

B: And what will be the form of these messages?

G: Ah, there's the rub. Some of them will quote me on this. It will need to transition from the spiritual to the material so as to have it effectively transmitted.

B: I still can't get my head, so to speak, around this material idea.

G: That's because it is not a concept but a thing.

B: I am no closer to understanding that.

G: It's all a matter of matter, you see, that will come down to operating biologically, chemically, and physically.

B: Same concern. That is not simplifying but complicating.

G: You'll see. One of them will make a similar point. I think I shall name him Ockham.

B: Am I to understand that action on our part will leave an impression on them?

G: That's right. Whereas your makeup suffers no diminution, theirs can, which is why all of us will need to be on standby to ensure that things do not go awry.

B: I have my doubts, but how will the messages get across?

G: As mentioned, they will leave an impression. Mortals will intuit what you convey.

B: I can foresee, sorry that's your jurisdiction, that there will be many hurdles in the transactions. And it sounds pedestrian when we have no obstacles in communication among ourselves.

G: True, they will not enjoy our powers, but think of the rewards when they come on board even with the limited faculties they will possess.

B: That sounds painful, more suffering than it's worth.

G: I realize, so we will need to ensure that it will be outweighed by our presence.

B: I suppose that's where we come in.

G: Yes, you will supply comfort to them when needed, for we will be impacted by their suffering as well when it occurs.

B: I can't say I am looking forward to it. Besides, how can we, being spiritual, affect something not, or less, spiritual?

G: I think it will have something to do with the mind-body problem. But it will work, even if the mortals cannot fathom how.

B: And where do you plan to put all these mortals?

G: On a planet.

B: Equally material?

G: The very same, and it will be spherical.

B: (Bartholomew was taken "aback"—but would not make an "affront"—by the potential attention these lower creatures might receive and was about to voice his disapproval, but then thought the better of it.) You're the boss.

G: There will be a great many of them; a vast multitude.

B: Mortals or planets?

G: Both. And also many stars, for they will need energy.

B: Okay, a little help here. No one could ever accuse you of not having enough vision, but no one could also plumb the depths of what you have in store.

G: That's the idea.

And with that, God created something called heaven and earth; not the kind of heaven Bartholomew was familiar with, but he would soon witness and marvel at what God had envisaged. Despite all the advice from the court to the contrary, God was "Adam"ant that the plan be put into action. Bartholomew and his compatriots beheld the grand design and could not help but wonder why God went to all the trouble, for much trouble there was, is, and came to be, but that is another "matter."

G: And they will also require sleep.

B: Which is?

G: A period of subconscious rest.

B: What for?

G: All their creative activity will tire them out and they will need rejuvenation.

B: Tire them? For how long will they be sleeping?

G: Roughly one-third of their lifespan.

B: One third? We would be reprimanded if we did that.

G: You are well adept at repetition.

B: I am completely nonplussed. Could you not just settle for us?

G: Oh no, not with this creative impulse.

B: I can see this ending in heartache.

G: Not just ending in it. If there are some of them who come on board, it will all have been worth it.

B: That's a lot of effort for potentially meager returns.

G: Just have faith.

B: I can envision that this could become problematic. Imagine if you will travelers who come to Earth from another planet, as you call them, and claim to an earthling that the travelers come from a superior solar system since much of the stellar systems in the universe you are about to unleash will be binary. That could give the earthling an inferiority complex, particularly if the travelers would give the earthling the raspberry for having but one sun to revolve around, in essence, "Our stars are better than your lone star." The earthling could then respond with the lame observation that more is not always better. The travelers' retort could then be such that it is in this case, for Earth's sun shines only in the yellow along with the ultraviolet and X-ray parts of the spectrum; to which the earthling could say, "It's good enough for us," get all hot under the collar, and warn the travelers that they should take back their remark. Next the travelers could scoff at them with "What are you going to do, chase after us with your internal combustion engines?" "They're jet propulsion, I'll have you know," could be the earthling's response, the travelers shooting back with "Oh why don't you just use a slingshot with a big rubber band for all the good your primitive technology will do you?" And among further charges of imbecility, the exchange would continue to devolve with increasingly overbearing remarks aimed at the other side.

G: I get the picture; have you been reading the blueprints? We will then need to keep them far enough apart for any interaction between them. I shall name therefore it the Babel effect.

B: How many of them do you plan to start with?

G: As many as are required for them to have the genetic diversity and variability not only to survive but to be a going concern with longevity—you will see what that entails, and they will be making more of themselves.

B: I thought only you could do that. We can't even do that! No fair!

G: I intend to confer on them this creativity as well.

B: Where do you obtain these ideas?

G: They just seem to come to me, and I figure that since I cannot have a bad idea, I had better act on it.

B: And let them come up with the bad ideas?

G: That is the risk I am willing to take.

And with that, God embarked upon such creative activity unequalled in material history, hardly taking a pause until completion, whereupon God stood back as many an artist would to behold the finished product. The trouble was that God would never actually be finished with this work of art, since it required continual refinements. Humans would see to that.

A Time to Speak and a Time to Sh . . . Refrain
(Based on Ecclesiastes 3:7b)

ON THE HEELS OF the previous discussion, I will let the reader in on a little secret. The inspiration for the writing material of the sort you have before you surfaces from whenever and whatever I come across in the everydayness of my life which not only piques my interest but arouses my ire. I never thought I would have anything to say; now I find I cannot resist. It seems, contrary to all health professional recommendations, that the more my blood pressure becomes elevated as a result of my reaction to ideas which I encounter, the greater my verbosity becomes. I suppose, or better yet sincerely hope, that my committing thoughts to paper is duly cathartic so that I can resume an even keel and approach the others in my life, who themselves have a stake in their own unhindered, unencumbered tackling of life's obligations with me in their vicinity, with a certain degree of equanimity. To do otherwise would not be equitable. Best, I imagine, not to linger for an extended period in environs where others might be affected, lest I begin to sniff out a bad review and am left to wrestle with the source of my irritation in solitary fashion. Some of the above wording is intentional, the purpose of which will be revealed forthwith.

I reckon the most apt way to commence explaining what I believe is to differentiate it from that of others, so here goes. I adopt the strategy of placing specific notions in my cross-hairs for critical scrutiny, to which I can only add, so as to reassure the reader that this investigation is not all about me, that I will invite onto the stage another descendant of *archaic Homo sapiens* to play the part of a foil to my outlook. Prior to doing so, I preface the current subject matter with a certain avocation of mine, namely numismatics (coin collecting). These hobbyists are a robust breed who perhaps obsess not only about particular coins but their all-important conditions. In an effort to adjudicate the grade of a given coin, there are two main features from which one initially selects, and they are whether the piece is in mint state or not. That is, can the specimen be evaluated as retaining its pristine status, which means never having entered circulation that would thereby present the customary wear that the numerous handling of grimy, oily fingers impose upon it? Either it has wear or lacks it, the latter understandably being the preferred condition. Also understandable is that it usually commands a much higher price.

To qualify as a particular grade, according to the hobby's (read business's) rules of engagement, certain elements of the piece must be visible and not worn off. This is the point where the rules do not serve us well, for the coin can be in great shape, but were it to lack those required aspects, it is given a lower grade. Another method of evaluation is which percentage of a copper coin bears a red lustre, which is the preferred color. Otherwise it is usually some degree of brown. One difficulty is appraising this percentage, for it is sometimes in the eye of the beholder. As I discuss below, then why not adopt the same, albeit imperfect, strategy when it comes to the percentage of the circulated item which has been lost due to wear, regardless of which specific aspects have succumbed? But first a greater explication is needed.

If in mint state, it retains all the details with which it has been struck, and even these can be imperfect, thereby issuing in another category, namely error coins. But if free from error, it might still bear blemishes, mostly scratches from having been bagged at the factory with many other coins and being transported in, shall we say, anything but five-star accommodations. The coin can also exhibit the kind of blemish called tarnish by those who fail to appreciate it and, euphemistically, toning by those who do. A coin, though, need not be in mint state to display toning, and with this I betray my position as in favor of it, for it can produce some beautiful rainbow coloring.

Yet if the coin shows wear, no amount of protestation will recover the details which it has lost from its having been wantonly fondled. Thus once it has marked its departure from headquarters and become assailed, or pawed, from hand to hand combat, it assumes some level of condition less than mint. The best of the mint coins have been separated from the rest and are without scratches, perhaps even given a polished mirror surface, and bear the highest grade known as proof. So coins may not only be lower than mint, they can also be higher. My point will be soon in arriving.

When a coin bearing any wear is graded, the approach taken is usually to inspect the highest point of the item, for this is assumed as the part of the coin first to reveal its handling. The trouble occurs when this is taken as the main or major, or at worst only, aspect of the coin to which appeal is made as to the ultimate grade assigned to it. It is possible, after all, for the coin to be handled in such a way that its highest point will not be the first or greatest part of the coin to be affected. Other parts might show the brunt of the wear if it has been handled unevenly. Secondary high points can become worn without adversely affecting the highest point first, or at least among the first. I have seen some evidence to this effect.

Nevertheless, grading is conducted according to the high points, hence if a coin has wear but the highest points are less or unaffected, it will score a high grade; alternatively, it can be an impressive, sparkling specimen, but if the highest points have succumbed to wear, it will be assessed a lower grade. I mention all of this to say that when we make evaluations in general, we can tend to focus much of our attention on one factor, prioritize it, and leave others well-nigh in the shadows. Numismatics is not the only arena in which this occurs.

This is the point at which I introduce a second member of the human race. There are four of us whose lives intersected at one university and our paths diverged from there. One of them is Bruce Toombs, who wrote the foreword to my first volume with Wipf & Stock, and J. Richard Middleton is another. Not only have our vocational trajectories differed, but so have our allegiances as well. Two of us have remained in the evangelical Christian camp, I have espoused a liberal stance, and the last has parted company with the Christian tradition altogether. My study concerns the second listed person, and in so doing I buck the journalistic trend of referring to someone by their surname and opt for, while we are on the topic, his Christian name, specifically Richard to those who know him. Knowing him as I do, he is a valued friend and scholar, but we come to our related subject matter differently, and the object of our scrutiny also differs. Mine is theology-philosophy and science, his is biblical studies, particularly the Old Testament (OT). Both of us focus on the Judeo-Christian sacred text, he more so than me, and his approach is markedly opposed to mine.

Holding membership as he does in the evangelical Protestant tradition, the methodology he adopts involves the foundational assumption that the scriptures are authoritative and must therefore be defended. The high points he treats are the biblical statements as they stand. I do this as well, but for purposes of suggesting that they are found wanting when comparing them internally, while he accepts and mines them in an attempt to draw out their proper use, an exercise termed exegesis, for passages could hold a meaning different from what was formerly proposed.

According to his tradition, the answers to life's questions are there to be found in the sacred text, so one must keep looking. He finds those pericopes (passages) and offers the appropriate interpretations through the academic tools he brings to the study, including intense life experiences, which can both speak to and assist in revealing alternate meanings, at times stemming from personal crises thought to mirror those of the characters in the text. While it might be debatable as to whether the newer interpretations contain the intentions of the original authors, they do serve the purposes of the church and meet current needs. For Richard and others, this makes the scriptures a living text, which can be applied to contemporary concerns when the need arises.

But our approaches militate against each other. My assumptions involve the viewpoint, opposed to his, that we do not require such investment in the text. I consider the scriptures to be a useful resource for beginning to come to grips with what life holds and affords wisdom to that end. The Bible, in my estimation, offers good advice and is a repository of wisdom (note, not "the" repository, for wisdom comes from the God who bestows it in any of its forms: "The fear of the Lord is the beginning of knowledge . . . [and] . . . wisdom" as the wisdom book of Proverbs declares [1:7])—the high points for me—which can speak to our life situation because others have wrestled with them previously with profit, propelling us to suppose (please pardon the plethora of *p*s) that we could do the same. For me, the text amounts to a set of recommendations, say, held out by health professionals that can promote health. Possibly, but not automatically. As I see it, the entirety of the text is open to not purely literary but also conceptual and coherence criticism. Circumstances with the characters in the text also may or may not parallel what we encounter, thereby further entailing correspondence criticism. Should there be sufficient overlap, then we are encouraged to apply them. Yet the text holds out little authority for me as such, little other than that which we give it and little more so than other extra-biblical texts that could have their divinely inspired moments as well, though not to the extent that the scriptures contain it.

Richard and I find ourselves on different positions in the spectrum of approaches to scripture ranging from the right extreme at which point lies the authoritative camp where answers to our life questions are to be found, for they might be concealed to the casual observer; to the left extreme where resides the naysayers though, at the same time, friendly critics. After much struggle with the text, say the devotees, if more appropriate interpretations surface only now, they could then reveal their riches millennia subsequent to their production. The view of this enclave is that these insights can emerge only with seeking the counsel of the Holy Spirit on a generational basis. Keep digging and God will eventually permit the revelation of long-buried gems, for the insistence is that they are there to be found and call for God's detectives to ferret out. The text amounts to a revelation from God and is therefore authoritative, since "men [hardly any women involved here] spoke from God as they were carried along by the Holy Spirit" (2 Pet 1:21b). The Bible then becomes a divine product.

At the left extreme, others view the text as a human product. Those can be considered the conservative and liberal ends of the spectrum, respectively. Humans, from the latter perspective, just like you and me, gave voice to their deeply felt and moving religious experiences. Employing human faculties of reason and cognition in the process, together with the powers of concept formation and articulation, language became the tool through which they attempted to make sense of these experiences to themselves and others. This approximation means they can err, and as such the text is not authoritative, resulting in a work reflecting the undoubted benefits in addition to the drawbacks of the endeavors of the authors.

To my thinking, the writings would not survive a non-confidence vote. There is no guarantee either that they did or that we will get it right. God speaks and acts, humans experience them through the grid that they hold up to the world, and we can merely hope that the attempts to convey what the divinity intends at a remove of at least two degrees of separation ultimately gets through. This approach assumes that the original experiences and the writings they and/or others left behind do not hold an appreciable advantage over the rest us who seek to contemporize, along with the same Spirit, its message for today. Neither the authors nor the text can be held up as residing on a level higher than ours and through which we must move in order to rise even further to reach the deity lying behind them. Each author retains the freedom to be in error, and about which God is neither ashamed nor troubled, for the "guid[ing us] into all truth" (John 16:13a) is not in haste.

This just makes God's task more involved, also something that does not deter God from executing it as though God nurses a tendency to shy away from additional expenditure of effort into reaching us. Now having mentioned all of this, in all honesty I must admit, even prior to the section dedicated to where I stand, that the position I hold and find myself in with respect to this axis has taken a more centrist turn. Should the mediating position be called the inspired approach, where both God and humans work together and God is pleased to employ the very gifts, talents, skills, and abilities that God has bestowed upon and invested in us, admitting that they can illumine our own native fragilities, frailties, foibles, faults, and failures (the five *f*s in increasing order of severity), then this comes a little bit closer to where I reside, for I have seen and felt a modicum of the same in my own life. That is the little secret I promised to let the reader in on. Please let the reader understand that this is purely an observation on my part. God then becomes a coach, instructor, or tutor who shapes lives and minds in attempts to get God's points across. If the message were to be so patently plain, then there would not be multiple versions of it in the Abrahamic traditions (Jewish, Christian, and Muslim expressions in chronological order). I have moved a little to the right in recent history, recognizing God's work of creativity operative in my own life, in a sense and intensity second only to the feeling of love.

Be that as it may, Richard and I would perceive the other's work as potentially undoing the efforts of each. When I read his writings, which are of high caliber, my sensibilities are sorely tried, perhaps even aggrieved and offended, for I think that his is precisely the tack I was hoping to impress upon my own readers as that which to avoid. I imagine he thinks the same about my work, should he even be familiar with it. We each have the high points that we emphasize, sometimes to the exclusion of the other's. I concentrate on those statements which seem to be contrary to other statements; he on the in-depth points which can allegedly corroborate others. He teases out meanings and implications from the valley floor; I compare statements that reach the mountain tops of systematic reflection. He believes there must be a resolution to the issues that arise from his pursuits; I see them as disclosing the messiness of the world, with the divinity of the text sometimes displaying similar vicissitudes as the other characters. He the text which becomes the focus of literary, in this case biblical, critical attention; me that which becomes, at times illegitimately, the theological-philosophical stuff of doctrine. I suppose the one could inform the other if the two disciplines were to converse. (And if we are not careful, in unguarded moments, the results of the two endeavors might actually converge.)

The state of affairs is that we have our own constituencies, which do not extensively overlap with the other. What this means is that we need to make room for both. Each of us is driven to do our level best in the proper deployment of the tools at our disposal; we just come at them from different angles. His approach is not for me, nor is mine for him. Neither's assumptions would resonate in the other's camp. This is acceptable, for God is not confined to one methodology. When it comes to adequately communicating God's message, God appears to be pleased to embrace multiple forms of "foolishness" (1 Cor 1:18, 21, 23, 25)—Richard's brand as well as mine.

Though since you might ask for specifics, let us launch into them. Initially, Richard, in his recent offering *Abraham's Silence*, quotes Woody Allen, as do I in my religion-and-science courses. For me, Allen in the 1975 film *Love and Death* disparages about the working of the world that "God is an underachiever," albeit for my purposes I make the distinction that the criticism is directed toward certain aspects of the God of the text that some biblical authors have attempted to capture, but in my appraisal their mindset or grid which they have placed upon the world so as to make sense of their experience of it has failed them when it comes to approximating what God is like.

Next, when Richard broaches the theme of the problem of evil, a.k.a. the theodicy problem, and entertains the "greater good" approach to resolve it, he does not mention how some of the textual champions of the tradition have added to the difficulty and, more significantly, how God did not step in to intervene so as to prevent the infractions from occurring. Moses, for one, committed murder. He slew an Egyptian who was mistreating an Israelite (Exod 2:11–12). At no time did God warn Moses, "Oh, no, no, that would be bad!" Or when David was about to commit adultery, God did not announce "Mustn't!" God, it seems, as a parent might, lets us make our own mistakes. This does not always constitute a greater good.

We are certainly prompted by Paul to "follow [his] example as [he] follows the example of Christ" (1 Cor 11:1). Point well made. Yet what is the extent to which we should do the same for all other biblical characters, especially if they are heroes of the faith? Do we declare that it would be safest to do so until we are cautioned otherwise and thus proclaim "Danger averted"? We ought definitely to follow these, albeit some of them fictional, characters to the degree that they are God-followers themselves and evade those instances in which they are not. But it seems that, firstly, God permits the transgression and does not prevent it from occurring, which God could arrange should God have seen fit; and secondly, these acts did not pave the way for some alleged greater good to take place, unless one intends the conviction of the heart when they are confronted with the misdeed and the humility resulting from it. I am not certain that the notion of a greater good should even be defended, for there may not be much in the way of it. Better perhaps to urge that in our having been fashioned the way we are, we have become choosers who can decide to act either in favor of God's purposes or not, God respecting our freedom of will and leaving us to our own devices, most assuredly in the hopes that we might come to see the light, but even if we fail to. And if the latter, then we will catch a glimpse of what life is like in God's absence, as in the Hebrew "Ichabod" meaning "the glory has departed" (1 Sam 4:19–22).

God and God's followers do look forward to a time, namely the end of history, when God will redress all grievances, though there is no guarantee that a greater good will actually manifest in this life. Think of the film *God on Trial*, where Jews in a Third Reich concentration camp decide to indict God for abandoning God's chosen people. After a mock court case, God is found guilty of negligence in protecting God's people and permitting an attempted genocide. Yet despite all of it, at the end of their heavenward fist-shaking for God's dereliction of duty, they come to the place where they recall that it is time to worship this same God after all. Perhaps they had in mind the conversation between the priest Eli and Samuel, where the former acquiesces that "God is God, let God do as God sees fit" (1 Sam 3:18b, my non-gender-specific rendition). This is not to be understood as a throwing up of one's hands in despair, but a recognition that this is God's rodeo, in which a this-life-greater-good may no longer be such a probable outcome, regardless if we would have it so or not.

Plus, if the above covers one issue, then the following could cover the other main one he focuses his attention on. Regarding "talking back to God" and/or negotiating with the divine, the insights sought for are in my view already contained in a way that is painfully obvious without needing to belabor the point in unearthing confirmatory evidence lying just beneath the textual surface from long ages past. Genesis 18:16–33, a passage he also cites, presents an episode in which Abraham enters into a back-and-forth with God about what the least number of righteous persons there could be in Sodom and Gomorrah at which point God would not exact judgment on them. Abraham and God agree on ten. Abraham should have continued the talks at the metaphorical bargaining table, for there were fewer than ten. We are not informed as to precisely how many, likely four, but the bar was lower than ten. God in this inter-municipal summit meeting neither berates Abraham for his impertinence or insubordination nor insists he cease and desist, but appears to welcome the intercession. And with this the bulk of the argument Richard wishes to put forward is settled without the requirement of two hundred additional pages of textual evidence. We "get it." Case closed.

Biblical-theological conservatives seem to require constant affirmation that they are on the right track, while liberals, presumptuously perhaps, assume it. Liberals cannot fathom how conservatives place so much stock in legend, since the OT text is not reliable historically, but was written from the perspective of those who had a stake in them and the text was then framed in such a way that it would serve the purposes of those in power—the stakeholders. This propels my disquiet, as the continual massaging sought on the part of the conservatives may actually point to a psychologically deluded condition. Health does not require a frequent religious or emotional fix. If it does, then it might actually be unhealthy. And instead of Jeremiah's calling out the Jewish people for misplacing their trust in what their hands have built rather than on the God behind it, in it, and with it, "the temple of the LORD, the temple of the LORD, the temple of the LORD!" (7:4b), the conservative clarion call becomes "to the Bible, the Bible, the Bible!" so as to shield themselves against the naysaying hordes.

Here are some of the low lights—for me the opposite of high points. In contemplating how and the extent to which we can and should engage God in conversation, Richard cites the book of Exodus where Moses interacts with God and appeals to God's sense of public relations by announcing that were God to do away with the Israelites, then the Egyptians would conclude that Israel's God had malevolently drawn them out of Egypt merely to cause them to perish elsewhere (32:12a).[1] This also points to another episode, not cited, where Moses implores the deity to "send someone else" to the Israelites more gifted in the art of public speaking (Exod 4:1–17), to which an exasperated God replied, "Oh, all right, fine." We can ask in response whether it would be becoming for a divinity to be concerned about the ancient tabloids? Indeed, who would desire to serve a deity who might have a press secretary in charge of "spin"?

Moses then pleads with God so as to change God's mind and avert God's wrath (Exod 32:12b–14),[2] setting up an ambiguity as to whether God relents from plans of bringing disaster or is committed to "staying the course" anyway (1 Sam 15:29; Ps 110:4). The answer is sometimes yes, sometimes no. God relents as in the Jonah episode, but is emphatic about the death of David's son from the illicit union with Bathsheba and repels all entreaties on David's part, who must then suffer the reprisal. If Richard is correct in that human intercession to alter God's mind "is what God wanted all along,"[3] then this makes God, should our motivation be God's marketing profile or image, out to operate like a manipulative mother; and in threatening to wipe the earthly slate clean of humans, save for a remnant, as God did in the Noah section, and begin populating again through Moses (in Num 14:11–12),[4] this makes it sound like God has a short fuse and could benefit from anger management or aggression counseling.

Further, the status of the prophet Elijah seems to take a hit and is taken down a notch in comparison to Moses, according to Richard's analysis, in 1 Kgs 19,[5] where Elijah complains to God that his life is in danger, though it is important to keep in mind that both Moses and Elijah appear with Jesus on the Mount of Transfiguration (Matt 17; Mark 9; Luke 9). Hence his status as being in the same conversation with Moses is nevertheless retained, and God simply puts up with insolence on the part of God's people (see the

---

1. Middleton, *Abraham's*, 46.
2. Middleton, *Abraham's*, 47.
3. Middleton, *Abraham's*, 47.
4. Middleton, *Abraham's*, 53.
5. Middleton, *Abraham's*, 60–63.

aforementioned film *God on Trial*), and recognizes it as such but does not lash out against any perceived insubordination.

Subsequent to these particular items, I have the following general comments interspersed with other specific ones. First, I am not certain that we should take our cues from those biblical characters whose walk, like ours, experiences frequent hiccups, since even the heroes of the faith bear feet of clay. This might be yet another way that God embodies longsuffering. We are encouraged in Eccl 5:2b, contrary to Richard's argument of expressing our complaint or lament to God, that this is actually God's preferred method of operation: "to let [our] words [to God] be few." At the conclusion to the book of Job where God finally enters the discussion, Richard sees Job's reticence to engage with an overwhelming barrage of instances of God's creative activity trained on Job as a failure on Job's part to participate in the exercise of proclaiming God's works. I view it as God's similarity to a parent asking a child who has perhaps spoken out of turn, "What have you got to say for yourself?" The expected response is that the child would have nothing to say in its defense, so it cowers and keeps quiet, awaiting a time when it is safe to raise its head and speak once more. Why should it be much different in Job's case?

Richard has also neglected to mention how utterly devastating the loss of Job's children was for him. He certainly was blessed at the end, but while their "replacement" was beneficial though not optimal, as a psychological point he would still be rocked by the multiple tragedy. What Richard and others need to keep in mind is that humans wrote these texts and God is one of the characters, meaning that the scriptures might not entirely depict what God is like after all, and no amount of special pleading (I am not accusing them of doing so, just issuing a caution) will counter this. The text is largely what the writer(s) wanted to convey, which does not always reflect what emanated forth from the heavenly "horse's mouth," and if this did not emerge that way, then what else did not?

An example of such a disjunct is what Luke, assuming he is the author of the book of Acts, wrote about what transpired after Paul's conversion experience, and what the latter, or his amanuensis (scribe), crafted in an epistle (letter) attributed to this very apostle in Galatians. Luke in Acts delivers an account treating Paul as having "spent several days with the disciples in Damascus. . . . After many days had gone by, the Jews conspired to kill him, but [he escaped]. When he came to Jerusalem, he tried to join the disciples, . . . But Barnabas took him and brought him to the apostles. . . . So Saul [Paul] stayed with them and moved about freely in Jerusalem, . . . [then] they took him down to Caesarea and sent him off to Troas" (9:19–30). This differs markedly from, allegedly, Paul's own report: "I did not consult any man, nor did I go up to Jerusalem to see those who were apostles before I was, but I went immediately into Arabia and later returned to Damascus. Then after three years, I went up to Jerusalem to get acquainted with Peter and stayed with him fifteen days. I saw none of the other apostles—only James, the Lord's brother" (Gal 1:16–19).

Both cannot be correct; in fact, at most only one can. Does that mean at least one of the accounts was drafted by someone who was knowingly being a false witness and uttering a falsehood? Or can the faulty account be excused since he was attempting to do God's work? Before you claim that God will not be assisted by what is false, recall the account in 1 Kgs 22:19–23, where lying was precisely the strategy God employed in carrying out God's purpose. There God placed "a lying spirit in the mouths of" the false prophets to give the king fatal advice.

A particularly blatant and flagrant instance of partisan methodology comes from Schonfield in his work *The Passover Plot*, where he does not even make the attempt to offer a dutifully thorough examination of his subject matter. As he states at the outset, "What is known can *only* be applied constructively when we are uninhibited by a religious compulsion to assume that the records about Jesus were divinely inspired."[6] Even if one were to share his personal view, this cannot occur in a dispassionate study, thereby making this an unscientific work. He has a vested interest and is out to confirm it, no matter what. As a result, we do not need to take him seriously, since he is not a serious scholar. I am not suggesting this is the methodology in reverse which the biblical authors adopted, at least not yet. But that could arise with time.

Richard, among many others, has a commitment to being faithful to the text; I, however, am under no such compulsion, but see my role as being free to criticize it, since, as mentioned before, it is largely a human product. It is not readily apparent how we can glean insights if not outright truths from what likely did not occur historically, and it would be hasty then to declare that "See, this is how or the way God acts." How would we know, simply on the basis of one writer's inclination? Besides, why should we strive to be faithful to what human hands have made? for it might not be what God intends (recall Jeremiah's warning not to put our trust in the temple of the Lord instead of God).

The way I would deal with the Gen 22 passage about Abraham's calling to sacrifice his son Isaac, the bulk of Richard's concern in his volume, would be to say that God would not ask us to do something that God is not prepared to do Godself, and actually did by way of the Messiah. And the

---

6. Schonfield, *Passover*, 6, italics mine.

passage in Heb 11:19 stating, "Abraham reasoned that God could raise the dead," in reference to Isaac, perhaps probes with a little too much speculation into Abraham's mindset at the time, and his thinking is ultimately unknowable unless it is divulged to us.

Some of Richard's statements also appear to militate against others. Was the plain text, for instance, ever meant to be a narrative that should be imaginatively entered into?[7] And if so, how would we then know if and when we have crossed the line into territory that is "read[ing] too much into" the text?[8] Plus, what safeguards are there to prevent this? Hence when do we appeal to the text as it stands and when to imagination? with the latter potentially turning assumption into the presumptuous. "We don't have access to [the] actual intent,"[9] then why so much space devoted to what might be? We are encouraged to "fill in the gaps" of the text, but are cautioned to "be reluctant to definitively fill [them] in."[10] Moreover, we should "respect the ambiguity" of the text and "refrain from making judgments about Abraham's intentions or state of mind," though he does not fully take his own advice when he qualifies the scheme with "except . . ."[11]

Since he introduces a comic strip to illumine his point, we can do the same. Recall the comic strip known as *Calvin and Hobbes*? Well, in it the boy Calvin explains the rules for a game to his "pet" stuffed tiger Hobbes, but modifies the rules as he goes along so as to suit his purposes, whereupon Hobbes christens the game with the name of "Calvin ball." Richard's approach seems to resemble it. With all the many, varied, and ultimately conflicting interpretations of the passages through the ages which he has in view, can we really say that the Spirit is leading into all truth (John 16:13)? I grow weary of being told that many a scripture passage should be translated differently or, more significantly, means something different than as stated, as though biblicists are engaging in apologetics whenever the passage does not support their study. It may very well not be that way, yet it seems so. Thus not only can we not have abundant confidence in the scriptures, but apparently we also cannot trust in the work of received translation work as not being wide of the mark, and this goes not only for disputed passages. I recognize that this work involves ongoing insights and discoveries to come to light, but then this complicates matters when we attempt to draw timeless truths from them for the church about which Richard is so concerned. On

---

7. Middleton, *Abraham's*, 173.
8. Middleton, *Abraham's*, 174.
9. Middleton, *Abraham's*, 181.
10. Middleton, *Abraham's*, 181.
11. Middleton, *Abraham's*, 181.

the one hand, how many truths are there, and on the other, when can we finally expect to get the meaning right?

Pressing onwards, Richard maintains that "genuine . . . trust in God" is not the product of "blind faith,"[12] but arises as the result of penetrating the surface of an encounter to determine if the experience has its roots in the divine nature and is not some type of counterfeit. One should not assume that an experience stems from the divine if the command is contrary to other biblical injunctions. Words to live by. This Abraham did in Gen 18 but not in 22. Richard's point is that biblical characters should apply this policy, and he focuses on the instance in chapter 22 where this does not hold. There is, however, another.

Noah in Gen 6:22 fulfilled all of God's instructions without giving them another thought. He knew why God was "going to put an end to all people" for all the rampant corruption and aggression in the world. It is regrettable that God had to deal with violence by throwing more at it. Yet Noah did not question God or attempt to intercede on behalf of the entirety of Earth's population, the reverse of which Richard considers laudable about Abraham in Gen 18 in reference to the sparing of Sodom (motivated perhaps more about the welfare of his relatives than the other inhabitants) though he did not in relation to the sparing of his son Isaac as a sacrifice in Gen 22. The inaction is more egregious in Noah's case, if the God of the text was expecting someone to "stand in the breach" but did not, for the simple reason of the proportionality of it, since the whole world of humans was at stake, not just one family member or a few cities. Not only did Noah not intercede, but he made no attempt to respond to God at all, precisely what Richard has misgivings about regarding Abraham in Gen 22.

Richard further insists that the kind of interaction God and Abraham were having in Gen 18 does not amount to bargaining, since that involves a back-and-forth of offers and counter-offers, settling finally somewhere in the middle. Abraham's series of requests to God in Gen 18, though, are in fact in the form of offers, which Richard recognizes,[13] but this makes the form of exchange a petition, and with that any difficulty of interaction identification should be resolved. (Even if the Gen 18 account is not a negotiation proper, Ezek 4:12–15 could very well be, where Ezekiel is commanded by God to bake his food over human excrement, Ezekiel objects on the basis of cleanliness and defilement, and God relents and permits him to prepare the food using cow manure. Interesting that appeal needs to be made to God on the basis of the danger of the food being unclean and running the

---

12. Middleton, *Abraham's*, 197.
13. Middleton, *Abraham's*, 202.

risk of the eating as defiling the eater. Did God need to be reminded, or was it allowed in this instance so as to make a seriously important point? It seems that this marks a place where God takes a utilitarian approach where the end justifies the means.) Beyond this, the outcome could very well have been a foregone conclusion on God's part, where the result might have been anticipated, but there is more going on here than just that.

Prior to this repartee, Abraham pleads the following: "Far be it from you to do such a thing—to kill the righteous with the wicked, treating [them] alike . . . Will not the judge of all the earth do right?" (v. 25). Abraham is appealing to God's sense of justice, with God perhaps inviting the interaction, even expectantly drawing it out from Abraham. Yet notice what God does not say here, "I'll have you know that justice, righteousness, and love are my, er, middle names." God does not take umbrage at what could be considered Abraham's insubordination.

If, as Richard suggests, God is waiting for Abraham's lights to come on or the penny to drop and act in Gen 22 as he had in 18, even though there are admitted imperfections in Abraham's approach and room for improvement in both according to Richard, then it seems to imply that God is playing a game of "hotter, colder" with human lives, who might never reach the target notion. Why would a divinity withhold something of such vital importance from one of the heroes of the faith? Does God permit those lucky unfortunates to miss the mark? How many of us fall victim to this? That may call for another investigation. Thankfully, the account is likely fictional and need not be the whole story.

Richard then cites the psychological trauma that could have ensued for all three family members of Abraham, Sarah, and Isaac in Gen 22 in the potential sacrifice episode (to say nothing of what Job would have undergone even more so with all of his offspring perishing on God's watch and clearance). Why, however, is no mention made, while we are on the topic, of the PTSD that no doubt would have been generated from the legendary account in the book of Joshua of the Israelite army taking the land of Canaan and "exterminating . . . without mercy" "anything that breathed" (Josh 11:11, 20), if one is concerned about proportionality, after all. If ever there was a need for an ancient version of psychiatric counseling, this was it. Finally, Richard urges that biblical exegesis must be "careful" and not rest on "the predilections of the interpreter,"[14] yet the text itself was originally framed in terms of the author's own preferences, which is difficult to avoid.

---

14. Middleton, *Abraham's*, 224.

Poor Richard's Almanac

FOR GOOD MEASURE, WE will also consider his previous offering, albeit in reverse chronological order of publication, its having only recently come to my attention. Its title is *A New Heaven and a New Earth: Reclaiming Biblical Eschatology*. The title I have chosen for this section centers on the type of text that informs us as to what has gone on before so that we can prepare for that which lies ahead.

The point is often made that after a lengthy period of the biblical myths of creation, fall, and the non-mythical redemptive work of God, the end of history will yield the city of the New Jerusalem as a product of heaven and transported to Earth. We are informed that this will be an improvement over the mythical Garden of Eden since Jesus has gone to assist in its construction: "I go and prepare a place for you, I will come back and take you to be with me that you also may be where I am" (John 14: 3). The trouble occurs when we consider the arduous route taken to conceive and complete it. If it were to have been in God's purview all along, then why go through the messiness of what led up to the city's shipment through the heavenly Amazon? Some refer to history's end as the eschaton (the doctrine of the end times or last things culminating in the final judgment and God's kingdom reestablished fully on Earth) or the consummation (as in the climax of the divine proceedings in the world). But if the end is superior to the beginning, then was all the (in alphabetical order) corruption, distortion, and perversion in between the two really necessary?

Further questions come to mind. Had the initial mythical human pair never sinned, would the City ever be dispatched? Or did the mythical Adam and Eve's sin set in motion God's salvation plan and history involving the birth, ministry, and sacrificial death of the Messiah? In which case sin and the curse would have been part of the plan from the beginning, thereby resulting in all the subsequent travail. Meaning the ugliness of sin and the cruel treatment of Jesus were not only expected but warranted, all in the service of God's plan and with the prospect of an even better future and the vindication of Richard's appeal to the greater good argument. Or was God simply throwing up God's hands and bemoaning "Oh well, let's put plan B into effect"? But if plan B is the preferred outcome, then why bother with plan A? Did the heavenly court then caustically remark "Hurry up and sin so we can get this over with," that which no one relished but was a necessary condition for the sufficient one to come "when the time had fully [arrived]" (Gal 4:4)?

Were this to be the portrait traditional theology is painting, then this consummation, employing related terminology and at the risk of sounding indelicate, is preceded by a type of divine-human courtship. But thankfully the Garden and fall are mythical accounts, though the curse might not be, given the divine response to human disobedience. Should this scenario be the case, then contrary to labels placed on certain consumer goods, the City would definitely be new but not improved, since there never would have been a Garden to compare it to.

I recognize that Richard is uncovering biblical themes, but to claim that God's purpose for the Garden was to launch humans on a trajectory intended to culminate in agriculture[1] overlooks the obvious anthropological fact that for the vast majority of our time on Earth as humans we were nomadic hunter-gatherers. Indeed, some anthropologists even lament that we settled down to build settlements and only then at about eleven thousand years ago took up agriculture, for this, they announce, was the biggest mistake in our history. Of course it afforded larger-scale culture and all of which that entails, but it also brought with it a cereal grain–based diet and increased our being more prone to ill-health. A healthier diet is the nomadic hunter-gatherer one which emphasized meats, nuts, seeds, berries, and other fruit and largely the avoidance of cereal grains, though there was some flour made from maize/corn and some tubers like yams. The de-emphasis on grains of all kinds as well as rice and potatoes makes for a healthier diet.[2]

Richard later cites a Jewish midrash (commentary) suggesting that God was uncertain as to whether Adam would fall into sin,[3] plus observes that "impediments [can arise] to block God's purposes."[4] These sentiments are problematic for theology and biblical studies. Were classical theology to

---

1. Middleton, *New*, 42.
2. For a fuller explanation of the health risks of a high fructose corn syrup component in our diet and how it is stored in the body as bad fat (layers of adipose) and hence detrimental to us, see the helpful volume by Daniel E. Lieberman, *The Story of the Human Body: Evolution, Health, and Disease*, especially pages 264–66.
3. Middleton, *New*, 62.
4. Middleton, *New*, 62.

be accurate and God is both omniscient of the type that includes the future as well as omnipotent, then there is no biblical room for God being either unknowing or powerless, though philosophically God cannot be both, since to know the future means one does not have the power to alter it, and to possess the power to change it means it will no longer be the future that God allegedly knows.[5] (Taking an example, for God to say "I never knew you" [Matt 7:23] is an odd statement to make for a divinity who is supposed to be omniscient and know every heart, but of course what is intended is that we have not fully permitted the Spirit to gain access and entrance into our own inner sanctum, where God wishes to set up camp and perform a work of transformation. It would be similar to a spouse saying to a changed, even demented and perhaps estranged, partner, "I don't know you anymore.")

Further, if the biblical account is accurate, then these theological categories will need to be modified. This is surprising given his evangelical commitment to be faithful to the sacred text, for then he could not be faithful to the highly though less important theological tradition. If he accepts the tradition as it stands without reformulation, he must abandon the biblical perspective, or vice versa. Moreover, if we are permitted to be incorrect about this doctrine of eschatology, as in church hymns,[6] promoting as many of them do the notion that our final destination is in heaven rather than on a renewed Earth, and still be Christian and not under God's wrath for it, then which other views can we be incorrect about? Can the same be said for our stances on scripture, anthropology, the virgin birth, the incarnation, the Trinity, etc.?

Speaking of last things, Richard later focuses on the final two chapters of the book of Revelation, namely 21 and 22. He begins with the caution that, given the prevalence of symbolism in Revelation, we are best to avoid undue literalism as we interpret the text.[7] This is wise counsel. I wish he would take his own advice. Throughout the book he has made no attempt to differentiate in the Bible a symbolic from a literal fall from grace, initially outlined in Gen 3. One wonders if his methodology might not also have come in handy here. There is no evidence of a Golden Age on Earth in which no death occurred, nor a time before which a curse is exacted upon creation and the natural outgrowth of the planet would become somewhat inhospitable. Hence the first two major themes of the overarching metanarrative of the scriptures involve creation, fall, eschaton (a large gap in time between these latter two), together with a series of covenants and the two

5. See Pickover, *Paradox*.
6. Middleton, *New*, 28.
7. Middleton, *New*, 168–75.

"re-s" of remnants and renewal/redemption. Of these six, the first two are metaphorical, and the lasting import they express for us, biblically and theologically speaking, is that we are therefore not without need of the last one.

Upon eating from the mythical fruit of the mythical tree in the mythical Garden, the eyes of the mythical first human pair were opened and they recognized their nakedness and were ashamed to have human or divine eyes set upon them (Gen 3:6–10). Consequently, the fall becomes a symbol of our moral nakedness before God (and how we cannot be trusted with anything resembling a Pandora's Box) from whom no one and nothing can be hidden, for this God knows and sees all that there is to know and see (which as I have argued at many a turn does not include the future, at least with certainty). Richard speaks of creation and fall with no qualifier, suggesting that we are to take these themes as undiluted events on the world scene, something with which at least fundamentalists would be comfortable. Additionally, he recounts the topics of the Garden at the beginning of biblical history (which is the only history on offer for this tradition) and the City of the New Jerusalem at its end as containing actual physical entities: after all, what would be tended, tilled and cultivated—something rural—but land, and what would be inhabited by a large community—something urban—but a city? Therefore, when Richard interprets the Garden, it bears bona fide terra firma components, and when he interprets the City, it evokes certain municipal constituents. Then when he mentions that there will no longer be any sea in the new Earth (Rev 21:1), why all of a sudden should this take on symbolic features?

Understandably, he correctly points out that sea in the scriptures does stand for "the forces of chaos and evil," for seafaring was a means whereby empires could exploit their own as well as other peoples and amass great wealth for themselves. Yet need this be the rendering in this case? for there are other ways to travel and exploit. A friend of ours was looking forward to there being no literal sea on the new Earth (he resided in the Canadian prairies where bodies of water are at a premium), for he was hoping to circumnavigate it unimpeded on his bike. I will invite Richard to break the news to him. Odd though that Richard insists on a real city of some description being shipped from a real heaven and placed on a real Earth where "no sea" means something totally different.[8] He admits, however, that the description of the City as a cube is simply intended to state that it will be enormous in size, though perhaps more planar than cubic, and will be able to accommodate all who are destined for it.[9]

8. Middleton, *New*, 169.
9. Middleton, *New*, 170–71.

And as if this were not enough, once the City, or at least the Garden surrounding it? is completely expanded (our original mandate) so as to cover the whole Earth (God's presence and rule),[10] and I do take solace in the prospect that there will be work to perform, then what do we do next with our everlastingness and all the free time on our hands? Understandably, expanding the renewed world will be a protracted undertaking, but what then? Forever would be a long time to be idle. Or will managing what has been established occupy the remainder? And manage from what—pests, inclement conditions, seasonal meteorological threats? Or will there be avocations aplenty with which to bide our time? (Insert favorite pastime here.) Yet this was not our initial mandate, for prior to Gen 2:15 from which this view is drawn, stating as it does that we were placed in the Garden so as to "work it and take care of it," Gen 1:28 delivers a two-pronged instruction, namely that we are to multiply and then rule over all animal life. Plus, in tending the creation, we, like God, bring order out of chaos and hence become co-creators with God, or at least, and perhaps also like God, arrange what is already there, the debate being whether creation is out of nothing (ex nihilo) or out of material eternal in its own right? The knee-jerk reaction on the part of evangelicals, to prepare the non-evangelical reader, will be to scoff that nothing can be as eternal as God, thereby putting to end any and all further discussion. We, however, are not at pains to do the same and are under no such restriction. Pardon the digression.

Next, we are urged to take another passage literally: Rev 21:24–26 claims that "kings and nations will bring their glory and honor into the city,"[11] intending by this to mean that human cultural achievements will find a place in the New City. This offers us a beautiful glimpse of not only how these achievements have enduring value but will also outlast the old Earth and will be invited into the new. This is curious, given that the average monarch does not ordinarily boast a blisteringly formidable track record when it comes to kingdom (or queendom)-wide unalloyed subject benevolence, thereby leaving their splendor a mite tarnished. Plus, as we are informed in Dan 11:20, royal splendor can often be at the expense of the taxation of those subject to the monarch. The trouble with this picture is that it is once again selected as holding a literal interpretation amid a multitude of symbolic material. Why this one and not perhaps several related ones?

Richard has decided that this passage, contrary to many others, also need not be taken symbolically. He finds support for this decision in Isa 60, which refers to a vision of a similar nature to the former. Granted the

---

10. Middleton, *New*, 175.
11. Middleton, *New*, 173.

thrust is suggestive for both passages, but permit me to comment. While the hope that the New Earth will have a United Nations flavor to it, since each culture has, by its very (human) nature something worthwhile to contribute and at least was grounded in God's original plan for it, this does not mean, first, that artifacts will gain entrance into it, otherwise I wish to apply for the position of curator for one of the perhaps multiple museums or at least archives there (one for each locale?), based on my skill and enjoyment of organizing (one affliction of having been reared in a German household), assuming this is where they will be "conserved."

Second, since we are already enlisting Isaiah in this investigation, then turning to 65:17, it states that in his vision of the New Heaven and Earth, "the former things will not be remembered, nor will they ever come to mind." Does this mean no artifacts? It depends on whether "things" refer to material items or foreign and domestic policies or something else. Does this mean that we will forget acts like the time Uncle Jake saved Billy from drowning? Probably not, for that is something God would likely desire to remember. It appears that the verse is explicated in Rev 21:4, where the "former things" in Isaiah becomes "the old order of things" in Revelation and constitutes the era in which there was "death [and] mourning [and] crying [and] pain." Elsewhere, "this world in its present form is passing away" (1 Cor 7:31) or fading into oblivion, so why concentrate on it so much? For now, then, artifacts may be safe.

As a side point, the beginning of the Rev 21:4 verse (together with 7:17) announces that God "will wipe every tear from their eyes," which prompts the question as to what is causing a person in the afterlife, especially there with God, to shed them. Perhaps it is either the blows, whether many or few, people will need to or have endured, alluded to in Luke 12:47–48, and only in Luke, or the anguish triggered by the realization that some may be separated from those they hold dear.

Third, does Richard run the risk (I trust that alliterations will also become time-honored) of his methodology becoming unfalsifiable, where nothing can count against his viewpoints or be allowed to undermine his interpretations if presented with disconfirming evidence (as I am in danger of becoming flippant with my word selection)? What is the extent to which he considers them air- or water-tight? That would normally be considered a negative thing in scientific undertakings. Thankfully, to his credit, he devotes two later chapters to those passages which could or have been put forward to detract from views of his kind, though he does find an interpretive way to avoid retraction, which prompts him to conclude that the "opposing" verses are but misinterpretations.

One wonders whether these topics can be considered workable theologically if not also biblically. The short answer is yes, though not in the same way. Since creation in six or so days, the Garden, the initial human pair, and the fall are not historical as such, the upshot, contrary to Richard's position, is that creation never did reflect the biblical will for it, since there was always aggression, violence, and death once there were predators of any kind in the biosphere, and these are not confined to the infra-human species world. Nor was there ever a single fall as such; instead, this is an experience we all encounter when we come face to face with our failing to comply with whatever standard we have set for ourselves—witness how soon it takes for New Year's resolutions to evaporate.

Thus, were we to draw a graph, the line of morality would not begin at a high point for the world followed by a dip once humans transgressed together with the curse applied to the world, only to rise again once Jesus inaugurates the kingdom with an increasing slope at the end of history where the endpoint will exceed even the outset. No, the curse theme could very well be salvageable, but perhaps the graph could theoretically give way to an ever-increasing slope leading up to the eschaton. Wrong again; this also does not take place, for we have not exactly been steadily improving ethically as a species. If anything, we have displayed our inability to learn from ours and others' previous mistakes. That leaves us with a horizontal straight line on the graph. Yes, there have been advancements when it comes to issues such as slavery, minority rights, and so forth, but we have also exhibited innovative ways to corrupt new phenomena, such as white collar crime, IT fraud, and so on. Hence the adage "If anything can be corrupted, someone will find a way" to mismanage it.

Therefore, our plight is similar to the biblical account at least from the point of the curse onward, but the trajectory is different. The movement is not from an outset of godly presence and rule in an untainted world, then to a loss of it, and finally to a regaining of it where the last or final condition is superior to the first, but a world *never having* fully reflected the divine will for it, but receiving God's incessant work in the world always with what is there—a diamond in the rough—and polishing it so that at the end it will sparkle with the divine brilliance. There have been, are, and will be many bumps in the road, the graph line will not always have an increasing slope, and, reminiscent of Richard's argument, the line will rise sharply upward at the end of history. The "renewal of all things" (Matt 19:28–30), then, will not be a reversal to a previous order having enjoyed the divine approbation, but, as some are in search of renewable resources of energy, God could very well perform a new thing with an old thing—God always having worked with a remnant of what was there before, the new being unprecedented in its radiance and splendor, like nothing we or the earth have ever seen before. Hence will there be a remnant in this case?

Also, albeit a minor point, Richard uses technical terms in a non-rigorous way, like "intervention" as a philosophical-scientific category, though he cannot be faulted for this, since we all do the same when touching on areas where we lack expertise. Were he to peruse my ventures into biblical material, he might very well place a palm on his forehead and shake his head at many a turn. Nevertheless, my constituency would not really have any emotional investment in his evangelical in-house debates.

I believe we have uncovered a further discrepancy in Richard's thinking. In the past, which is where the subject matter always is when reporting on something having occurred before the present, Richard has been of an opinion, nor have I any evidence of him having changed his position, concerning a passage in Matt 24. In the pericope referring to signs and events surrounding Jesus' return (vv. 36–51), verses 40–41 teach about those who will be either taken or left at that time. Richard has understood this passage as referring to the contingent having been taken in the negative sense—it is a bad thing to be removed from the scene, and those who are left as in positive terms, since being left on Earth reflects God's will for us and it, God being invested in the world, intending it to be restored to health and our managing it so that it remains in this way. Yet on page 202 he makes reference to Enoch in Gen 5:24 who "walked with God; then he was no more, because God took him away." In this instance, being taken is a good thing. Then in 2 Kgs 2:1–11, Elijah is spoken of being "taken" from Elisha, the term occurring four times in the passage. In verse 11, Elijah is taken "up to heaven in a whirlwind" with the assistance of a "chariot of fire," and so as not to give the New Testament (NT) an inferiority complex, "the Spirit of the Lord suddenly took Philip away" (Acts 8:39), again in a positive sense.

Speaking of heaven, there is no way in heaven or on Earth that these events could be understood as negative, aside from the apprentice Elisha missing his "master" Elijah. So here we have multiple references to being taken as beneficial, whereas in Matt 24 Richard and others understand it as detrimental. If his methodology is to disclose themes which have a continuous, unbroken line of similar meaning throughout the scriptures, then this should be one that calls for consistency. Thus is the rendering in Matt 24 off the mark? Richard is committed to claiming it is not. Remaining on Earth seems to have God's approval. Thus we have instances in which the point Richard wishes to make about having been taken does not apply. In his favor, though, Ezek 33:6 does provide an example of a passage in which being taken away is used in the negative, thereby leaving us with a scriptural ambiguity. In how many other cases, then, we might ask, do themes where we would like to see consistency not obtain? As it is exceedingly unlikely that there ever was a Golden Age and the Earth was entirely bereft of a pre-curse period, how can we have confidence in what the scriptures teach about, from our perspective, a nebulous end of days when the Jesus of the text here in Matt 24 even takes the existence of the era of Noah as authentic?

But back to the issue of Matt 24 itself, when Jesus speaks of those who have been "taken" versus "left," the disciples ask where the former might be and Jesus responds with "Where the corpse is, there the vultures will gather" (Luke 17:37 in his parallel version). He refers to the Noah episode where the wicked generation was *taken* away by the flood waters. As for where vultures gather, this could just as readily mean where those who are *left* are deposited, for they could be left on the ground where corpses are *left* for carrion. The implication is that the meaning appears to be ambiguous. While this admittedly does not square with the Noah passage, neither does the *taking* of Enoch and Elijah agree with it, since Enoch was *taken away* by God and we are not informed where, but presumably where God is, and Elijah specifically "went up to heaven in a whirlwind," one reason why we imagine that heaven is overhead. (The taken or snatched away in the Philip episode could be similar to Paul having been caught up to the third heaven as related in 2 Cor 12:2. This third heaven "is a Jewish expression for the immediate presence of God, and for Paul a phrase to convey the idea of the most sublime blessedness"),[12] while the first is the sky and the second the realm of the stars.

In the German of the Revised Luther translation of the Bible, the term for "left" is rendered as "*preisgegeben,*" the past tense of "*preisgeben,*" meaning "abandon," which would correspond to throwing corpses out on the ground as refuse for birds. Hence the taking away from this would be a positive thing, and thus the meaning of having been taken is not the same across the board as would be conveniently consistent. Richard makes reference to all three passages, but he does not connect them and thus overlooks the fact that they do not mutually support each other. The point that needs to be made is there might not be as firm a footing here as Richard perceives there to be.

And in his reference to 2 Cor 5:1–10, Richard reckons that there is no "intermediate state" for any immortal soul, but as we are clothed with our *current* corruptible bodies here in this life, so we will be clothed in new imperishable resurrection bodies *then* with nothing in between. Yet we must ask when Paul makes reference to "the earthly tent we live in" (v. 1), what is this "we" that live in bodies? For Paul to take seriously the notion that in

---

12. Guthrie and Motyer, *New Bible Commentary*, 1086.

between the two clothings there can be a naked unclothing, then the plain text implies that there is some disembodied existence, which some refer to as this intermediate state or "personal survival at death," or alternatively a "soul sleep," in which the soul survives but is unconscious of its state or surroundings in terms of time or place.[13] Nor is one automatically cognizant of any elapsed time between one's demise and the resurrection. That would make sense of the idea that "the dead know nothing" and there is no knowledge in the grave (Eccl 9:5, 10).

Further down in verses 6–9, Paul states that we can either be "at home in the body" or "away from" it and in the Lord's presence. Again, what is the "we" that can either be in or out of bodies? It does not say that we would be in a new body, just away from the old one somewhere and for some time, both undisclosed. Nor has he explained what "out of the body" would then mean in 2 Cor 12:2–3. Plus, in Phil 1:23–24, it "is far better," Paul maintains, for him to remain "in the flesh," but what is the "I" that undergoes this remaining? The soul need not be immortal, only survive the first death in some capacity, long enough either to be subjected to the second death (Rev 20:14–15), in which case, should that death be an annihilation, then that soul would be mortal, or if not, then it would be united with a resurrection body. As the shade or spirit, note not a soul, of Samuel can be consulted by King Saul, Samuel considering it a disturbance (1 Sam 28), and perhaps even suggesting that knowledge can in fact be stored in the grave though not accessed until the spirit is raised, so it might be best to understand the "I" or "we" as a spirit instead of a soul to resolve the issue, and in which case the scriptures would already have done for us. What stands in the way appears to be our aversion to further subdivide the human person into additional components. If so, that may reflect a failing on our part.

Lastly, Richard adduces two of the following three passages as implying the resurrection indirectly: Matt 22:32; Mark 12:27; and Luke 20:38, stating that God "is God not of the dead, but of the living," Jesus specifically having the patriarchs Abraham, Isaac, and Jacob in view. Yet Richard avoids elucidating where or in what way they are alive. He is surprisingly silent in this. It would have been useful information with much bearing on his argument. The difference between pre- and post-resurrection human vessels does not appear to be night and day as we would anticipate from Paul's description in 1 Cor 15, for Luke's resurrected Jesus is indistinguishable from other pre-resurrection males (24:13–43). Evidently, the approximately thirty years' time frame between these two writings was long enough to make a shift in theological viewpoint emerge.

13. Middleton, *New*, 235–36.

If I might be so bold and candid (as though I have not been already), some of Richard's parallels do appear to be a bit of a stretch, especially when he compares the souls under God's altar in heaven (Rev 6:9–11) which ask, "How long, O Lord?" to the blood of Abel which cries out from the ground (Gen 4:10). It seems more likely that he is doing in-house apologetics from one evangelical to others so as to prompt them, as he himself did, to "repent" of their previous ways of believing that heaven is our final destination.[14] The bottom line for me is that God is not required to conform to our biblical interpretation despite "reasons exegetical, theological, and ethical."[15] Our reasons might not be God's.

Regrettably, Richard might be a candidate for the charge of arbitrariness when it comes to what is to be taken literally versus symbolically in the book of Revelation and elsewhere. I find it disingenuous of him when he appeals to the "plain reading"[16] of the text when this is precisely what I was hoping he would carry out in several other instances. Then on the following page,[17] he engages in the souls to Abel's blood comparison, as per the aforementioned. He admits that the interpretation of the one passage "might lead" to a similar one for the other. Conveniently, the "plain reading" is inapplicable here, seemingly not adequately serving his purposes. He agrees with John W. Cooper, despite the latter's allegiance to a dualistic understanding of humans, that the Revelation passage does not corroborate a dualist position by reason of "the imaginative nature of apocalyptic symbolism," as put forward by Cooper. As long as the meaning is reinforced, it does not matter from what quarter its provenance, apparently. This breaking news flash just in—spoiler alert—Abel himself is an imaginative figure! So why does Richard not interpret him as such? Be consistent—take the plain reading of the Revelation passage.

Should the reader be experiencing brain pain or other discomfort at this point, I offer the following to lighten the load prior to resuming this topic.

---

14. Middleton, *New*, 237.
15. Middleton, *New*, 237.
16. Middleton, New, 231.
17. Middleton, *New*, 232.

That's Using Your Head

AUTHOR'S NOTE: THE SETTING for this tale is the southern British prehistoric remote past, approximately the time when *Homo sapiens* became behaviorally modern, fifty thousand years previously having become anatomically modern, fodder for those suspicious of these all-too-convenient fifty-thousand-year increments. Yet the group in view here belongs to *Homo neanderthalensis* and their dominance in Europe, much earlier than the setting for this tale, before the invasion of *Homo sapiens*. The comedic element vehicle is the incongruity of assigning sophisticated language forms to a pre-linguistic people on their behalf. The question can also be raised as to whether or not the non-linguistic sounds we utter and the physical gestures we make have a referent in our distant forebears or their Neanderthal cousins.

Fifty thousand years ago. August. The twentieth. Wednesday. 7:42 p.m. Greenwich Mean Time.

In the beginning, or at least closer to it, before there was Homo, meaning human, there was Australopithecus, which apparently does not, but means southern ape, proto-human, on the way to becoming human, having already taken the step, literally, of walking upright. They could not see far off in the distance what they would become or yield, though perhaps aspiring to it. Hence their plight was taken up with the Department of the Inferior, suffering as they did from genus envy. Alongside *Homo sapiens* was *Homo neanderthalensis*, shorter and stockier, albeit of larger brains. They were the first people to inhabit as far north as southern Britain, which did not become an island until less than ten thousand years ago owing to melting glacial ice. This is where our tale commences.

A band of primitives completes its domestic obligations and gazes longingly upon its surroundings, amply be-foliaged as they were, though with clearings upon which to erect a series of huts as well as lean-tos at forest's edge. The band members were wishing there might be recreational activities to engage in as their daily energies waned. Unable to muster the requisite inspiration, they sought the assistance of a black monolith, a shorter version of that much later to appear in the film *2001: A Space Odyssey*, though the reference would have been lost on them, and despite the anticipation on the part of those filmmakers that the moon would already have been colonized by that date. The larger versions considered the shorter to be the runt of the litter and referred to it as "Mini-us."

Reticent to approach the dwarf-like 1 x 4 x 9 (1^2 x 2^2 x 3^2) hand-breadth entity in what could be regarded as an unworthy manner, one bold primitive marshalled the nerve not only to draw near but also to touch it, thereby producing what could only be described, had they the wherewithal to do so, as an electric shock, which enabled him to hit upon the idea of an athletic group pastime. This seed thought began to germinate in, what should he call it, the neuroanatomy housed in his cranium? Yeah, that's it. He was all a-flutter with devising the rules of a game, which of course must be adhered to should the event commence and continue in an orderly fashion, for one mustn't simply participate in a contest willy-nilly or, heaven forbid, higgledy-piggledy, as that would produce the merely chaotic. No, there must be a proper conforming to a standard of conduct, which made him cogitate, "perhaps in my spare time I should apply a similar code to acts outside of avocations in general; but then again, nah, who's got the time?"

Days afterward, he was ready to present the concept to other members of the group, arriving as he did with the object of play, not knowing how well it would be received. He gestured to the leader, known respectfully as Gronk Number One, with his hands, the group being at the pre-linguistic stage, but at the same time masters at charades, as to how this object originated and could be utilized. This highest-ranking band member, for one did not want to usurp the official pecking-order, pointed to the object of play with a resounding "Huh?" when presented with it as if to ask, "From whence came this sorcery?"

The subordinate band member, understood as Gronk Number Two, employing the middle and index fingers, not as yet having come to symbolize peace, motioned in response to a deer in the nearby hills and then to the region of his own mid-section, technically known as the belly button, whereupon the higher-ranking member rubbed his tummy (excuse the jargon) and licked his lips uttering "Mmmm," as if to acknowledge, "Yea, fine sir, I concur. Their musculature when served smoked with herbs is most pleasant to the palate." To which the other waived his hands palms outwards from side to side, shook his head and uttered, "Uh uh." Not a sophisticated expression, mind you, but a vocalization nevertheless, as if to protest, "Nay, good squire, you misinterpret. I speak not of gustatory delights but the anatomical provenance of yon spheroid, namely lower in the intestinal region of the animal, where may be found the admirable quality of fortitude, demonstrated as it is in the resilience of this object of play." Gronk One, let's call him Hector for ease of reference, then responded with an "Ah" of feigned acknowledgment. Gronk Two, similarly let's call him Benson for the same reason, both of whom peered about in wonderment when their names were mentioned, then permitted the object to drop according to the eminently dependable law of gravity, whereupon the deer's bladder orb, pneumatic as it was, bounced from the ground and he kicked it up to himself with a satisfied grin, signalling a sense of accomplishment.

Let the reader understand that this grin was indicative of an additional form of communication, whereby alternately pursing lips, moving either or both corners of the mouth, raising eyebrows, flaring nostrils, and wiggling ears, all complete with inflection and emphasis, constituted a system of facial signs now lost to history. Just as well perhaps, we might intone, for it would prove impractical for, say, a baseball manager to utilize—is he giving signs or merely swatting away mosquitos?—except of course for shrugging the shoulders, which is still with us today.

The leader then took the object in his hand reassuringly. Once again, Benson exclaimed, "Uh uh," as if to dissuade him and announce, "On the contrary, my dear compatriot, the rules of the game as I have established them are such that they do not permit the handling of the object with, what else, the hands and arms, notice—hands which handle, hence the derivation of the term. Never mind. Instead, only the other body parts are allowed to make contact with it." Looking inquisitively about, this prompted Hector to utter a guffaw, as if to lament, "Rubbish, we possess perfectly good upper appendages which could also be employed in the game." Astounding the detail these short grunts connoted. Benson shook his head as if to pontificate, "Even so, that would detract from the beauty of the sport," only much later to be called the beautiful game.

Undeterred, Hector growled, grabbed the object, tucked it firmly in his hand by his armpit and extended the free arm straight outward as if to fend off would-be attackers, believing opponents would seek to dislodge the object from his control. Benson, who would not be prevailed upon, simply shook his head as if to bemoan, "See here, that will never work. Who would engage in a sport like that?" Insistent on the superiority of his idea, Hector motioned to have Benson attempt to prevent Hector's progress in carrying the object. Benson was unwilling and held his hand up as if to say, "Most appreciated, but I elect to pass." Hector redoubled his efforts to have Benson comply, subtly reminding him of the present rank differential, but he was firm in motioning, "No really, I simply must protest that I would rather not."

Yet Hector would neither cease nor desist, prompting Benson to imply by his facial expression to assert, "Very well, my fine friend, I shall take you up on your provocation and resist with all the means at my disposal and I intend to reduce you a whimpering mass." And with that, the video component of our tale turned black and the audio presented the noise of motor vehicles in collision with hubcaps sliding along the pavement; curious metallic and asphalt sounds for the group, mired as they were deep in the bowels of the Stone Age. Once the light was restored, Benson was found atop Hector in pick-a-back fashion, tongue firmly on the outside corner of his mouth and rubbing his knuckles on the top of Hector's head in an early ancestral form of "noogies," entirely failing therewith to halt the advancement of the object-carrier.

Believing to have proven his point, Hector proceeded to metaphorically throw down the gauntlet, should he have been in possession of such an anachronistic item and about which Benson could only shrug, and spiked the object in a fit of peevishness and challenged the latter to a team duel. Hector promised roundly to defeat him at his own game's devices, to commence at 1:15 the following day, despite having insufficiently developed gestures with which to convey it. Somehow the intent was communicated and the challenge accepted (we would not have much of a tale had he declined), provided of course the domestic chores could be completed in timely fashion—he would need to check his schedule.

The next day (see, the meaning did get across), Sunday for those keeping track, when all good sporting contests occur, was suitably dry for it. Hector was preparing his troops as a player-coach would, instilling in them, even prior to the time there was anyone identified as a "Gipper," that if opponents should come at them from the right, then they were to move left, and vice versa, to which the players rolled their eyes as if to drone, "This is insipidly obvious; what else you got?" The first order of business was to set some ground rules. The length of the field was to be one hundred steps, the members of the group all operating in base ten owing to their ten digits and toes. One works with what one has. The goal line at each end one hundred steps distant, where the object of play must cross for a goal to be counted, was to be bordered by a skull on each side, eight steps apart, in direct defiance of ten or multiples thereof. And should there be a penalty kick, it was to occur from the eleven step line. Ditto.

As for the duration of the contest, an official Gronk indicated that a sundial would mark the beginning, to be alerted by the sounding of a skull struck with a bone. As explained to both sets of competitors, the next such sound would signify break time, communicated by the gesture of the head tilted and a cheek placed on the back of the hand, implying that one could sleep during this time if one so desired, and to which the teams gave an emphatic "Hoorah." Play would resume for an equal amount of time as the first, what would come to be known as a "half," once the skull was struck again. The end of the match would be signalled by a final skull strike at which point full time would be reached and a winner declared.

The players took to the field at the end each would defend. But before the game commenced, a female—Gronkette One, let's name her Tamsin—strolled out onto center field. The crowd gathered there stood at attention as she voiced, naturally without words though making an "Ah" sound with each "note," the first few "bars" of what would much later be known as the British hymn "Jerusalem." Struck by the lofty intent of the piece, some removed their head gear, placed them over their hearts, and were observed to have quivering lips, during which time a player—Gronk Three, let's call him Delbert—not as yet having lost his epidermal pigmentation as a holdover from an out-of-Africa group, and politically incorrectly referred to as dark-skinned as opposed to a person of color, took a knee as other sports figures of a later age, and fretfully sniffed the air in protest of the hymn. As this was an egalitarian enclave, no one strenuously objected. (Apparently, his direct ancestors in Africa within their group did not get invited to the best parties and decided to leave in a huff out of spite, so he came by way of his orneriness honestly.) Tamsin the vocalist then strode off the field waving to the crowd amid enthusiastic applause.

As the contest progressed, spectators were still tardily filing in to the grounds while a fourth Gronk, let's call him Clive, was stationed at the entrance to accept admission, consisting of a colorful feather, considered valuable in that society and somehow held to forecast auspicious occasions. Upon recognizing someone attempting to sneak in without paying, Clive, as an apt sentry on duty might, placed his hand on the other's shoulder, pushing him back and objecting, "Ah, ah, ahuh," syllables gaining considerable mileage at the time, and simultaneously waving a raised index finger, intending by this to mean, "Not so fast my intrepid knave. How dare you deprive the governing authorities the resources applied to infrastructure projects aimed at the benefit of all concerned. How could you place yourself above the needs of the collective?" Despite the remonstrance on the part of the other that he did not have the means to enter but wished desperately to witness what could most likely become an historical event in the burgeoning annals of sport, he was rebuffed for his efforts in an inconsistent turn as to what precisely constitutes everyone's benefit, and Clive pointed a harsh finger in the opposite direction, thereby implying, "I am completely unmoved by your protestations and highly recommend, nay urge, you to turnabout and take your appeals elsewhere," thus unwittingly lapsing into laissez-faire free market capitalism. The irony was lost on him.

Meanwhile, an impartial group member with a talent for whistling was brought in to ensure the rules of the game were being followed. He perceived early on that two players, one of whom was Benson, were battling for ball possession as Benson pushed the other over and knocked him down. The impartial one immediately put to use his whistling penchant and halted play, despite the shadow of the sundial moving relentlessly forward, and held up a bone to signify that a major infraction had just transpired, much later to be understood as the objectionable conviction of being "red-carded." The convict attempted to explain his version of events by pointing his index finger at the impartial one, being careful not to touch the one held in such high esteem, and uttering the sound "Bap," signifying the meager amount of contact he dealt out onto his opponent, and followed this up by raising his hands, flailing them about, and, as later physicians would request, "Stick out your tongue and say 'Ah,'" portrayed the feeble nature of the offense and lack of sturdiness on the part of the player to withstand it, as if to say, "Be not fooled by the antics on his part with such a lame display as though felled by little more than a twig, for his is but histrionics." Other members of the same team went to Benson's defense, holding their hands palms upward, pleading with the impartial one to revisit the offense and perhaps reverse his decision, their mode of expression potentially compounding the offense. Alas, the efforts were to no avail and the convict was sent off the field, leaving his team one player short, with the partisan segments of the crowd either voicing their disapproval or cheering in hearty agreement.

As pertains to the crowd, all standing, which is why it is called in the stands, yet another Gronk, let's name him Cedric, moved through it with a portable concession stand—a mobile refreshment unit—consisting of wooden cups on a wooden tray held over the shoulders with a leather strap. Tasty drinks were on offer. A spectator signalled by raising his hand toward the vendor that he wished to sample the wares. Cedric approached and accepted from the spectator a stone in payment for the liquid refreshment. Cedric held the stone up to the sky as though to examine it for possible evidence of counterfeiting. He soon recognized that this examination would prove inconclusive, given that the stone possessed neither transparent nor translucent qualities, and knocked it against the edge of the tray instead, trusting that this assessed it as legitimate, and returned two pebbles to the customer in change. He handed over a wooden cup, the man took a swig, turned around and let out a sizeable belch, whereupon the woman he was with looked around in disgust and mumbled something inaudible about desiring to be rescued from the embarrassment. She looked about as perplexed as someone attempting to remove a boundary stone telekinetically.

While the action on the field was nearing its conclusion, with the score still deadlocked at what would later be described variously, and in alphabetical order, as bagels, donuts, or Life Savers, the players sought for any possible edge. In an attempt to remedy the scoring drought, one player endeavored to apply his head to the difficulty, literally, by using it to deflect a pass toward the goal. The projectile orb trickled across the goal line, marking what would be the only goal of the contest. Bravo. The proud scoring player then assumed an arms-folded-looking-off-into-the-distance pose and was flanked by two cheerleaders stroking his forearms and making an exclamatory "Oooh" sound. They then noticed the aforementioned Delbert on the sidelines stereotypically kicking a spare object of play deftly upward with his feet and knees, never allowing it to touch the ground. In a fit of flavor-of-the-month-flash-in-the-pan-fifteen-minutes-of-fame fickleness, these same two went over to him instead and made an even greater cooing display. Sometimes our behaviors do have a long history.

The shadow on the sundial advanced ever nearer its endpoint, the crowd exhibiting increasing looks of anxiousness as it did so, and the scoring team wondered if it could survive a late barrage from the opposition. At last the official sounded the skull and the impartial one gave a last resonating whistle, signalling the conclusion had been reached, hence bringing the contest to a close. Final score: one-nil, the latter concept essential for the higher mathematics of a future age. The prevailing side was jubilant; the losing side either despondent or disconsolate, whichever is worse. The crowd dispersed; some to the glory of victory, others to the humiliation of defeat.

Some group members, buoyed by the success of the event, approached the short black monolith in search of the inspiration for further novel occurrences. One fearless individual—Gronkette Two, let's name her Pippa—touched the diminutive edifice and was immediately taken aback by the tactile encounter. A hush fell over the crowd as it turned around to witness what might transpire. The brave group member bent down to scrutinize an even more puny, diminutive, itty-bitty plate on the depository-and-dispenser of novelty and sought to convert the symbols into sounds, thereby embarking on a journey leading to the onset of linguistics. Those gathered recognized that an unprecedented event was to be generated.

Initially her lips moved but nothing audible emerged. She then shed her inhibitions and let loose with unrefined vocalizations. Out came "M-m-m, ma-, mad-, made, i-, in, cha-, chee-, chi-, chin-, china. Made in China?" The crowd looked around at each other and ran off in frenzied terror this way and that, not knowing whether it feared eventual language exams or what was to befall humanity in terms of the source of nearly all manufactured consumer goods in the distant future. Or both.

A further development was such that this linguistic capacity became contagious. Not long after the first words were spoken, other group members engaged in vigorous discussion using their new-found abilities about what the sport having recently been observed should be named, humans becoming adept at naming animate entities and inanimate items in their environment. Some chose "soccer" since the object of play designated a "ball" was socked in a kicking action, completely overlooking the fact that it could just as readily be called "kickball." The others pointed to their lower extremities as the determining feature of the name and referred to it as "football." A chorus of song then broke out as each side promoted its term as the one to be assigned. Competing ideas about the object of play were committed to lyrics: "It is a soccer ball," versus "No, it is a football, er, ball." Neither a musical masterpiece, but definitely melodic. They were found to have instrumental accompaniment in the way of a beat supplied by those energetically striking skulls with a bone.

Concurrently, and surfacing entirely outside the bounds of physical law, a film crew arrived to capture the event. Some group members became amused when they perceived artificial lights employed for the production, even in broad daylight. Inexplicably, this overshadowed the very astonishment their arrival elicited. The person in front of the box with a dark interior, named a "camera," sought an interview with Benson and commented, "Sounds like you've got a real controversy on your hands about reaching a decision concerning the name of this sport." Benson looked at his hands to determine if something were literally attached to them and concluded it was merely a figure of speech. The interviewer spoke into a "snow cone" or "lollipop," for lack of a better term, and pointed the business end of this, let's call the small receiver-recording device a "microphone" if you please, into the interviewee's *face*, quite rudely invading Benson's imaginary *space*, though at the same time imparting into Benson's mind the germinating idea of what could constitute a rhyme. Startled by the strange individual, and in a flurry of verbal activity, yet not always certain as to what he was saying, Benson chimed in with, "That's right, Biff. This is a debate that will no doubt rage for over fifty thousand years. Wait, how did I know that?"

Contrary to this euphoria, Hector nursed a grudge about the popularity of the sport in competition with his and which he regarded as inferior to his own and thought, "A pox on your blasted contrivance. Commit it to the flames." He thus sought the assistance of the mini-monolith for injurious purposes. He did so, moved by the realization that inspiration could also operate in a nefarious or pernicious fashion, whichever is worse, and intended to apply his new-found powers not for "pleasantness" but "selfness." He located a stick with a sharp end and elected to introduce that end to the surface of the soccer/football ball so as to puncture it. Mission accomplished: it worked. Gleeful about the damage he had just inflicted, and consequently ushering in a dark period in human history, our tale ends with his jumping in the air in response and clicking his heels over his detrimental achievement, preserved in perpetuity through the film crew's technological miracle of "freeze frame."

    Introducing Winthrop the Mini-monolith
    Sweat Lodge courtesy of Lapland Industries

By Way of Comparison

I KEEP ON WRITING because I continue to be perturbed. I just do not always know where to begin. Organization, Herb, remember that is your strength from your German upbringing (is it healthy to speak of yourself in the second person?). Allow me, then, to interject with an anecdote. From a Canadian perspective, we have found it interesting that some Americans at least were not sufficiently familiar with global geography or even their own national geography; at the state level, however, they are quite aware. This has been changing on both sides of the border. It thereby gives me no solace to regale you, dear reader, with the following observation. I once placed a long-distance call from South-Western Ontario, where we reside, to the Maritimes, what we call our East Coast. I contacted someone in Halifax, Nova Scotia, about a certain military museum in Cape Breton, on the northern side of the province. The woman at the other end of the line asked, "Where is that?" She did not even know her own relatively small province well. I was crestfallen at our lack of provincial and, probably, national knowledge. Oh the shame of it. Our American counterparts are becoming more aware and we less. Hence the gap between our nations is narrowing in this respect.

As for racism, the racist gap is not as prevalent or divisive in Canada as in the US, though, regrettably, we do have our unfortunate moments as well. In particular, our record with First Nations people is checkered at best, deplorable at worst. I broach this topic for purposes of illuminating where our two nations are similar. We both contain in our citizenry those who consider themselves entitled, wallowing as they might in their vanilla-covered privilege. Not only this, but they may also seek to safeguard their station by ensuring that powerful politicians and smart law-makers are put in place to preserve it (fans of alliteration too, no doubt), for, after all, that's both the North American and Christian ways, a natural law even. Heck, God's law could be used in support of these actions should we ever be called to account; we are certain of it, they would assure us. The Protestant

Work Ethic ensures that those holding this viewpoint will be blessed, but the mindset has drifted from being entirely ethical. This is a repugnant view of personal rights and Richard is correct to criticize it. (See, our views do overlap somewhat and we do have some common ground.)

The story is told (a second anecdote) of a businessman who was further adding to the plight of the downtrodden and disenfranchised for his own financial gain. When asked why he, a religious man, was behaving this way, he responded with, "I am saved. Nothing can take that away from me. Now I can do what I want." See, it does matter what one believes, not just what one does. As it turns out, there are about as many biblical passages in favor of this doctrine, known as the perseverance of the saints, as there are those warning against the facile presumption of it—a topic I have treated elsewhere.[1] The Bible's position on the issue is ambiguous—it could be one or the other; this man was placing his bets on the self-interested one. Does one really want to rest content with a position of eternal safety and safe journey to one's buddy Jesus when he returns when there are passages like the following? "We have been made holy through the sacrifice of the body of Jesus Christ once for all," but "If we deliberately keep on sinning after we have received the knowledge of the truth, no sacrifice for sins is left . . . How much more severely do you think a man deserves to be punished who has trampled the Son of God under foot, who has treated as an unholy thing the blood of the covenant that sanctified him, and who has insulted the Spirit of grace?" The former passage prior to the ellipsis is from Heb 10:10 and is reassuring, the latter from verses 26 and 29 of the same chapter is a stern warning that, contrary to the "once saved, always saved" notion, those who rely on it while through their lives exhibit the very opposite are equated with "the enemies of God" (v. 27).

If this were not enough, 2 Pet 2:19b–21 hammers the point home: "a man is a slave to whatever has mastered him. If they have escaped the corruption of the world by knowing our Lord and Savior Jesus Christ and are again entangled in it and overcome, they are worse off at the end than they were at the beginning. It would have been better for them not to have known the way of righteousness, than to have known it and then to turn their backs on the sacred commandment that was passed on to them." We therefore can lose what we have already attained, so what kind of lives should we lead? Richard's prescription is directly on the mark. Kudos. But enough of this love fest.

As for myself, I view the imago Dei, the image of God, to consist in: (a) our self-reflective capacity, particularly in reference to our relatability to

---

1. See my *God Only Knows*.

God; (b) our faculty for participating in God's moral attributes (also in my view, ethics is the system whereby we adjudicate whether an act is right or wrong; morality is how well we comply with the former); and (c) our participation in God's creativity and kingdom rule for the purpose of expanding it in both this world and the next. Richard, in this his second volume under study here, emphasizes the third, referring to it, as mentioned, as the original mandate. Questions I have include whether there are gradations of "imagehood" ("imagity?" "imagitude?"). That is, can we be more or less image-bearers? Are atheists any less image-bearers? Or just less in expression (I suspect that is his position)? If the image can be distorted, surely theirs is less of one, having in mind Oscar Wilde's *The Picture of Dorian Gray*.

Developing this theme further, on the heels of speaking about what constitutes the imago, we turn our attention to a follow-up task that combines the topics of theological anthropology and the atonement. Where, we might ask, do we find the imago, or, alternatively, are we as *Homo sapiens* the only ones ever to have possessed it? Let's focus on the "if not" side of the ledger first. If we were not the only ones, then one implication is such that bearing one does not guarantee longevity. Admittedly, other human species have lasted longer than we have to this point, we for a mere two hundred thousand years so far, at least in the modern sense, while others for hundreds of thousands of years longer. Yet they all went extinct. Hence God must not place a great deal of value in the imago, at least not a sufficient amount so as to sustain the others as going concerns.

Another issue is whether these peoples were able to avoid transgressions. If so, they would not have required a savior; if not, were multiple saviors required, say one for each of the human sub-species? Or was Jesus' sacrifice sufficient for any and all of them? Which in turn affects the doctrine of salvation (soteriology), for Jesus must be our representative and substitute (to be elaborated in due course). The latter part is covered, but the former poses some potential questions. Was Jesus' representation on the basis of being a human in general or a *Homo sapien* in particular? Additional particularity in terms of ethnic group does not play a role, for despite Jesus as having come specifically to the Jews, thankfully his sacrifice goes well beyond those borders. Plus, would the law or some other moral code have been delivered to other sub-species verbally, since they are expected to have been illiterate, since they left no written documents? And what about those prior to the onset of speech? Did God then resort to charades to get the covenantal point across? Or were pictographs on cave walls sufficient?

Considering next the "if so" portion, if we and our sub-species were the only ones ever to have borne the imago, then does that mean God waited patiently but with anticipation until such time as there were no other sub-species left standing before an imago became present? In any event, the "if so" means that we have non-imago blood in us, for Neanderthals interbred with us, which now forms small amounts of our own genomes (1.5 to 3 percent at last count). Are we then tainted by this (not thereby intending that sinfulness is transmitted genetically or through the blood)? After all, we have reptilian features in our brains, but that does not make us reptiles; we have long since diverged from their and our common ancestor.

As yet another issue, is the imago something that developed in evolutionary terms or was it, like Alfred Russel Wallace claimed, over against Charles Darwin's view that everything has a natural explanation, parallel to the human mind, which is the only aspect we bear that is a direct divine deposit (the three ds)? Important too, to keep in mind, after having introduced the topic of mind, is that classification schemes are human mental products, and the assignment of certain sub-species to the genus Homo may be wide of the mark. The designation "human" may warrant other characteristics than how we moved about, what we fashioned with our hands, and how big our brains were. In all, these notions have theological import, so we would do well to consult anthropological, archaeological, and biochemical genetic works beside our biblical and theological ones so as to be more fully informed. A similar form of reasoning would likely occur if we were to substitute intelligent-life-possessing-an-imago-on-exoplanets for the present exercise, unless the "ancient astronaut theorists" are correct that we are human-ET hybrids. No comment.

Also, given Richard's rejection of the "us versus them" mentality in some Christian circles,[2] he ends the chapter with the subheading "The Hope of the Kingdom,"[3] concerning the idea that we are not in a position to assess which areas of life are, and who is, fit for the kingdom, as every activity and vocation and every person is a candidate. The issue becomes whether we approach our tasks obediently or not, whether we work in such a way as to submit every area of life into the expansionist program of God's kingdom and partner up with anyone whose pursuit is the same, leaving no one and nothing out, and leaving it up to God to decide on the extent of the authenticity of the allegiance.

This all-inclusivity is a theme which the metaphysics of process thought also champions, though with a different focus. There are those in the process camp who would contend that were it not for the process strategy, which some Christians would term heretical, or "us"es calling the others "them"s, they could not consider themselves holding membership

---

2. Middleton, *New*, 275–81.
3. Middleton, *New*, 281–82.

in the Christian fold specifically or even theism generally, process thinkers referring to themselves as a halfway house between theism and atheism. Would Richard either enthusiastically or reluctantly accept these folks in their own purported Christian walk? Or would they be regarded as yet another group that amounts to a mission field wherein the adherents simply need to be converted?

As for another religious body, Unitarian Universalism, to be outlined below, what would be the perspective on U.U.s, who in their drive for social justice can out-Christian some Christians? While they might not consider themselves Christian, their having drifted from their roots, are we willing to make room for them, or have they crossed the religious line from insiders to outsiders? If pressed, Richard may be hard-pressed to acknowledge that despite their, what to his camp would be, kingdom work, they ultimately do not belong, since they themselves would testify that they do not, for the most part, seek to belong, nor would they take umbrage at the charge, only to those doing the charging. After all, "whoever is not against us is for us," since they may have done many things in Jesus' name (Mark 9:38–40; Luke 9:49–50).

Here now are some general comments about his earlier book, albeit treated second in our investigation. On the one hand, we learn that God is invested in the world (an overlooked aspect of John 3:16), yet on the other we are informed not to conform to its pattern (Rom 12:2). We understand from Richard's work that God's intention is to bring the fullness of God's kingdom onto a renewed Earth. I am interested to know how much we should be invested in this world, asking it from the perspective of some of those in the evangelical tradition whose investment is seen as indifferent, and you know which portion you are. I suppose that God observes how well or poorly we care for this world as a rehearsal for the new Earth to come.

By pouring our efforts into the current world we display how serious we are, but at the same time we are not to be overly concentrated on it, for that would be idolatrous and it will be superseded. This idolatry is more implied than explicitly asserted on Richard's part; I merely point out the corresponding emphasis from his early works, and of course it is possible to obsess about anything. Some, however, would consider these to be mixed messages in his treatment. Attend to the world, but be not of it, together with be not so heavenly or new earthly minded that we are no this-worldly good. The two can be held in fruitful tension, but the two sayings can also equivocate on the term "world." In the first instance, the stress is on the Earth geologically, geographically, together with the biosphere; in the second, the concern is more the Zeitgeist—the spirit of the age or time, which can often be corrupt.

Jesus himself used this kind of literary vehicle when in a boat with his disciples. The latter bemoan that they forgot to take bread on the journey, whereupon Jesus says to "Be on your guard against the yeast of the Pharisees and Sadducees" (Matt 16:6), which in Luke 12:1 he identifies as "hypocrisy," intending by this also to mean their teaching, which can reach one's innermost parts and when "fully baked" can produce a loaf of bread or human vessel which might very well be a caricature of God's intention—emphasizing what is secondary in God's sight over what is primary. We can apply this to our very planetary home—it is currently of secondary importance when compared with the one to come, as are our physical bodies.

The world to come should be the one occupying our attention from the standpoint of the length and breadth of what we are to take as our treasure, for it is not to be this Earth, and our heart should be directed to the next, since "where your treasure is, there your heart will be also" (Matt 6:21; Luke 12:34) and vice versa. The thrust, of course, is that God's kingdom should be our treasure, the first installment of which is right here. Jesus himself mentions that we can store up for ourselves "treasure in heaven" (Luke 12:33); and the issue is whether that is where it will remain and we will join it, or if it too will be transferred to the new city where it will meet up with us. Nevertheless, I wonder whether the care this world warrants (and my hope is that alliteration will have a place in the next) removes our sight from the next. I am not suggesting that we should not gear our efforts away from the lesser since God's program will yield the greater, but are the efforts ultimately worth the effort if one is to give way to another? I do not need convincing, but others do.

This becomes an additional concern to the one with which Richard opened his volume, namely an indifference toward this world, since the mentality is "it's all going to burn and pass away anyway." That mindset is rightly rejected, yet it seems possible to look forward to a renewed Earth instead of the mistaken view, in opposition to his affirmation that our final destination will be a renewed "here" and not a heavenly "there," while simultaneously backing away from contemporary planetary stewardship. Richard envisions that our future citizenship on a new Earth might possibly inspire us to be proper custodians and managers of the one we currently have. I fear this is not automatic. We can be on board with Richard's distillation of the divine program and still have our vision set on what is to come and relatively ignore the present one. The mentality which holds, as Sarah Palin has said, "drill, baby, drill," could have the same result as the mindset which understands even a renewed Earth as sufficiently foreign to what we could accomplish, so that God would be renovating the current one in any case, or is this age merely practice for us? The situation appears similar to home sellers who debate how much in the way of resources they should invest into renovation prior to listing the property so as to make it presentable for showing to prospective buyers, only to learn that potential new owners would be interested in gutting the place anyway, resulting in wasted efforts and resources on the part of the present owners. Why then go to the trouble as tenants and stewards of the planet in cultivating the creation or even manicuring the landscaping when it could experience a divine facelift as a matter of course, thereby potentially negating our efforts? I am not recommending this course of action, only casting doubt on the stated logic.

Hence Richard's prescription might not be remedial, for the Earth will be scrapped, not in favor of heaven but a renewed Earth, which will still amount to a scrapping, since the slate will be wiped clean, which is not radically different in outcome from those holding the initial burn idea. We could stay the course unabated and the renewed Earth would still arrive; despite admirable action on our part, how much of it would survive? If we will be significantly changed beyond flesh and blood (1 Cor 15:50–52), this could be similar for the planet as well. How far then do we go as caretakers of this world before it crosses the line into idolatry, something Richard is justifiably at pains to avoid? And similarly, how much do we have the future Earth in our cross-hairs before it too becomes idolatrous and we neglect our current "digs"? It appears both "here" and "there" can be idolized. We can buy into Richard's appraisal and still not avoid idolatry—rendering devotion to something that should be reserved for God alone.

The inner logic of Richard's scheme, either stated or implied, can backfire, at least the implications to be drawn from it: (a) our citizenship will be not in heaven but on a renewed Earth; (b) thus a mindset of being free to trash the current one is illegitimate; (c) so we should cultivate (literally) a planetary consciousness and be proper stewards of it; (d) we should be committed to this task but not so invested in it that it becomes illegitimate in the opposite direction, for what is "here" will be replaced by what is presently "there"; (e) since we should not be unduly invested in the "already" but have our sights set on the "not yet," the importance of this world is actually secondary, not primary; (f) therefore our view can become "it's all going to be replaced anyway" instead, which is not what Richard intends. There is, thus, a flaw in the logic.

In both Richard's and the fundamentalists' accounts, neither world survives into the next, although in Richard's rendition those who manage the Earth well can be trusted to manage the one in the new era. Nevertheless, I fail to see how a person would be convinced to treat the world with utmost seriousness if the present Earth is to be replaced with the new. If that person has the perspective that this world is of secondary importance after all, then one danger is we may imagine that the more environmentally conscious we are now, the less "replacing" will need to be done later; yet if it is bound to be replaced anyway, then why bother?

And while we are on the topic, if God did not begin with the secondary Earth but the primary, perhaps as a trial run or dress rehearsal or apprenticeship, then did God also do the same with humans? As stated, there was never a Garden nor a sinless undying adult human pair, but God fashioned both the world and its contents, including us, with the intention and hope that they would ever progress toward the place where they would shed their usefulness and be catapulted to an advanced version through a break with the past. This scenario would be marked by a single discontinuity while Richard's would have multiple—the fall and curse, the Noachian deluge, and the eschaton (the second more a remnant than a discontinuity). In the single version, life is a training ground or probationary period to determine fitness for the new and improved to come; in the multiple scenario, we have been placed on probation due to a felony, the judge being lenient because it was our first offense.

Yet the bottom line appears to be, as Richard's interlocutor expressed in the introduction to the earlier work, perhaps this friend had the scripture passage in mind when he lamented regarding the fate of the world and all within it, that "it's all going to burn" (2 Pet 3:10–13). These are verses which Richard must respect and one that supports his friend's view, but we may conclude that the passage contains, as I maintain with regularity, a both-and rather than an either-or approach. The all-consuming fire will include the entirety of creation *and* there will be "a new heaven and a new earth" (v. 13). Thus both Richard and his compatriot are partially correct, together comprising a whole as a type of complementarity of unanticipated components.

I repeat, I am not attempting to dissuade readers from endorsing Richard's program, for it is a noble and commendable pursuit (and further, he approaches his subject matter as ardently as I do mine). More than that, it is a trenchant calling we all should heed. My disquiet is the route he takes to get there, for the way is strewn with obstacles which need to be cleared first. Nor am I the one who needs convincing, but for the circles in which I travel, should appeal be made, say, to biblical writings which Richard cites that are attested to be from Paul but are likely not, then the thrust of Richard's argument will run aground for them, for they could very well suspect that these forged, fraudulent documents might not even be worthy of authority.

So Richard's message, as I have stated, is for evangelical eyes and ears and may not make a significant dent in minds to the left. In response to his offering, I can say well then, if no aspect of life comes out from under the umbrella of God's claim over it, and there is a Christian way to conduct any and all vocations so that they submit to God's calling for them, some requiring more significant *reform*ulation than others (the first part of the term is italicized as a nod to the Reformed tradition from which it stems, though Wesleyan thought has adopted it as well—see, not everything about me is leftist, for we can heed that call too), it makes sense then that the world itself is part of that calling and *ought* to be managed accordingly (and by employing this italicized term, we have entered the ethical domain). And as I have alluded to in a previous volume, I part company with that type of dualism, so too Richard, which elevates the metaphysical and denigrates the physical, though not all dualisms are required to be Platonic or Gnostic, and mine is not. Those who reason as Richard does have their hackles raised every time they hear the term, but more about this below.

Recalling the analogy with which we began this examination, how would the two of us, Richard and myself, grade coins? I suspect he would concentrate on the standard high points, the traditional ones that have become accepted as the norm as the initial features to show wear. Having said this, he would also bring our attention to those which have been overlooked and really ought to come into play to render a thoroughgoing appraisal of the item. I, on the contrary, would emphasize that a coin has two sides that should, against the norm, be accorded equal weight, not just the side usually labeled "heads," that by convention informs us as to which side constitutes the most important one.

I would further stress that, high points aside, focus should also be placed on those parts of the coin that, without which, the item would not stand out as much, be they facial features of the person's image on the portrait, his or her vestments, if any, and those which could detract from the overall eye appeal of the specimen (please do not misunderstand this as an exercise in judging by appearances only). Possessing two sides means that both need to be taken into consideration, despite one side often being more significant than the other, thereby entailing a duality of weight attached to them. The relevance of this analogy to biblical and theological categories is suggestive.

As mentioned, it is possible for a coin to have the high points intact but to have other spots worn, resulting in a higher grade according to accepted grading practice, though for little good reason. Even though hyperbolic, in the extreme the high points would be visible while the remainder of the coin becomes a slug. More precisely, the coin would then be graded as lower condition having higher condition details. In order to qualify as a certain grade, a coin must exhibit certain agreed upon visible features; the trouble is that some of these are arbitrarily chosen and there could just as well be other aspects, should consensus be reached on them too, or instead. This could be analogous to observing the letter of the law legally but coming up short in terms of the spirit of the law morally.

For those keeping track, there is a task I have left undone. Thus far there was a fourth member of our quartet at university who has remained unnamed. I did not want to neglect him by leaving him out. For ease of reference, let's call him Gord. He is the other in our group who has remained, at least since last notice, evangelical. This citation is in his honor. A habit which both he and Richard have fallen into, or victim to, on occasion is the application of the biblical witness directly to our own lives, whether warranted or not. The tendency is to locate an episode in the scriptures which mirrors one's own and claim the outcome of the textual situation as something which God has intended for God's people in similar circumstances. This is a hasty strategy and is part of what prooftexting means.

Scripture contains a record, a sometimes fanciful, fictional, legendary, and mythical account of what transpired in the lives of God's followers, and even for some who have declined the offer to follow. In another attempt to engage in a back-and-forth with God, as Abraham did in Gen 18 and about which Richard endeavors to explicate, defend, and apply to our contemporary context, the methodology is periodically employed when beseeching God with requests, such as, "See, as you have been pleased to be active in the life of (here insert the name of the biblical character in question), we ask that you do the same in what we currently face as mightily as you did in the original event."

The trouble, once again, is that there is not a one-to-one correspondence of what we are encountering with theirs, nor is the resolution necessarily reflective of God's activity elsewhere (and elsewhen?). But if we are insistent that the strategy holds in all comparable cases, then we in our investigation can do likewise. To the extent that the Bible, for instance, is looked upon by the evangelical camp as an instructional manual delivered from heaven to our doorstep, then the scheme could further play out in the following way. We are informed in the book of Revelation (20:12) that there is a heavenly book wherein is written the names and perhaps even the histories of the saints, but the passage states that there are additional books. Should the book of life not contain biographical material, then one of the others might.

One of, if not the, most recent books of the OT is the book of Esther, and 6:1 records how King Xerxes of the Medes and Persians (1:3) in a bout of insomnia had "the book of the chronicles, the record of his reign, . . . brought in and read to him," sure to put one to sleep, it seems. The point is, applying the king's situation to the heavenly, when God, who neither "slumber[s] nor sleep[s]," and keep in mind this is in reference to "he who watches over Israel" (Ps 121:3-4) as a collective, a nation, and not automatically in the same way in the lives of each and every follower throughout history, may at times be particularly downcast, say when God is misrepresented as "hat[ing] fags," then God might need a little pick-me-up and will call in members of the heavenly court who will not want God to remain in such a morose state, to read to God the accounts of the saints, leaving God's spirit uplifted as was King Xerxes' and reminded that there indeed have been, as well as will be, better days ahead.

The God of the text delivered Daniel from the lion's den (chapter 6) and his compatriots from the fiery furnace (chapter 3), but God does not typically operate this way, though can and does surprise at times. Hence if these mishaps befall others, the expected, or at least hoped for, deliverance will not automatically take this shape, and Daniel's three friends take their stand that God can deliver them, but even if not, they elect to defy the king's decree (3:17-18). If not in this shape, then perhaps in others in the ongoing sagas of the saints. Incidentally, in Dan 3:25 the fourth one in the furnace "looks like a son of the gods." Then in verse 28 this person is referred to as an angel. Perhaps Paul had this passage in mind when he thought, as some have asserted, of Jesus as having first been an angel (Gal 4:14) (though 1 Pet 3:22, as a way of determining how scripture interprets scripture, reads "angels," not "angels other than himself," as the extent to which the exalted Jesus enjoys dominion over all other authorities, save the Father). And the German term "preisgeben" is also used in this same verse and is translated as "give up," that is abandon, once again contrary to Matt 24:39-41 where those who are left are abandoned, and also contrary to Richard, since in Luther's German translation, to be left is a negative thing, while for Richard it is positive.

These heavenly books in Revelation are hopefully massive tomes, even multi-volume works. Gord introduced me to books, his own library in particular. I availed myself of them at the time. Here's to you, Gord.

That Makes Two of Us

I NOW WISH TO examine two other works whose authors treat similar themes as does Richard but make no reference to him. The first comes from NT historian Bart D. Ehrman's recent volume *Heaven and Hell: A History of the Afterlife*. Jumping right in to his treatment, Ehrman is of the opinion that "God is not even present" in Sheol,[1] but in so doing overlooks Ps 139:8, which teaches that one cannot hide from God even there, since God makes an appearance there as well, with the difference that in Sheol humans might not actually have access to God. That God is in heaven, from the first part of the verse, is not ground-breaking, but that God also has a sticker on God's suitcase announcing "Sheol y'all" may come as a surprise, though Ehrman suggests that the enlightened authors of Hebrew wisdom literature might have left such untutored beliefs to the common folk,[2] but, drawn as they are from poetic material, not necessarily intending that they be taken literally.

Ehrman makes statements similar to those of Richard and others regarding the redeemed as having their place on a renewed Earth, according to God's initial plan,[3] and that God will prosecute it in renewed bodies[4] of some description. Never mind merely intervening in the world, God will invade and occupy it as an imperialist with expansionist tendencies would.[5] All of this sounds strikingly similar, at least on this score, to Richard's appeal, without actually citing his work, meaning an interpretation of this kind has not escaped some authors in this field of scholarship, even if not widespread. Yet Ehrman's take on the makeup of humans is distinct from Richard's in that, initially, "first a body is made, then the breath of God is

---

1. Ehrman, *Heaven*, 86.
2. Ehrman, *Heaven*, 89.
3. Ehrman, *Heaven*, 103.
4. Ehrman, *Heaven*, 108.
5. Ehrman, *Heaven*, 117.

breathed into it and it comes to life"[6] (Gen 2:7), and latterly, he informs us that "son of man," used often in Ezekiel, simply means "mortal,"[7] its way of saying "Dude!" For certain Jews anticipating a resurrection in the distance, "the 'soul' or 'breath' that enlivens their body is [removed] at death. But at the resurrection it will be returned, bringing the body back to life."[8] So, contrary to Richard, there *is* something in addition to the body. As for where this breath is headed upon death, both authors might do well to revisit Eccl 12:7, informing its readers that "the spirit returns to God who gave it," where spirit here means the life force.

Furthermore, Ehrman, again unlike Richard, is not prepared to excise dualistic language about the intermediate state in Paul's epistles, as in 2 Cor 5:1, but permits the text to speak as it stands. As he does so, however, he runs the risk of implying that the eternal home of humans is in heaven after all, unless the scripture passage is qualified as such.[9] Yet the bottom line for Ehrman seems to converge with Richard's view,[10] hence it is a wonder why they do not interact, at least in a way that we would notice, whether or not in the journals.

Ehrman's emphasis, though, differs in terms of who will be the beneficiaries of this renewed world. Whereas Richard asserts that it will be for the few who are chosen as a subset of the many who are called or invited (Matt 22:14), Ehrman concentrates on those passages, all from Paul, which proclaim that mercy and life come to all people (Rom 11:32),[11] albeit the offer might simply be a demonstration instead of a settled fact of acceptance, the transaction still needing to be completed. And in Rom 5:18–19, whereas the first verse uses the language of "all people," the second reverts to "the many," leaving us uninformed as to whether the two are to be taken as equivalent. In any case, I would add to the list those passages, purportedly also from Paul, that make a stronger point to the same end: Jesus "gave himself as a ransom for all [people]" (1 Tim 2:6) (perhaps extrapolating the offer from "many" in Mark 10:45), and "we have put our hope in the living God, who is the Savior of all men, and especially of those who believe" (1 Tim 4:10). This might appear like moving the goalposts of salvation with each rendition.

Distinct also is Ehrman's take on death and its aftermath. As for rewards and punishments, particularly the latter, a concept often employed

6. Ehrman, *Heaven*, 99.
7. Ehrman, *Heaven*, 99.
8. Middleton, *New*, 160.
9. Ehrman, *Heaven*, 184, 187–88.
10. Ehrman, *Heaven*, 224.
11. Ehrman, *Heaven*, 280.

by exegetes is that of Gehenna, understood to be a garbage dump set ablaze and which constantly smolders, as a depiction of the fate of the ungodly, but actually refers to "a place where children had been sacrificed to a pagan god," and therefore "was a place of unfathomable cruelty . . . an unholy, blasphemous place."[12] And as for the passage in Matt 10:28: "Do not be afraid of those who can kill the body but cannot kill the soul. Rather, be afraid of the one who can destroy both soul and body in hell," there are multiple items for consideration. First, Paul's view of the body is such that its unregenerate aspect is called *sarx* in Greek, which Paul calls the flesh, while the regenerate aspect is known as *soma*, or body, that which will rise and be transformed at the resurrection with no *sarx* characteristics remaining in it.[13] Second, Ehrman believes the term "destroy" in the verse can be translated "exterminate" or "annihilate."[14] As per the former point, he places Luke and Paul in opposition, for whereas Luke sees "the body that went into Jesus's tomb [as] the one that came out of it—a view that actually contradicts Paul," who insists that his "body was completely glorified and transformed," since "flesh and blood cannot inherit the kingdom of heaven"; not so for Luke, whose Jesus has a resurrected body that "is a revivified corpse."[15]

And as per the latter, it highlights the debate between the side that takes punishment to be eternal and the side that judges it to be temporary, even momentary.

On this last score, Ehrman holds to the idea of annihilation, as mentioned above, where the lake of fire will cause those in it to be extinguished.[16] Here he seems, however, to be at odds with the bulk of biblical statements, mainly the parable of the rich man and Lazarus in Luke 16:19–31, where the rich man's fate gives no indication that it is set to terminate, and Mark 9:48–49, taken from an earlier writing, namely Isa 66:24, in which "their worm does not die, and the fire is not quenched." On the one hand, one can have either a fire or gorging worms but not both, since worms will not survive a fire; and on the other, as with Rev 14:10–11, confirming that "the smoke of their torment rises for ever and ever. There is no rest day or night," in reference to those who side with the beast, the outcome appears self-explanatory. Ehrman, though, finds this as playing right into his hands, for while the fire is admittedly ongoing, the notion that those in it are eternally suffering is not established, and hence we are free to question it

---

12. Ehrman, *Heaven*, 158.
13. Ehrman, *Heaven*, 240.
14. Ehrman, *Heaven*, 160.
15. Ehrman, *Heaven*, 195.
16. Ehrman, *Heaven*, 139, 223.

as theologically definitive.[17] A point I wish to add is that an oft-overlooked verse is the second one of the Mark 9:48–49 reference, which maintains that being "salted with fire" is a fate no one can avoid; plus, Jas 2:13: "Mercy triumphs over judgment,"[18] should further be kept in mind to the end of softening extreme views. Lastly, Ehrman alerts us to a discrepancy in Rev 22:2, where the leaves of the tree of life "are for the healing of the nations." The concerns are what these nations are and what would require healing if all things have been renewed (Matt 19:28)?[19]

Nevertheless, contrary to the view of some evangelicals, who appear to require their position be massaged more so than others—we all do, but they a more steady diet of it—this exercise illumines that one can be an atheist (by Ehrman's self-identification) and still perform responsible biblical exegesis, to the extent that some of Ehrman's progressive perspectives can even be found among those in the evangelical camp. And perhaps counterintuitively, he vigorously defends there actually having been an historical Jesus.[20]

The second study, to which we devote a longer treatment, comes from the late Terry Nichols (also having been a personal acquaintance of mine), a conservative Catholic theologian. When comparing his work to the other two, it becomes evident that most academics do not boast multiple areas of expertise: theologians would benefit from biblical scholarship and vice versa. Studies like ours tend to highlight the lacuna between them. Regrettable that we have but a single lifetime to work with. One thing I am convinced of, with the wide range of positions on biblical and theological topics in church history, is that a representative of God will not meet us upon entering the afterlife with a questionnaire or checklist determining whether our beliefs could be considered orthodox or not, for there are other more pressing matters.

Nichols deals with much the same terrain as the previous two and comes to similar conclusions, but, as intimated, his biblical work is not of the same depth as these other two, nor, as one might expect, is the theological work of the other two of equal caliber to his. Nichols interprets the same passages as does Richard but has a different perspective on them. Whereas Richard excavates the texts for deeper meanings, Nichols takes the plain text, which Richard is reluctant to do, despite Richard thrice insisting on the natural meaning. Hence Nichols adopts a hermeneutic of "natural

---

17. Ehrman, *Heaven*, 224.
18. Ehrman, *Heaven*, 290.
19. Ehrman, *Heaven*, 229.
20. See his *Did Jesus Exist? The Historical Argument for Jesus of Nazareth*.

reading[s]," which then afford us, and with this we commence our investigation into his thought, the meaning that personal identity subsists into the grave—Sheol in OT Hebrew thought.[21]

As in 1 Sam 28, where King Saul approaches the witch of Endor to call up the shade of the newly deceased prophet Samuel, she does so and Saul has no difficulty in recognizing him, entailing that the apparition is not immaterial but bears some physical features. The wraith is not bereft of physicality.[22] Nichols, contrary to Richard, holds both to an enduring existence beyond death, though not in the sense of a Platonic dualistic immortal soul, and hence an interim period without an immediate resurrection. This is albeit, as he admits, what remains has both immortal-like and soul-like aspects,[23] which Plato would endorse.

He adduces the parable of the rich man and Lazarus in Luke 16:19–31 as instructive in this regard. The following points emerge: the rich man has died yet is sufficiently conscious so as to have Abraham as an interlocutor, in apparent opposition to the view that "there is no knowledge in the grave" (Eccl 9:10), even though the grave for him is already in the rear view mirror. This account was not considered scandalous to its audience in the sense that common, if not prevalent, notions were such that survival of personal identity occurs prior to the resurrection; and the rich man, while specifically in Hades, apparently subsequent to a short stay in the grave, petitions Abraham to warn his brothers of his plight (in which he is consciously suffering), necessitating that they are still alive and that the resurrection has not yet occurred.[24] What is more, Lazarus is transported by angelic couriers "to Abraham's side," indicating once again not a lengthy tenure in the grave. Hence on the one hand, there does not seem to be an extensive interim period, yet on the other, our final fate is entered upon even prior to the end, thereby confounding a straightforward time line of afterlife events.

Luke 24:36–39 is also presented as an attempt by the gospel author to instill in his readers or listeners the thought that resurrection bodies will be physical of sorts and thus has the resurrected Jesus invite his disciples to a tactile encounter, confirming that ghosts do not possess physical features as such, and suggesting that this experience was both contrary to their expectations and perhaps an intentional foil to the Platonic dualistic understanding in which his audience, likely gentiles, might very well have been steeped,

---

21. Nichols, *Death*, 20.
22. Nichols, *Death*, 22–23.
23. Nichols, *Death*, 129–33.
24. Nichols, *Death*, 129–33.

together with offsetting Paul's conviction in 1 Cor 15 that it is precisely flesh and blood which are unable to inherit the kingdom (v. 50).

The other Synoptic Gospels, Matthew and Mark, do not contain Luke's account, but do present the episode of Jesus walking on water, where the disciples confuse him with a ghost (Matt 14:26; Mark 6:49). Luke does not have a corresponding passage to this, yet accomplishes a similar feat, namely that Jews at Jesus' time held to disembodied existence, and neither the earthly Jesus (in Matthew and Mark) nor the risen Jesus (in Luke) was an instance of it.[25] This, of course, does not mean that their view was correct, nor does it offer us an indication as to how to reconcile Paul's position with Luke's. Furthermore, we are not guided in knowing how selective we are permitted to be with literal biblical interpretations; if we are afforded the opportunity to adjudicate on the issue, then would we rule that we have lost the chance to be surprised by the text?

Additionally, Nichols militates against Richard's view in another passage from Paul. In 2 Cor 5:1–8, Paul interjects a further stage between this life and the resurrection. Paul proposes that there is a phase humans undergo between being declothed in the earthly sense and reclothed in the resurrection sense, and this Paul refers to as being "found naked." For Nichols this is clear evidence of an intermediate state, while Richard does not follow him in this. Paul reckons that the interim period is superior to the earthly stage but inferior to the resurrected, for to "be away from the body" is to be "at home with the Lord."[26]

This reasoning applies also to the Rev 6:9–10 passage where the souls of martyrs are under God's altar in heaven, though, once again, Richard does not see it this way. His strategy is to campaign for an anti-dualist posture by emphasizing a term which incorporates body and soul into one, and believes he has found one in humans as being "psychosomatic unities": *psyche* as Greek for "soul" or "mind," and *soma* for "body." Interesting that he uses a term derived from the Greeks whose concepts he distances himself from. My comment is that one does not unify multiple concepts or initiate a merger between two distinct items, one abstract, the other concrete, simply by giving the unity a new term; to think this way to me is merely wordplay. Nevertheless, Richard is required to argue against what he regards as dualistic passages since he has already committed himself to this psychosomatic unity position. He can do no other; he is locked into this strategy. Nichols is one for whom the interim stage does not result in Platonic/Cartesian (Descartes) forms of dualism, since the Bible "constantly looks forward to

---

25. Nichols, *Death*, 48.
26. Nichols, *Death*, 50.

the resurrection of the whole person. It is the soul that carries the personal identity of the dying person beyond death to the resurrection of the body in the last days."[27] While I agree with this aspect of Nichols's approach, my question is, despite how transitory the status of the naked soul period may be, how in Harry Houdini does this fail to qualify as dualistic?

Another way to think of the interim period is in terms of what is referred to as "soul sleep." The interval between being declothed and reclothed becomes a time similar to deep sleep when we are taken aback that an appreciable amount of time has elapsed without our conscious awareness. And like we are not non-existent when in deep sleep, so we will be in the grave.[28] The disadvantage of this strategy is that there appears to be no functional difference between a temporal gap from grave to resurrection and no gap at all if personal identity survives but lacks awareness. Where there is consciousness, the person who survives without a life force is not asleep as such, hence why invest so much effort into defending a claim which posits this type of lacuna?

Further passages suggesting a dualistic understanding include the statements of Jesus in the Gospels. One is "What good will it be for a man if he gains the whole world, yet forfeits his soul? Or what can a man give in exchange for his soul?" (Matt 16:26); another is Jesus on the cross promising the co-crucified supplicant thief that "today you will be with me in Paradise" (Luke 23:43), though the interpretation very much depends on how the sentence is punctuated and whether the comma should appear prior to or after the term "today." Were it to be pre- as in the text, the transition to Paradise would be same-day; were it to be post, it would signify the point at which Jesus is informing the thief, namely that very day, which hardly needs to be mentioned. In any event, as Richard would appreciate, the most natural interpretation might not be the most accurate one, nor does something being widespread guarantee its veracity, for the majority can in fact be in error. Contrary to Richard's view,[29] Paul in 2 Cor 12:1–4 speaks of himself in a thinly veiled way and equates paradise with the third heaven, which implies that paradise is not on Earth, and offers us another point in favor of the idea that one can be absent a body and still be conscious, meaning the thief will be with Jesus in a paradise of some level of heaven, perhaps even that same day, though once again this is not the way Richard sees it.

---

27. Nichols, *Death*, 51.
28. Nichols, *Death*, 71.
29. Nichols, *Death*, 234–35.

Nichols argues that the soul should be understood as a "subject-in-relation" to the body.[30] The difficulty with this stance is that if it were to be the case, then the soul cannot exist on its own, for the intermediate state occurs without a body. Nichols confesses that he is not certain how God accomplishes this feat of placing the soul in a type of holding pattern in the interim period, but postulates that it might simply persist in the mind of God.[31] We could also ask, therefore, whether the soul that survives is the one that obtains at the point of death. If so, then the ones which Alzheimer's patients carry are impaired. Does God intervene to siphon out the soul that most closely reflects the pattern indicative of the kind occurring over the course of one's lifetime?

Plus, the issue arises as to how far back in our evolutionary history we need to travel before we no longer find soul-bearing humans. Does the genus Homo cover all those possessing it but not Australopithecus, or are some Homo species also lacking it? Science, of course, in this case anthropology, and by its own admission, would not consider itself as in a position to comment on when a soul first appeared, since it has no place for one. This also elicits the thorny question as to how a soul could emerge where there was none before. Was Alfred Russel Wallace, a contemporary of Charles Darwin, correct when he supposed that the human mind/soul was the only feature we boast which does not have a natural explanation, and in saying this he was opposed to the majority view at the time, but is a direct divine deposit?

The scenarios appear to be the following: Either the bodies of the initial mythical pair were the spiritual bodies of which Paul speaks in 1 Cor 15, for which there can be no archaeological evidence, and the fall amounted very much to a fall to ordinary physical bodies, an event about which we are unambiguously biblically uninformed, and for which there can only ever be archaeological evidence, or bodies were only ever physical as anthropology describes. There was, however, no time in which we have or can have evidence for such an apparently abrupt change from not-human to human in the archaeological record. Or were the bodies of Adam and Eve (assuming for the moment that there were such for purposes of debate) ever of resurrection quality, though the hypothetical movement from immortal to mortal bodies may suggest otherwise, and human history is but a choreography leading to an improved but still material-spiritual physicality, which could have been the initial state of humans had God willed it, and one wonders why God did not?

30. Nichols, *Death*, 129.
31. Nichols, *Death*, 131.

As mentioned, history may be a probationary period for us so as to earn our spiritual spurs, and please no letters or emails about our alleged inability to merit salvation when we have accounts like Luke 19:1–10 before us, where Zacchaeus "give[s] half of [his] possessions to the poor" as well as promises to give back fourfold to those he has cheated, if any, to which Jesus is pleased to announce that "Today salvation has come to this house." The other difficulty is exactly how presumed immortal bodies could become mortal upon a transgression when we have scriptural evidence mostly for the reverse, omitting the transgression for argument's sake. It might not be more arduous for God to do one over the other.

Back to Nichols, nor can he fathom how free choice arose were it not for the God-human relation.[32] This of course is neither an argument nor is it undermined by his admitted inability. From my perspective, the capacity to relate to God is through the spirit God bestows, which is more than a life force—it is also a conduit for relationality. Hence, in deference to Wallace, it seems like God injects something into the proceedings after all. One must also keep in mind that death is not a prerequisite for a resurrection body. That this idea is false is patently plain, for both Enoch and Elijah were taken by God, thereby avoiding the ordeal altogether. First Thessalonians 4 also maintains that those "who are still alive" will be "caught up" in the air with the ones who have already risen from the dead so as to greet the Second Coming (v. 17), see? some of us *will* get out of this alive. Moreover, at the Transfiguration (Matt 17:1–8; Mark 9:2–8; Luke 9:28–36), Moses and Elijah appeared on top of a mountain together with Jesus—the first of whom being the lone individual of the three having undergone death to that point. While these were not necessarily resurrection bodies as such, one could say that the Transfiguration pre-figured them.

There are also certain disconcerting items to note, one each from Luke's and John's Gospels. In the Emmaus road experience, Jesus' two interlocutors were "kept from recognizing him" (Luke 24:13), but the issue is not whether Jesus could have passed for someone else, the concern is that a resurrected, renewed "spiritual body" (1 Cor 15:44) is indistinguishable from the old form and did not raise any eyebrows. Such a body can vanish from sight (Luke 24:31), but could otherwise seemingly not be picked out from a lineup. John's Jesus can also pass through locked doors (20:19), yet still bears the marks of having been crucified (v. 27). I see a spiritual body as alternatively the Great Oxymoron and the Great Paradox, where the terminology is oxymoronic and the concept paradoxical.

---

32. Nichols, *Death*, 132.

So much for the notion that these new bodies would be a healed or made-whole version of the former ones. Just how different, then, will the hereafter be?—the term is apropos since the "after" will be "here," but one would have thought that the after picture would be noticeably different from the before, even from our current perception. The transfigured bodies of Jesus, Moses, and Elijah, contrary to expectation, would then, perceptibly at least, beat the daylights out of resurrected ones, as per the information which the accounts afford. One would have anticipated a little bit more glory for the latter.

What is more, we are told that at the moment of Jesus' death there was a resurrection of the bodies of other holy people, even prior to Jesus' own (Matt 27:51–52), meaning he might not have actually been the "first fruit" of this event, the same verb form being used for both, namely "raised" for the others (v. 52) and "risen" for Jesus (28:6). One final thing: if at the end persons will be separated as the sheep are from the goats (Matt 25:31–46), and if it is prosecuted along the lines of those who are selfless versus selfish, respectively, then exemplary individuals from some other religious traditions could be candidates, since obviously they too can be selfless (alongside, of course, the essential belief-in-God component [Heb 11:6 and many others]). As a bottom line, Nichols follows Walter Eichrodt who claims that "What survives, therefore, is not a *part* of the living [person] but a shadowy image of the *whole* [person]."[33] The point "remains," though, that there appears to be some remainder which endures beyond death. And not only this, but it is interesting to note that Richard has an atheist in his corner and a Catholic colleague partly outside it.

On a personal note, there was a time, early on in my socialization into Christendom, when I would read little, unless required to, that did not originate from evangelical presses, intending thereby to remain unsullied by forays into what I regarded as unwashed ideas. Now it is the reverse—I read little that comes from these evangelical publishing houses for fear of eye strain as they roll in their sockets. I make exceptions for Richard and Nichols, for instance, by reason of appreciation by association. Plus, it gives me more to write about with little danger of suffering reprisals at the hands of acquaintances, not least of which is the cause of the passing of Nichols, who is perhaps currently determining what is actually definitive about his afterlife postulates. Be well.

Time for another tale.

---

33. Nichols, *Death*, 195n16.

The Plain (or Plane) Truth

BENELUX IS AN ABBREVIATION of the three countries comprising what is known collectively as the Low Countries: in order, Belgium, Netherlands, and Luxembourg. They became settled in the fifteenth century, but prior to this time the inhabitants had little clue as to what lay beyond their immediate environs. Recall that this is fiction. So a group of adventurers decided to explore the area in the event that it would feel the need to expand its territory, given the rise in population, for interest in arable land not already being encroached upon by others. Their desire was that neighbors be neither seen nor heard, especially during weekend times of dissipation, you know, raucous carousing and the imbibing of libations, together with the cranking up of music. Those involved were the two "ads": ranging from adolescents to adults, painting the area red with various and sundry samplings of whatever wine could be made from. A local favorite was dandelion and rosehip, the latter already being red.

The aforementioned group was not composed of tee-totalers, mind you, though they preferred the fruit of the barley and hops. Wine versus beer—a clash ever since. These sudsy souls sought solace (one would not want to be in the line of fire when they uttered this alliteration unless one had a shield for protection, given their juicy lisping dentition) in the prospect of securing ample fieldage for their beloved grain. Their expedition brought them to a scene containing a novelty in the terrain, whereupon they hid behind a tree for fear of being spotted, though the purpose was defeated as they insisted on standing abreast, where at most one would be occluded from view. Yet there they stood, spears at the ready, the sun glinting off the spearheads, which, if viewed from above, traced out an undecipherable message in Morse code. They were reticent to advance.

Jan (pronounced "Yun," and whose brother's name was Hither): What is this I see in the near distance?

Jean-Claude: It appears to be a rise in the terrain.

Jitse (not all their names began with the letter *j*): What is a rise? Everything around us is flat.

Albert (see?): It is like if you were to ride on horseback.

Leopold: Or be on the tops of trees.

Jan: Precisely. But can the ground do so by itself? Does it enjoy this amount of power?

Jean-Claude: It looks rounded in front. I wonder what it looks like from the back.

Jitse: In order to be scientifically thorough, we should not assume it looks the same until we have observed it so as to determine if there is any difference from back to front.

Albert: Science does not give clearance for investigating without protective equipment, for recall asbestos—you don't want to come near it without a mask, otherwise it can lead to mesothelioma. Anyway, who is brave enough to observe that entity from the rear?

Leopold: Quiet, it might hear us and attack.

Jan: Or run off.

Jean-Claude: It seems stationary to me.

Jitse: Is that stationery with an *e*?

Albert: No, the handy rule of thumb is that if you are going to write a letter, then you will need stationery; that is with an *e*, as the term "letter" contains two of them.

Leopold: It's confusing, given that they are homonyms.

Jan: Quite so, but back to the issue at hand, I wonder if it means well.

Jean-Claude: It doesn't appear threatening.

Jitse: Yet not knowing what they are like, they could act benign but then turn on us.

Albert: Best to be cautious.

Leopold: Any takers for advancing?

Jan: Should we rush at it, spears drawn?

Jean-Claude: We could simply meander toward it as though not noticing it, and then pounce; after all, we outnumber it.

Jitse: A fine ruse, but we do not know what it is concealing or what it is capable of, pardon the dangling participle. It might be more powerful than the five of us combined.

Albert: We could send out a scout.

Leopold: And risk the loss of a compatriot? There is safety in numbers.

Jan: Let's all walk toward it with our spears behind our backs so we do not arouse alarm.

Jean-Claude: Then company advance. No movement on its part as yet.

The Plain (or Plane) Truth

Jitse: Steady as she goes, Mr. Zulu. I don't know why I said that. I think it has something to do with being enterprising.

Albert: Coming into clear view.

Leopold: It has for a while now.

Jan: Approaching the anomaly. Proceed to orbit.

Jean-Claude: I can confirm that the base is circular. Also same in back as in front as we suspected.

Jitse: Always best to be certain with empirical evidence. For instance, I do not assume that a chair will bear my weight every time I use it. We have no justification that it will do the job on the next occasion, so better approach it gingerly each time so it could hopefully surprise us with its durability. If so, it's a relief to me and I am elated every time it works. Anyway, the object before us seems to be a good three forearm lengths in elevation, though I could employ a different system of measurement involving another body part, namely four feet.

Albert: What is this elevation of which you speak? you who are so wise in the ways of mathematics.

Leopold: Think of the aforementioned rise discussion.

Jan: It does not make any sound.

Jean-Claude: Maybe it's asleep.

Jitse: Should I poke it with my spear?

Albert: Better let sleeping dogs lie.

Leopold: It does not resemble a canine in the least.

Jan: This could go down in the annals of cryptozoology or -botany. I shall name it the pimple.

Jean-Claude: I shall call it the bulge.

Jitse: Honestly, dear friends, we need not do battle over it.

Albert: Climb on top of it.

Leopold: You climb on top. It might react aggressively.

Jan: Well it's not doing so with all the noise we're making.

Jean-Claude: Perhaps it's limited in its sentience.

Jitse: What are you doing?

Albert: I am waving my hands in front of it to determine if it can see.

Leopold: Why are you assuming where its eyes might be?

Jan: Maybe it has a compound eye like a fly.

Jean-Claude: Well somebody needs to take the reins.

Jitse: Are your insurance premiums paid up?

Albert: He made it to the top unmolested.

Leopold: Brave man.

Jan: How's the view from up there?

Jean-Claude: I can see clear to . . . as far as . . . about the same as ever.

Jitse: Curious creature, doesn't stir at all.

Albert: Of what substance is it? What's it made of?

Leopold: Doesn't appear to be much different from the surrounding land.

Jan: Better not disturb it, otherwise we might be charged with substance abuse.

Jean-Claude: I should stand guard over it here while you search to determine if it has confederates.

Jitse: What for?

Albert: In case it tries to escape.

Leopold: Or call for backup.

Jan: What would you do if it tried something?

Jean-Claude: I could poke it with my spear.

Jitse: That's the second time this has been suggested it. Would that make it pop?

Albert: Only if it were actually a pimple.

Leopold: On the contrary, that could also occur if it is pneumatic.

Jan: Or even if it's filled with air.

Jean-Claude: If it were, I could probably bounce on it like a trampoline.

Jitse: And give it a headache?

Albert: There are several terms in use here with which I am unfamiliar.

Leopold: Best not to inquire.

Jan: I wonder if it objects to this treatment.

Jean-Claude: I am uncertain as to whether it has formed an opinion of any sort on any matter, quite frankly.

Jitse: Maybe it is just playing possum.

Albert (returning): After a thorough search, I can confirm that there is no sign of any others.

Leopold: I say we level it for its insolence in differing from the rest of the terrain.

Jan: I say we erect a structure on it, like an observatory. We'll never be any closer to the stars.

Jean-Claude: Why disturb it at all, instead of simply enjoying it for its anomalous nature?

Albert: That's much too radical for me. What are you, some kind of bulge-hugger?

Leopold: I don't like your tone. Let's try for some other recommendations.

Jan: We could decorate it with art works.

Jean-Claude: Need I remind you that we always need to think in financial terms and make sure we obtain ample returns on our investments, like selling it to a traveling carnival show for its freakishness.

Jitse: I think we should just concentrate on beautifying our surroundings.

Albert: And we need to protect our environment from corporate interests.

Leopold: We're forgetting what we came here for in the first place.

Jan: Of course, you're right, we could use it for beer storage.

What I (Tentatively) Believe

If I criticize the faith positions of others as I did above, then it is only fair that I lay my own on the table for public scrutiny and evaluation. One way to reveal this is to submit both what I believe and what I do not, in addition, of course, to what is outlined above. For me, the best way to inform readers as to what I believe is to differentiate it from the positions and commitments of others.

I consider myself to be a Unitarian Universalist (U.U.) of sorts, but with qualification. Taking each of these two terms in their turn, I do think there is but one God yet with multiple functions. God the Father is creator who holds a claim on all of creation, meaning the entirety of the cosmos. This role also pertains to the providence God bestows upon the world of nature as well as individual and collective human lives, and thus God the Father is also sustainer. God in the capacity of Holy Spirit then draws the misdirected world unto Godself and has visibly done so through the Messiah as an inauguration of what can be expected to reach its completion in the end. As Martin Luther translated the passage 1 Cor 5:18–19: "God was in Christ reconciling the world to [God]self," a variant of the verse as stated in the majority of biblical translation traditions: "God was reconciling the world to [God]self in Christ." A different emphasis, one in which I hope Luther was correct even if not in precision of translation, for even Germans can be "disprecise." Then in taking on this mission (as the Ultimate Missionary) through the Messiah, God becomes redeemer.

As for the second term, I do not hold that all paths lead to God but that, once again, multiple ones do, specifically the three Abrahamic traditions of, chronologically, Judaism, Christianity, and Islam (though I suspect Muslims would likely switch up the chronology so as to place themselves first). I perceive Christianity understood in broad terms as the most direct route but with the other two in parallel. The apostle Paul bemoans that his own heritage, namely Judaism, is not precisely on target. He regards their program as "zealous for God, but their zeal is not based on knowledge" (Rom 10:1–2).

This passage harkens back to Prov 19:2, which states that "It is not good to have zeal without knowledge, nor to be hasty and miss the way." Paul might have had the Proverbs sentiment in mind when he wrote his missive (letter) to the Romans, but what is noteworthy is that the verse in Proverbs was written by a Jew (or Jews) whose perspective was Judaism as constituting that very way, while for Paul it was the Way—that of God's Messiah. And to the extent that "zeal" in both passages can be interpreted as "heart," fortunate then for us that God is invested in and evaluates the heart more so than the head: "the word of God . . . judges the thoughts and attitudes of the heart" (Heb 4:12), heart here functioning as mind does for Westerners like us operating in our inherited Greek tradition.

The U.U.s themselves, however, would bracket these two features as in general they have shed the need for a divinity in the first place, having moved significantly left from their origins, and correspondingly dispensed with the need for a path to it in the second place, both points having progressed well beyond the point of simply being moot. I speak from experience; I have borne the brunt of their misgivings toward divinity when I am invited to speak to them about versions of it. This of course does not stop me from making the attempt. One wonders, then, why they continue to ask.

Correct doctrinal formulation is one thing; proper inclinations another. What would prevent one from reconciliation to God is neither theology nor religious affiliation as much as a heart tuned in to God's frequency or bandwidth. In any case, thank God that God is merciful (Luke 6:36). The standard U.U. may not intend these tenets of faith, but I do, at least provisionally. I have had students who claim that we should use the whole Bible when making a biblical point, but a passage that inconveniently does not buttress one's view is still part of the whole Bible, so what do we do with it if we need to be thorough? What students may intend by this is that we should prioritize the statements or elect to go with what the Bible states the majority of the time, perhaps having in mind that by doing so they are more in a position to bolster their own stance, but that is not utilizing the Bible in its entirety as they claim. In my estimation, the gospel message comes through and I render my allegiance to it despite the inadequacies of both the biblical text and theology in this regard.

Yet, regrettably, what I also believe is the following. If you recall the satirical 1963 Stanley Kubrick film *Dr. Strangelove: Or How I Learned to Stop Worrying and Love the Bomb*, the title character who makes his initial appearance near the end of the film is Peter Sellers, who plays three roles in the film, one of which is a German scientist confined to a wheelchair. When he becomes excited about the nuclear threat that would impact the globe, he has difficulty restraining his arm which seems to have a mind of its own and by reflex will render the Third Reich salute, despite repeated attempts to keep it in check. My impression with the fundamentalist, if not also the wider evangelical, community is that it might also have difficulty keeping in check mentally conjuring up the thought, if not also physically making the sign, of the cross employing the two index fingers held perpendicular to each other and intersecting, when confronting any notion that even sniffs as though it is contrary to cherished beliefs. Even God can work through iconoclasts, signed I. Conoclast.

A Slightly Systematic Look at Theology

Moreover, I do not regard Jesus' alleged divinity as a necessity, though he most definitely needs to be human. The former might very well be a theological requirement, but it is not a biblical one, though it is suggestive—a topic I shall return to forthwith—and theologies do not have the same status as the scriptures themselves—no one I know proposes that "the gospel according to Calvin and his *Institutes*" should realistically become part of the canon of scripture. I believe that Jesus was and is the Son of God, but there were others: Israel in Hos 11:1, Solomon in 1 Chr 28:16, and the Caesars, for instance; he was and is Messiah (the anointed one), but there were others: the kings of Judah and Israel as in the accession to the throne ceremonies outlined in Ps 2, and Cyrus king of the Persians as in Isa 45:1, note—a non-Jew in a non-Jewish land; and Son of man, though this is also spoken of by God to the prophet Ezekiel many times: eighty-three by my reckoning (a prime number for the numerologists among us). What makes Jesus unique in my view is his willingness to undergo suffering and "give his life as a ransom for many" (Mark 10:45), whereas others like the Buddha seek to transcend suffering.

Why not, then, rank the various theological categories according to relative importance? Well, I suspect that most doctrines are non-essential for salvation, though they will differ from one denomination to another. Please be aware that this outline is merely a sketch (I was contemplating using the term "adumbration," whose meaning is as per the foregoing, but my mammy told me never to employ a term with the word "dumb" in it, in the event that it would reflect poorly on its user. I'm glad I listened. Thanks mammy.), and there are many more and complex contours to each of the themes presented. These are not exhaustive but will suffice for our purposes. The least significant, in my appraisal, would be church government—the way in which a church setting is structured in terms of its hierarchy of authority and the extent to which decision-making power rests at the ministerial staff and/or the congregational levels, together with regional bases within the denomination. Next comes the sacraments and how often, say, communion is participated in and whether baptism is for infants or adult believers.

Then is the question of what comes after us with respect to the eschaton and issues like the rapture, tribulation, and intermediate and eternal states, for not all of these categories will be accepted by all denominations, and in any case the end will come to pass regardless of what we believe about it. Each denomination understands its theology as the true version and those of other denominations are wide of the mark—few would knowingly hold to the wrong one. Odd, then, that each sees itself as the actual recipient of the Spirit's leading into all truth. How can this be, one can object, if the truths led into are so different? While in the context of the Lord's Supper, Paul's diagnosis that "No doubt there have to be differences ["divisions" in the previous verse] among you to show which of you have God's approval" (1 Cor 11:18–19), could also be applied to our current concern here, for this is precisely the point—is it obvious as to which ones demonstrate being led into all truth if all sides claim to be in possession of it?

Hardly a rung higher than the previous two is the authority inherent in the scriptures themselves. This itself yields a continuum with the right extreme holding to the Bible as a divine product, the left as a human product, and in the middle a position on its inspired status, where the sacred text is a divine-human collaborative effort: the divine component imparting wisdom to those who have ears to hear; the human as exhibiting gifts, talents, skills, and abilities along with, as stated, fragilities, frailties, foibles, and, yes, faults and failures (the five *f*s) of authorial composition. I personally hold a position left of the midpoint, and correspondingly place this issue near the middle of importance.

Following this is what occurred at the beginning and whether creation was out of nothing or a preexistent chaos, as well as the rate at which it was completed in terms of days or eons. Next in line would be what we believe about ourselves and whether we were specially created or arose through a lengthy and gradual evolutionary process, plus whether we are mono-, di-, or tripartite (or more), that is, how many parts go into our makeup—body, spirit, soul/mind? Nor does there seem to be a time before which our natures were tainted or stained, unless by this is meant the era prior to our having become a member of the genus Homo.

Then come the most significant categories for me, namely (and not whether there is a Trinity or not) the work of the Holy Spirit, or that aspect of God overseeing this, in our regeneration and transformation in the

Christian life; and the person and work of Christ, not so much his alleged human and divine natures but the efficacy of the atonement achieved by his life, death, and resurrection, or that aspect of God effecting it. To elaborate on the latter, the standard belief in soteriology—the theological doctrine of salvation—is the idea that Jesus must be both a representative of humans as well as a substitute for us, sacrificing himself in our place, for had we done so it still would not have amounted to much, since our sacrifice would have been blemished by our transgressions of God's law. Just as with the blood of lambs, bulls, and goats, atonement in the OT needed to be made annually for humans since animal sacrifice is insufficient to make the efficacy permanent. Well Jesus can certainly fulfill the sacrificial aspect, but as for the former, he definitely was human, yet this is not all he was in the traditional sense. If Jesus was like us in every way, then was he also under the curse from Genesis chapters 3 and 4? Or escaping this, were he to have any transcendent component at all, then the requirement of his being just like us (Heb 2:17) is unsustainable.

To have a divine nature means he is not merely a human, which theologically he needs to be. This is an example of a theology forcing us into a position that we would rather not hold, for it means he cannot then function as a savior. In my estimation, it is sufficient for him to be a human and a substitute; we get into trouble when we insist that he must also be like us, for divine persons are not. Plus, we then become committed to the position of his sinlessness (Heb 4:15), whereas no other messiah ever was, nor were they ever sacrificed for us. From my perspective, he needs to have fulfilled God's mission, which he did admirably, not that he ever transgressed. Can it really be said that, knowing both children and adolescents, he never disobeyed his parents? Perhaps so, and maybe as an adult he accomplished this feat, but all we have is some accounts which take a stand without ironclad evidence, such that his life must conform to the theological grid we have imposed upon it. The question this leaves us with is Would Jesus recognize himself in the theological contortions we have placed him in?

Jesus himself, in an apparent retreat to humility and the desire to remain inconspicuous, sternly requested that those whom he healed from infirmities would not broadcast the event to others. The Gospel of Mark is known not only for its use of hyperbole, in its describing the movement of the action in his account with terms of exaggeration, such as "people . . . came to him from everywhere" (1:45), and the transportation of persons from one place to another "immediately" (2:8), as examples, but also employing a strategy known as the "Messianic secret" as in 1:43–45. The purpose of this may have been that Jesus intended to forestall word of his healing reputation to precede him when visiting subsequent towns and villages, otherwise people might become more interested, knowing what we do about human nature, in what he could provide for them rather than hearing the gospel message he came to convey. Their attitude could readily have become "Yeah, yeah, kingdom this, kingdom that, let's all dig for clams at the pearly gates. Heal my aching feet would ya? And I've got this cold sore . . ." To which he may very well have responded not with "I got this," but "Seek ye first, dude" (Matt 6:33; Luke 12:31).

And most importantly, continuing with our list, is not so much the attributes assigned to God but our commitment to God's existence (Heb 11:6) and our following whatever manifestation of God that God orchestrates, convinced that God has set up camp with us in our innermost being, amid the taunts of the atheistic crowd (Ps 42:2–3), revealing that both theism and atheism have long histories.

In a subsection that could be titled "Papers Please," there is more to say about the work of the Holy Spirit. There are five passages I wish to put forward, the first three being preliminary. We are instructed in 1 Cor 6:18–20, in the context of injunctions against sexual immorality, that we should avoid physical indiscretion because our physicality is not only claimed by God but is actually inhabited by the Holy Spirit, thereby becoming a temple of God's presence with us. (BTW, is there a temple in heaven [Rev 7:15; 15:5, 8] or not [Rev 21:22]?) Our very selves and in particular our bodies are not our own but are contested ground for which spirits vie, they being very territorial. This means we are not in a position to do with our bodies as we please, and the decisions we make about them need to be made in accordance with this same Spirit in mind. And within the concentric orbit of the Spirit's influence occur additional passages referring to the extent to which we can self-identify our own spiritual allegiances, and some of them are unsettling. They are about as difficult to corral as gerrymandering electoral districts is easy.

Next, in the context of having established for oneself a position on certain issues, in particular one's diet, including what one considers clean and unclean food and drink, this becomes generalized into the statement "everything that does not come from faith is sin" (Rom 14:23b). Before proceeding, we would be remiss if we did not emphasize that the corollary to this helpful rule of thumb is patently not "everything that does in fact arise from faith is entirely acceptable, even encouraged, so feel free to go right ahead and vilify those not completely entrenched within your belief structure," something that needs to be said though ought not require it, for it is not as obvious as we might expect. Does this also extend, we may ask with perplexity, to difficult ethical decisions which we are fearful to make lest we mean well but may err unintentionally? Plus, the Jesus of the text breaks the stark news to us that "Not everyone who calls me Lord, Lord" (Matt 7:21–23) is guaranteed not to be in the enemy camp, for that may be the very place in which we reside unawares should our spirituality be rendered suspect. This theme will be elaborated upon in due course.

For the time being, corollaries are wonderful things: like the yin and yang, they reveal the counterparts of issues which together comprise the whole and which might otherwise go unnoticed. Yet their strength can also become their weakness, or undesired consequence. Take for example how Jesus enjoins us to sell our possessions and give to the poor (Matt 19:21 and parallels)—a noble, commendable, and admirable pursuit—but there is a concern. Should we undertake it, then we are unintentionally making the purchasers of our goods the very types of persons Jesus was speaking about who will now in turn need to sell their material goods as well in a type of "hot potato" scenario. We are thereby contributing to their delinquency and placing them in Jesus' bad books, though I dare say this ought not prevent us from taking Jesus' advice despite the potentially unwanted results.

Also, from a scientific angle, the default drive for the history of our planet is glacial periods alternating with usually briefer periods of warming known as interglacials—indicating the dominance of ice ages. We are in one of those interglacials and no matter what effect we have on the Earth, we can still expect an ice age on the horizon. Not as readily as without the industrial revolution, mind you, but soon from a geological framework and on a similar time scale. Hence the contrary to warm and cozy in the planetary system is uncomfortably cold, which is more of a threat to life (how many of us could huddle together at more equatorial climes?) than we could ever throw at the world from the opposite direction. Once again, this topic will be developed further below.

Then, having covered the preliminaries, we focus specifically on the Synoptic Gospels—Matthew, Mark, and Luke, since they can be "seen together." Matthew 12:30–32 and Mark 3:28–30 warn us (the term "caution" being insufficiently urgent) that anyone who "blasphemes" (in Mark) or even "speaks" (in Matthew) "against the Holy Spirit" has crossed the line into unpardonable terrain. This offense is the lone one about which no one can ever be absolved. Never. Ever. Period. And the reason Mark broaches the topic is that the religious authorities at the alleged time were insistent that Jesus was able to perform the exorcisms he did by the very power generating the possession in the first place (3:22). Jesus countered by stating that it makes no precious sense for an evil force to "drive out" that same evil force, in essence performing his exorcisms by the power of the very spirit he exorcises, if that evil power seeks to set up camp and reside in such a human abode (3:23–27). In diagnosing that Jesus thereby "has an evil spirit" (v. 30),

Mark maintains that these religious figures have attributed the work of the Holy Spirit to the Adversary (1 Pet 5:8–9 KJV) or Accuser/Satan (Job 1:6). This is inexcusable, and the fate of those who have uttered this blasphemy is assured. They are now beyond redemption as a direct result of their appraisal. No hope remains, and absent hope does not augur well for one's future status. Plus, one figures that it would be strategic on the part of the principalities and powers to tempt people to commit it, for if people do, then the powers win, and as we see even the pious can transgress in this way.

So it is not enough to call Jesus your Lord, it must be done in the right way; and he can forgive everything, except of course the lone offense which cannot be (even if he helps us come to see the error of our ways and, naturally combined with the Spirit's assistance, willingly reverse course? We do not know how far God's grace and mercy extend.). Furthermore, on the one hand, unless we deny ourselves and carry our crosses and follow Jesus we cannot become his disciples (Matt 10:38; Luke 14:27), and on the other, God shows leniency in permitting a multitude of persons from other faiths and traditions to be in attendance and appear before God's throne at history's close, despite not strictly having been followers of Jesus. Representatives from every and all peoples will be found there (Rev 7:9), suggesting that they would be considered honorary Christians. In one case, allegiance to Jesus must be acknowledged outwardly; in another, it is not so much as even mentioned and is accredited to others who might never have heard of him. My position—this one life made all the difference in the world.

When Words Are Not Just Words

Hence, in my estimation, and more often than not, most theological doctrines are of the non-essential type, but the ones that are essential seem to be non-negotiable at least from the scriptural perspective. Nor can the work of theology inevitably ever be complete, since we do not possess all of the works worthy of inclusion into the canon and therefore are not aware of what they may have contained, such as Paul's epistle to the Laodiceans as stated in Col 4:16, as it is no longer extant. One point of qualification, though. Colossians is not widely accepted as authentically from Paul himself, so perhaps we are also hasty in considering the Laodicean epistle referred to in it as potentially canonical. Or does anything purporting to be from Paul, whether authentically or not, automatically warrant canonicity (including, say, previously uncovered directions to the nearest recommended tentmaker in a church's locale)?

Moreover, try this analogy on for size. As CDs can be burned from a vinyl/LP source, and barring the CD from being digitally remastered for the moment, the quality of the material on the CD will only ever be less than 100 percent of what was originally on the record album. Something will always be lost in the translation. You can probably forecast where I am headed. Likewise, in the movement from one language form to another, the translation is not a straightforward one-to-one correspondence, but there are subtleties and nuances not brought forward or at least not properly conveyed. Biblical exegetes appreciate this and so should we.

The exact meaning of a passage is always a matter of interpretation and the interpreter always brings his or her perspectives and presuppositions along on the trip. Each translator adds color to the task and these can and do distort the meaning. Scholars do not shy away from this important job but do recognize the difficulty in being definitive when there are both different and disputed readings. The fact that there are preferred as well as downplayed texts only adds to the concern. And competing translations not only affect biblical studies but can also encroach on the theology drawn from them. In spots this can make a difference. One more obstacle to overcome in attempting to arrive at a conclusive interpretation. This is an ongoing endeavor. We can only stay tuned in the hope that meanings will become clearer with time.

Whereas Richard is counseled, and himself seeks, to remain faithful to the scriptures, my pursuit is to test even those same scriptures against the courts of reason, experience, and common sense, and should they not align, then so much the worse for the sacred text. Besides, the notion of being faithful implies that we are actually serving this text. For me at least, the Bible assists in our becoming "transformed by the renewing of [our] mind[s]" (Rom 12:2), but they too contain thoughts which need to be "take[n] captive" (2 Cor 10:5), contrary perhaps to the perceived self-appointed gatekeepers of those scriptures. They tend to come to the sacred text with the mindset of "if there is anything evaluated as amiss in them, then it is superficial only and there is a reasonable explanation for them, and it is only a matter of disclosing them; so fear not, for we need merely to suspend our judgment until such time as the true meaning rises to the surface by the divine's own supporters."

I commend them on their faith, misguided and unfounded though it may be. They appear to stifle logic when convenient. It is like Thomas Kuhn's diagnosis of how data anomalies are dealt with: they can be ignored or shelved until they can properly be addressed (with the hope that this time will never arise); but rarely are they taken seriously during the confident period of paradigm consensus but carry weight only in periods of crisis states.[1] And not only that, but the position of biblical-supremacy-no-matter-what might well-nigh, in Karl Popper's estimation, be unfalsifiable to boot, for their adamant stance appears to be unshakable and no evidence could count against it, no counter-offensive could ever make a dent in their biblical appraisal. Instead, they must make claims which, if refuted, would undermine their theory, but they make their position invulnerable to it, and that makes it a position not worth considering.[2] Of additional concern is that they imagine they are simply being courageous as opposed to stubbornly naïve.

I myself was once a defender of the scriptures and would fight tooth and nail against all naysayers, and were there to be discrepancies contained in them, then much like Scully in *The X-Files*, I would seek what I assumed must be a logical explanation for them, until such time as the very rationality which I sought to reinforce them failed to materialize and counterevidence reached a critical mass and actually undermined them. Symptomatic of my disquiet is the following syllogism. Premise 1: We are informed in Prov 10:19 that when the verbal becomes verbose, therein lies foolishness; premise 2: The Bible contains many words; conclusion: Why should the Bible be immune from this malaise? To deny this would be contradictorily tantamount to saying "I am way more humble than you." The biblical authors were not seeking philosophical rigor, but we can still apply it on their behalf. This is not to say that they no longer convey wisdom, it is just that the inconsistencies are what we need to live with amid the wisdom. In fact, in spiral-like fashion, sometimes wisdom is required to unravel the wisdom embedded therein.

As a personal admission, there are moments when I struggle with what it means to be "like Christ" in a specific sense. Consider this: the figure of Daniel spoke to a superior "with wisdom and tact" (Dan 2:14). Good strategy when approaching those in power over us. Jesus' own tactics included remaining silent before both Jewish and Roman authorities immediately prior to his crucifixion. Yet in the company of common folk, he did not always display tactfulness. Instead, in Luke 4, at the time of the delivery of his reading in the Nazareth synagogue, for which, by the way, there is as yet no archaeological evidence of such a structure, he impressed those gathered there and was even praised as having "gracious words" (Luke 4:22). But this was quickly lost as he needled the crowd by interjecting two examples in Israelite history when God favored gentiles over the Chosen

---

1. See his *Structure of Scientific Revolutions*.
2. See his *Logic of Scientific Discovery*.

People. Understandably, this did not go over well and the people sought to throw him off a cliff (vv. 28–30). Evidently, the camel express did not get through with the message that this was not good public relations, not that that mattered to him. And the same one of whom it is said "a bruised reed he will not break" (Matt 12:20) also cursed a fig tree (Matt 21:18–22; Mark 11:12–24) (done, of course, for its literary effect, foreshadowing as it did the destruction of the temple).

All four Gospels also note that he "made a whip out of cords" and cleared/cleansed the temple area of all those treating it as a marketplace (John 2:13–17; Matt 21:12–13; Mark 11:15–17; Luke 19:45–46). This was meant to antagonize and make a distinction between true and false followers. Jesus was no stranger to hurling (justified) insults, even at those who invited him as a guest to their home for a meal (Luke 11:37–54). Subsequent to dismantling Pharisaic egos, he turned on the experts of the law who bemoaned that they too were insulted by Jesus' tirade. What followed was his way of saying "Suck it up, princess." He could have used diplomacy and said, "Well now, there are multiple ways of looking at this," but he did not. Nor are we informed that such heated exchanges are ungodly in nature.

He did manage to attract a following, but do not expect your beliefs to be massaged there in the inner circle. He went so far as to call Peter, his main disciple, "Satan" (Matt 16:23; Mark 8:33) for his misinterpretation of Jesus' mission. One could imagine Peter having thought, if not verbalized, the Aramaic equivalent of "Chill dude." Jesus did not care whose views he debunked. All of this combines to inform us that Jesus is not the best source on "how to win friends and influence people,"[3] for he was not out to, say, campaign for public office. Hence despite the usual characterization, amounting to a misnomer, he was not always "meek and mild," as in his vituperative "Woe to you" sections—certain to make enemies—the largest of which is Matt 23:1–36. That in itself could be enough to get one killed—a strategy, incredulously, the religious authorities saw as their only recourse (when in doubt, snuff out, I suppose—now there's an admirable role model for all of us to aspire to [to be read sarcastically]). Are we then to follow in his footsteps in this way as well? Is this what the accounts are advocating? We may feel justified in doing so, yet Paul cautions us that "my conscience may be clear, but that does not make me innocent" (1 Cor 4:4–5). Jesus certainly came to serve (Matt 20:28) and washed the disciples' feet (John 13:5), for instance, but he also came to bring a sword (Matt 10:34) to divide those who are his from those who are not, definitely the opposite of the instruction we are given in 1 Pet 3:8–22 about being a witness to the faith

---

3. The title of a book by Dale Carnegie.

we have and to do so with "gentleness and respect." This opposite is also the portrayal we obtain from the canonical gospels. Or is Jesus the only one authorized to address others in a shake-em-up fashion as a type of foretaste of the judgment to come?

I further believe that the language of those books attributed to Peter, John (both of whom were in Jesus' inner circle), or James (purportedly one of Jesus' brothers) are, at least suggestive to me, far more sophisticated than ordinary fisherman with their limited vocabulary and little awareness of koine (common) Greek could achieve, and it does precious little good simply to declare that the Spirit supplemented their efforts. They were uneducated and likely illiterate (Acts 4:13), so some educated, literate people or persons must have written the works for them or on their behalf. Nevertheless, the Bible can indeed be mined for its rich resources; it is a gift that keeps on giving. It has an inexhaustible wealth of wisdom to offer; it is the most important writing in human history to my thinking, despite its inadequacies. It is not without its faults, largely because the humans who drafted it are not without their faults. And the Spirit can speak through it, for God is not averse to employing all manner of foolishness to get God's point across, and God does so to good effect. We can peruse it with profit and it rewards the diligent seeker.[4] Nevertheless, to "coin" a term, the scriptures are not omnihelpful in this regard.

My bottom line about Richard's material is this: from the scriptural standpoint, where did we get the idea that we go to heaven upon death, and why do we think that there is some sort of existence or survival post-bodily death and pre-resurrection? Because that is where the souls of the martyrs linger—under God's altar in heaven (Rev 6:9, a similar episode occurring in 20:4), and that is where a vast number of persons are gathered, a great throng "from every nation, tribe, people and language, standing before the throne" (7:9) prior to the time of the resurrection.

And now for something completely despicable. The history of Christendom is punctuated with pernicious acts for which we—do not imagine that anyone in the fold can evade it—can and should be justifiably excoriated. Banish the assumption that Protestants are in the clear because the worst

---

4. Speaking of false attribution, I am also suspicious of texts such as the book of Mormon, allegedly delivered to them through the angel Moroni. One must ask about the legitimacy of a spirit offering a revelation concerning Jesus having visited the shores of North America after his resurrection. Why not Europe? The recipient of the information, coincidentally, is an American. But then again, do we end up doing a similar thing with the legendary aspects of our own scripture? And is the fallen angelic domain having a laugh at the Mormons' expense with the name of this spiritual entity? My uncle told me, "Never trust a religious movement with the term 'moron' in it somewhere." I am glad I listened. Thanks uncle.

offenders are Catholics; make no mistake, for the former are in the mix too. The church sought for some persons to be scapegoats for the economic and other ills it was facing. Its methodology was to vilify some people, simply on the basis of preferential hearsay, as those responsible for the difficulties, and in its wisdom—led by the Spirit it assured itself—was misled into torturing and burning witches, among others, and were egregiously self-congratulatory about it. This occurred on both sides of the North Atlantic. Europe and New England are to be discredited for their repulsive enforcements of these policies.

And who can forget the Crusades?

Canada has its own activities in the Aboriginal school system to answer for, in contributing to the deaths of thousands of children merely for the crime of not being sufficiently Christian, that action plainly being un-Christian. We, contrary to the view of some politicians, even the descendants of those perpetrating these acts, bear the shame. Even were we to be generations removed from the events, that does not render us guiltless. Even God nursed a grudge against the Ammonites and Moabites long after their offense (Neh 13:1). Can we escape a similar fate despite arriving on the scene late in the game? And I suspected that, two millennia after the outpouring of the Spirit at Pentecost, we would see much more of our being led by the Spirit into all truth (John 16:13). Evidently not. While it may not be in haste, what is taking so long? We are poor judges of our own and others' spiritual status. Rather, it is before God that we stand or fall (Rom 14:4). This I also believe. (Parenthetically, hence the parentheses, my pappy cautioned me about false advertising when it comes to national names and announced that Canada, being unintentionally Portuguese for "nothing there," is a complete fabrication, for there is much that our land has to offer. I am glad I listened. Thanks pappy.)

I would be remiss if I did not include reference to the following item of concern, and it also does not speak well of human nature. Consider this example: were we to have been among the allied nations in World War Two, we would likely have championed the effort to repel the axis powers. Had we at the time compiled a list of the worst evils in the world, the Third Reich might very well have been in first place. We might also have invoked God to address the ghastly problem, and there were and are those who believe this strategy was effectual. We now find ourselves multiple generations removed from the Nazi scourge, meaning our list of the worst evils has altered—it no longer places the Third Reich at the top spot, for this has been remedied (except for Holocaust victims and survivors) and has become history. Perhaps what was in second place then has become promoted to the gold standard of evils that we wish God would do something about. Should our mindset be that God should at least give attention to the very worst of evils, well if our reckoning is correct, then God may in fact have already done so at the time of WWII.

Here is where the human condition surfaces, to say nothing about how much it was on display in both the axis and allied nations. We have replaced one evil with another, imploring God to act on our behalf. The point is that our view of the worst of evils is time-dependent. God may very well have been active in eradicating evil, but we see only the worst evil at any given time. We tend not to acknowledge the potential eradication programs on God's part because there is always a worst evil ever before us. It becomes a what-have-you-done-for-me-lately attitude on our part, a there-is-no-time-to-concentrate-on-the-past-when-the-present-is-risky-and-we-wish-God-would-shift-focus-from-oblivious-to-helpful-since-we-sure-could-use-it-now mentality. We forget about the past and are never satisfied about the present. And we think God is the problem for delaying intervention, regardless if we also happen to view an interventionist divinity as objectionable and less than scientifically compelling. We would hope for it were we to be in those metaphorical foxholes. Recognizing God as having been instrumental in the eradication of past evils, I suspect, is for those bearing eyes to see. Given what we have observed about human nature, it does not instill confidence that we readily come with the requisite ocular equipment.

Infrequently Asked Questions

Developing the topic even further of what the present author holds to be true religiously, and in the interest of biblical literacy, I offer the following exercise in a Q and A format, some of which we have already broached. There are some of the faithful who treat the Holy part of the Holy Bible a touch too seriously, as though there were a holy quaternity: after the Father, Son, and Holy Ghost comes the sacred text. The Bible is an excellent book, but it is not worth worshiping, and any one denomination does not speak for all of Christendom. Evangelicals tend to venerate the text as the Pharisees venerated the law. But what the evangelical group often does have over some others is a deeper knowledge of the scriptures. Liberals tend to take the writings at face value for better or worse; do with them what you will, but let us be clear as to how they read.

As an example, I do not consider Ezek 23:20–21 to be holy (a passage revisited below). I believe the Bible should be honored as a distillation of God's revelation conveyed to those having had such religious experiences, committed to writing for posterity, and thereby benefiting those who follow in time. But what is holy is to be revered and venerated, and this does not include the scriptures, for that would include all their discrepancies and inconsistencies. Worship, rather, is to be reserved for God alone, quickened by the Holy Spirit, in the name of God's Messiah, and to the glory of God, who is greater than the Messiah (John 14:28b), as the divine chain of command. (Note that the passage does not read "while I am in this temporal frame.")

With this in mind, I find these two verses not only particularly pernicious but also out of character for God to support: "A day of the Lord is coming when your plunder will be divided among you. I will gather all the nations to Jerusalem to fight against it; the city will be captured, the houses ransacked *and the women raped*" (Zech 14:1–2a, italics mine), apparently the only instance that the term "rape" is employed in this sacred text. Now the prophecy related in this chapter has a happy ending, for afterward "the Lord will go out and fight against those nations, as he fights in the day of battle" (v. 3), and "The Lord will be king over the whole earth. On that day there will be one Lord, and his name the only name" (v. 9). Though our focus, no doubt as is true for women in general, is on the rape. Perhaps this is not something that God ordered outright, but, like an air-traffic controller, has given clearance on the runway for it to occur, or, more than that, is calling for it. This may not be God's explicit but permissive will, hopefully with epic reluctance. In any case, it is not normally something we expect from the divine method of operation, yet there it is in the Bible, that "holy" book.

As a side note, I also wonder about the part of the Lord's prayer which requests that God "lead us not into temptation" (Matt 6:13; Luke 11:4), as though this would ordinarily be God's method of operation had God not been petitioned otherwise. No doubt the principalities and powers lead astray and into temptation, as Jesus was to discover and which God might very well have used as a type of rite of passage (Matt 4:1–11; Luke 4:1–13), but oftentimes we and our hearts and their inclinations become the authors of our own undoing. (Perhaps these principalities and powers get blamed or credited for too much.) God, though, may indeed test us and our mettle, and should we persist in rebuffing God's attempts to redirect our course aright and try God's patience, we may be abandoned to our own devices so as to illumine what life might be like absent God.

We continue in our Q and A with the question as to what the term "messiah" means. At least some translations or versions of the Bible contain footnotes, and when the term "messiah" is employed a footnote alerts the reader that it intends those who are anointed by God for a certain role or task. How many were there? The most important one is easy for Christian respondents: it is Jesus as stated in John 1:41 and 4:25. One mention of his having been anointed occurs when Jesus is in the synagogue reading from the scroll of Isaiah and quoting the passage where it states "the Lord has anointed me . . . " (Luke 4:18, quoting Isa 61:1), but this is self-referential, hence it is not confirmatory as actually having occurred. Another passage which is conclusive comes to us from what some regard as Luke's second volume of scriptural witness, namely the book of Acts. In 10:38 Peter attests that Jesus was in fact anointed with the Holy Spirit by God, likely at the time of his baptism, but does this suffice?

Before we get to other messiahs, we pursue the Jesus case. When was he anointed and with what? If one seeks to convert Jewish persons, they would insist that he be anointed with oil as this has been the practice in our OT. Where and when did this occur? All three Synoptic Gospels (by parsing the term, as mentioned, it means they can be "seen together," that is, the Gospel material can be placed in columns side by side and compared) agree that Jesus was anointed with oil by a woman (Matt 26:6–13; Mark 14:3–9; Luke 7:36–39), the former two on his head and the latter one on his feet using perfume, which can readily contain oil of some description. One wonders if some Jewish people would object to the use of a woman to this end (some people are never satisfied). Psalm 2 assists us here for it is a coronation ceremony stating that Jewish kings are God's anointed ones, applicable also to high priests. Thus the question as to how many messiahs there were can now be answered: many. Counterintuitively, were there any outside of the Jewish people? Yes, as mentioned, Cyrus—a Persian no less!—who permitted the exiles to return from Babylon to Jerusalem and is called God's anointed (Isa 44:28—45:1), though there is no mention of oil.

Contrary to a previous contemplation on my part, Jesus could not have been an angel since he accepted worship (Matt 28:9 for example, and several others), which angels are not permitted to do, and Rev 22:8–9 warns us to this end. Perhaps the biblical author mentioned it because it had become a concern. As well, there are certain things Jesus could only have known, assuming it was not merely speculation on his part as a human, from a time before his incarnation, as in Mark 12:25 about the state of humans in the afterlife, particularly their not marrying, since "they will be like the angels in heaven." Note that he did not also say "like me and the other angels." I further have a question about the preparatory procedure Jesus underwent prior to his baptism and temptation, making him ready to embark upon his ministry. There were rabbinic schools, but he probably never attended one, yet was called Rabbi (John 20:16 for instance, and several others), perhaps because of his extensive knowledge of the scriptures and lived wisdom. It was likely more than simply the evangelical panacea of "read (or listen to) the Bible and pray" until he reached the age of thirty (Luke 3:23).

On a related theme, who are God's sons and how many of them are there? As you might suspect, once again the most important one for Christians is straightforward—Jesus as stated at his baptism, agreed to by all three Synoptics (Matt 3:17; Mark 1:11; Luke 3:22). In the first of these, the announcement from God is directed to those gathered there: "This is my beloved son," while the latter two are directed specifically to Jesus himself: "You are . . . ," implying that Jesus required some convincing? And as with messiahs, Ps 2 informs us that kings are sons of God as well.

Furthermore, King Solomon is singled out as God's son in particular (2 Sam 7:14), and Hos 11:1 proclaims that Israel as a nation is God's son—a male. Therefore, the answer to the second question is similar to the first, namely there were many sons. Lastly, does this gender specificity on the part of Israel persist into the afterlife? To the extent that the church is the new Israel, the New Jerusalem then becomes the bride of Christ the Lamb (Rev 19:7; 21:9-10)—and brides are typically female. Does this entail that there was some gender-reassignment surgery in the interim? And while Jesus is greater than both Solomon (Matt 12:42 and parallels) and Jonah (v. 41), he is not equivalent to but lesser than the Father (John 14:28b), even though the two are one (John 10:30), that is, in accord or purpose.

Bringing together two themes, a coin that has high points present but lacks it in other portions due to wear will be assigned a low grade but with high details, thereby acknowledging the senses in which the coin has eye appeal but cannot measure up to a higher grade. Such a coin is one in which the grade is technically correct, though would be undesirable at a higher grade despite its bearing details in other areas, nor would it be generally marketable given the consensus of grading standards according to which set conditions must be in place, hence the coin would earn the adage "It may grade that way, but it won't sell that way." Analogously, in terms of the doctrine of atonement and Jesus' requirement to be both a representative of humanity and its substitute, such a stance can back us into a corner if we insist on its theological import. As can happen, and theologically speaking, this doctrine is one area where theology commits us to endorse a position we might rather not hold. Yet applying the logic of necessity instead, if only God could bear the burden of taking our place for it to be efficacious toward all of humanity past, present, and future, then out of necessity it need be the case that the human-divine line be transcended. Since only God is big enough to cover and encompass the entire world and its estrangement from God, then Jesus cannot be absent a divine component. Neither a mere human nor an angel could accomplish this. The exercise we have just undertaken is not a theological but a philosophical one and displays that a position on Jesus' dual nature can be rational. We will return to this theme presently.

In hyperbolic terms, and this is why I venture all of this coin information, the rest of the coin can be as flat as a pancake, but if the high points are intact, then it grades highly in details. This of course is not the case, but it highlights the fervency with which graders insist upon the details which must be present in order to qualify as a specimen of a certain grade. That seems odd, but the analogous situation which we have drawn throughout also appears to be in place, where biblical emphasis and theology have gone awry. As long as the high point, so would say some who call for biblical and theological rectitude, of "believe on the Lord Jesus Christ and you will be saved" is the shibboleth (Judg 12:6) of the movement, then the remainder can nicely be subordinated to secondary material. Yet the sheer amount of times that the Jesus of the text refers to the shape that the life of faith should take in order to qualify as discipleship, it would seem that carrying one's cross becomes the deciding factor in our soteriological (salvation) status. What constitutes heresy from an orthodox standpoint, salvation is actually and in fact *merited* based upon what Jesus states we must do. This is not the argument Richard intends to make, but becomes the prior one even before we can contemplate the notion of our resurrected life.

Full disclosure: I have had all I can stand when it comes to the liberties taken with the scriptures. Below please find a partial listing of what the Jesus of the sacred texts instructs us to fulfill. Most certainly we are called upon to believe, but this is not all. There are many other passages from other portions of the NT, but we will focus on the words of the Jesus of the text. Those which stress faith and belief are meager at best: Matt 17:20, Luke 17:5–6, and Mark 1:15. That's it, and the last of these combines them with repentance, and Mark 16:16 includes baptism into the mix, together with coming to Jesus and repenting in Matt 11:20, 28–30, yet repentance and baptism are non-negligible acts in their own right to be performed beyond belief, for there are some who believe but continue on in, what Paul would refer to as, their unregenerate living. Notice that John the Baptizer never once uses the term "believe" when people come to him asking what they must do to be saved. He gives practical guidance in addition to "Produce fruit in keeping with repentance" (Matt 3:8; Luke 3:8–14). Not to belittle the role of faith, for it can be both curative and salvific (on healing: Matt 9:22, 28–29; 15:28; Mark 5:34, 36; 10:52; Luke 17:19; and on saving: Luke 7:48–50 [the degree of forgiveness as directly proportional to the degree of love shown]; 18:42); however, the list gets longer for other aspects of the Christian walk and which it ought not to do without:

Matt 5:3-12 on what we are to do and the kind of people we are to be as conveyed in the beatitudes;

v. 16 on our good works are to be visible to others, yet visibly practicing piety and almsgiving for our own gain are to be avoided (6:1-4), and the same goes for prayer (vv. 5-7) and fasting (vv. 16-18);

5:21-22 on shunning anger and insult, as well as lust (vv. 27-28), taking oaths (vv. 33-34), retaliation (vv. 38-39), but loving your enemies (vv. 43-44) and giving to the needy and praying and fasting (6:1-18);

vv. 19-21 on not seeking treasures other than the kingdom, and not pursuing or serving wealth (v. 24);

vv. 25-34 on avoiding anxiety about personal needs, and not judging (7:1-2);

v. 12 on the golden rule about what matters most is how you treat others;

vv. 13-14 on taking the narrow path, your doing must not be from power but the will of God, and act on the words you hear from God, whereas fools do not (vv. 24-27);

10:32-33 on acknowledging Jesus, loving Jesus the most (v. 37), and taking up your cross and following him (v. 38; Mark 8:34);

Mark 9:35 on being servants to all people;

Matt 18:21-22 on forgiving;

Luke 10:29-37 on loving your neighbor;

12:1 on avoiding hypocrisy;

v. 48 on giving God returns on God's investments (along with Matt 25:14-30 and Luke 19:11-27 on the parable of the talents, which, it must be stated, is couched in very monetary terms and should not be taken as referring to talents of personal abilities only);

14:7-14 on giving to those who cannot repay and humbling yourselves;

v. 33; 16:19-31 on giving up all your possessions;

15:7, 10-32 on repenting but also about the presumption and hypocrisy of the Pharisees (and Matt 20:1-16; 23:1-36; Luke 16:14-15; 18:9-14);

18:1-8 on praying and not losing heart;

19:8-9 importantly on giving half of one's possessions to the poor, righting fraudulence, seeking restitution, and making reparation *as translating into salvation*;

21:19 on enduring to the end *so as to be saved* (also Matt 10:22; 24:13; Mark 13:13)—which implies that our salvation is not settled before the end?;

Mark 13:33-37 on being aware, alert, watchful, awake, and on guard;

Matt 25:31-46 on service to others is needed;

Luke 15:7, 10 on repentance being important, but verses 11-32 on some need to repent but their piety stands in the way;

Matt 28:18–20, and only there, on making disciples of all nations;

and Luke 22:19, and only there, on taking communion in remembrance of Jesus.

Get the picture? This is not an exhaustive listing, and there are some parallels of them in other Gospels, but these make the point that the mindset of "turn from sin and you're in" is lacking, for there is much which that entails as qualification and to which I must say God help us in this.

Looks like we are on a roll, so let's keep going. What is the difference between resurrection and resuscitation? In the former, a person is clothed with an indestructible body, outside of being "thrown into the lake of fire," (Rev 20:15), which is not the kind of thing one can recover from; in the latter, one can expect to pass away a second time, unless of course one happens to be alive at the time the Messiah returns (1 Thess 4:13–17).

What is the most famous resuscitation? This of course is Lazarus in John 11:43–44, who was raised to life by Jesus. One wonders, though, given that raising someone from the dead is not a daily occurrence, one might even venture that, likely on most systems of measurement, it is an earth shattering event, why then it was not included in the other three canonical Gospels. Why did it not make the editorial cut? Did the other Gospel writers agonize over it and conclude "nah, let's opt [say] for the pericope on paying taxes to Caesar instead, since everyone has vested interest in their purse strings, right? Early marketing strategy suggests and recommends that this is bound to capture a larger audience (Matt 22:21; Mark 12:17; Luke 20:25). Additionally, Jesus must no doubt be advocating for the separation of church and state to boot."

Matthew 27:52–53 also informs us that upon the moment of Jesus' death, "The tombs broke open and the bodies of many holy people who had died were raised to life. They came out of the tombs, and after Jesus' resurrection they went into the holy city and appeared to many people." The same commentary applies to this as well: why would a monumental occurrence such as this be found in only one of our four Gospels? (Besides, if they are likely resuscitated as opposed to resurrected, did they rise only to die again? Hardly an enviable proposition.) If this sounds suspicious, one may be on to something. Best sometimes to focus on those passages attested to by multiple Gospel sources. Here is something that *is* multiply attested: the Messiah is the firstborn from the dead (Rom 8:29; Col 1:15, 18; Rev 1:5) (despite Colossians perhaps not authentically from the apostle Paul). That much is indubitable, which means it can't be dubited(?)—that's just science.

BTW, FYI, I also happen to like the much overused John 3:16 (where would it be without sporting events for broadcasting it?), for it tells us that God is a "world-o-phile," who in the attempt to redeem it considered the

Messiah expendable. God is exceedingly invested in this world and luxuriantly given to life forms. What I remain agnostic about, though, is why certain groups place so much energy and effort into the authority, even inerrancy or infallibility, of the scriptures when they contain obvious, even glaring, discrepancies and inconsistencies. Perhaps it is the trepidation at least on the Protestant end that, having shed the need for popes and church councils, taking away the Bible's authority, as the lone remaining one, would leave them without the spiritual security afforded by the scriptures, which they desperately seek to perpetuate and cannot seem to do without. Nor am I certain as to how this insistence fails to amount to bibliolatry and how groups like these can fail to recognize it.

Inspired by these sentiments, for more than the Bible can inspire, we can rephrase such biblical statements as John 3:16 and Mark 2:27–28, Jesus speaking in both, and please excuse the gender specificity in the latter: "The Sabbath was made for man, not man for the Sabbath. So the Son of Man is Lord even of the Sabbath," into the following: "Jesus is for the world, *and* the world for Jesus"; "the Code/Law/Torah is for humans, not humans for the Code/Law/Torah"; and "the Bible is for humans, not humans for the Bible." To reiterate, we do not serve the text; we were made neither for the law nor the biblical text. Hopefully this covers it.

Despite being one of the greatest gifts ever bestowed upon humankind, there is something "wrong" with the law (Heb 8:7): it is "weak and useless" (7:18) because it "made nothing perfect" (7:19), which in turn makes it "obsolete" (8:13) compared to the new covenant. This gift is flawed in that it is "powerless" to save (Rom 8:3), for it only revealed sin and never removed it. That required an even greater work of God—the one who not only talked the talk but walked the walk, showing us how it's done. The law's delivery is also less exalted than the one who delivered it, and by itself lacks the impress to widely take captive the hearts of persons, otherwise there would be many more in the Jewish fold. The supplement it needed was the story of the one who fulfilled it, for that's the impressive part.

Nevertheless, whatever criticisms we bring to writings in general and level against them can and should also apply to the scriptures, since it is not immune from conventional criticism, given that conventional humans crafted it. The Holy Spirit might very well be a co-author, but once concepts are framed in ordinary language, they suffer from being lost in translation as the sublime must work with and be subject to the mundane, which is where we meet those ideas. In this way, the glories of the holy, when communicated into how we should live, take the shape of ordinary law, though it implies something more transcendent.

If the scriptural authors were "carried along by the Holy Spirit" (2 Pet 1:20–21), though the passage is specifically in reference to prophets and prophecy, then they were also driven into inaccuracies, for instance comparing the aforementioned difference between Luke's account of the aftermath of Paul's conversion in Acts to Paul's own report in Galatians. Evidently Luke the amateur historian did not have access to this Pauline epistle, or if he had he ignored it for agenda purposes. Plus, "no prophecy of Scripture came about by the prophet's own interpretation" (v. 20) does not guarantee that the next phase of committing the prophecy to writing was flawless. And the writer of these verses himself might not be a witness above reproach, for it is unlikely that the apostle Peter ever penned or dictated these words, nor would he have lived long enough to do so, given the estimate of when his epistles likely arose together with his assumed lack of multilingualism.

Admittedly, the Bible is useful for discernment, among other things (2 Tim 3:16–17), though at times I find that I still have some difficulty, as another admission, discerning the difference between God lighting a fire under me and my own impatience. I am also suspicious of those who might claim that they are led by the Spirit, while others making the same claim about something in opposition to the former must then be in error. This is definitely something we want to get right, for some have acted on their belief in being Spirit-led with devastating results. Witness the blood spilled (or other obscenities) in the name of multiple religious postures. We do not want to be found presumptuously with this blood on our hands. Forever is a long time to reflect on it.

Why then am I liberal? Because I do not have confidence that the scriptures are offering the straight goods; or maybe there are not even many to deliver. Too many human hands have been involved in the composition of the biblical books for there not to be human elements in it, and at that point we are well within our rights to ask if there is corresponding distortion. As I alluded to earlier, scripture even militates against itself. There is a development from conservative views of a one-to-one correspondence between actions and just deserts, as in the books of Psalms and Proverbs, to a much more complex assessment of "the wicked get what the righteous deserve" and vice versa, as outlined in the books of Job and Ecclesiastes. Which in itself begs the question as to whether divine justice policy has an evident rhyme or reason in our present sphere. What then can be said about the Spirit leading into all truth (John 16:13)? Is there less of it to be had in some books in the wisdom literature section of the biblical canon than others? Half the truth perhaps? And what becomes most perplexing, to which evangelicals must give an answer, is God in the habit of telling half-truths?

I am not denying God, only disapproving of the biblical and theological portrayal of God, but not of course in its entirety. Rather, to reiterate, I advocate for God, just not in the usual fashion. While the depiction of God in the OT includes essentially showing no mercy as in the book of Joshua, specifically 11:11, 14, and 20, the NT is often though not always expressing God's merciful side, as in Luke 6:36, prompting some to announce that we have before us two different divinities, although this need not be the case. We are biblically advised not to "believe every spirit, but test the spirits to see if they are from God" (1 John 4:1), after all, and by all means. For there are some spirits that are not from God, especially in the scriptures, Jesus having encountered one in the desert (Matt 4:1; Mark 1:13; Luke 4:2).

If we are to follow God's example, then are we to lie when divinely directed to do so, as was the lying spirit dispatched by God (1 Kgs 22)? And keep in mind that the God of the text is not above and beyond employing "a messenger of Satan" to torment the apostle Paul with "a thorn in [his] flesh" lest he become conceited about all the revelations he was receiving from God (2 Cor 12:7–10). If not, if there is something amiss with this strategy, then is the God of the text the complete role model for us? I am a champion of the cause, but the biblical cause is sometimes wide of the mark, meaning it is acceptable to be sceptical when approaching material that does not sit right, for we are, after all, enjoined to "Test everything" (1 Thess 5:21). As outlined above, the Christian life is not always a one-to-one correspondence in terms of biblical-situation-to-contemporary-application, but is seasoned, *even tempered*, with reason and experience through God's spirit to assist us in being *inter alia* (among other things) *even-tempered* about the faith.

The difficulty with our use of the Bible is that we come to it with preconceived notions and make the text conform to the scheme or grid we have placed upon it, to the point where it can no longer surprise or challenge us with the depths of its wisdom or how we are to apply it to our contemporary circumstances. My attempt here is to illumine those passages—the highlights of the contra-party line—which could work toward the shattering of our preconceptions so that we could hear anew what they have to say to us. With our grids firmly in place, we have distorted the message and have become unteachable. I have seen this in some of my students as well as in some fellow congregants. Being subject to the dismantling of our views can be daunting, but, like a bad tooth that needs extraction, it is worth the momentary discomfort.

Besides, we are enjoined to contemplate on that which is commendable (Phil 4:8) (presumably together—and this is the more difficult part—with the corollary of avoiding entertaining the opposite), which is neuro-anatomically and -physiologically prescient, for a change of mind will cause different dendritic pathways to form in the brain, and they will be reinforced with repetition, to the extent that the idea of "the power of positive thinking" actually has some merit. If we modify the way we think, we can alter in a non-negligible way who we are. Both Rupert Sheldrake, as outlined two volumes ago, and Norman Vincent Peale in a limited way are insightful in this regard.

Back to the issue at hand, theology is worse off than the scriptures, for theology is not even sufficiently biblical. Despite its difficulties, the sacred text has no inclination to pursue the Greek interest or penchant for systematization, so systematic theology does not even rise to the level of the scriptures from which they seek to draw. As it stands, as mentioned, I find it curious the fervency, nay zeal, with which these ancient documents are defended, as though one's faith hangs in the balance. There are those of us who do not resort to special pleading, that is, treating the text as though it were above criticism, failure to do so amounting to a heresy charge. In itself that would not be such a bad thing, for a few of those heretics might actually have stumbled upon something worthwhile. Liberals can still have a strong faith, even if not in the text.

The Parabolic

I wish to proceed to what Jesus was exceptionally good at, namely the telling of parables. Two of which I have in view come from Matt 13:44–46: "The kingdom of heaven is like treasure hidden in a field. When a man found it, he hid it again, and then in his joy went and sold all he had and bought that field. Again, the kingdom of heaven is like a merchant looking for fine pearls. When he found one of great value, he went away and sold everything he had and bought it." The first thing to notice is that in the former, the purchaser did not inform the owner of the field that it contained treasure, and Jesus, perhaps in an ancient form of "finders keepers" did not chide him for it, but probably considered it a shrewd move on his part.

Nevertheless, these two short parables emphasize the great value of the kingdom, ranking it as of top priority for those who have been given the good sense to perceive and pursue it. In the first, discovering the treasure is unintentional; in the second, locating a prized pearl is intentional.[5] Yet their interpretation should avoid the two extremes of spiritualizing them, such that one ought to give one's entire life to God, for while true is not their intent per se, but is more akin to the counsel given the rich young man/ ruler in Matt 19:21; Mark 10:21; and Luke 18:22: "If you want to be perfect,

5. Guthrie and Motyer, *New Bible Commentary*, 834.

go, sell your possessions and give to the poor, and you will have treasure in heaven. Then come, follow me." To insist, therefore, that the parables must have an immaterial emphasis and can only mean the capitulation of one's inmost being and not one's assets would in my appraisal be a distortion. Having said this, however, the other extreme of actually placing a price on the attainment of the kingdom (as in Martin Luther's invective against the perverse church policy of the selling of indulgences for blessings to be bestowed upon those who have passed away), despite its sounding on the face of it like an admissions ticket to it that can actually be purchased, would be hyperbolic.

In any case, and completing our look at generosity and obedience, notice in the parable about the two sons whose father told them to "go and work . . . in the vineyard" (Matt 21:28–32), the son who declared he would not follow his father's instruction but did so anyway is said to have fulfilled the will of the father. What we are not informed about, however, is whether that son did so without grumbling, since that is what the heavenly Father also wishes, and if the son did grumble, was his act still accepted? To claim that he carried out the task willingly is speculation—a Hollywood script with a happy ending—yet could still be true. Bottom line: as Paul asserts, "God loves a cheerful giver" (2 Cor 9:6–7).

Since causes have effects, then of course comes the corollary, as intimated above, in that the ranks of the imperfect would increase had the rich young lad accepted Jesus' instruction in the way of those who would purchase the former's possessions in question, who would then in turn need to dispense with them so as to lift themselves out of the hole they have dug for themselves by their purchase, and about whom the parables give no noticeable accommodation. Or do they simply become more of the living dead about whom Jesus spoke (Matt 8:21–22; Luke 9:59–60)? (While we are on the topic, is the corollary of 3 John 11, stating that those perpetrating "evil ha[ve] not seen God," that those who instead do good have in fact seen God?) These parables should not desensitize us to the fact that one man's gain does not make attendant problems disappear but might actually compound them, and they can generate a ripple effect whereby the number of those who need to hear the parable's message will multiply. Some might even be inclined to complain, given that an itinerant ministry requires financing and therefore does not proceed on its own, that Jesus' needs were provided for by privileged women in his entourage from their own resources—some of whom did have the means to do so (Matt 27:55–56; Mark 15:40–41; Luke 8:1–3), thereby making his statements about austerity measures carry less weight, though he does announce that he has "nowhere to place his head." Or, who knows, Jesus might have spent his artisan/carpentry vocational years saving up for just such an eventual ministry (the Bank of Galilee at the time hopefully offering a competitive return). After all, he waited about thirty years before he undertook his commission (Luke 3:23).

In a contrary vein, the same Jesus who was concerned for the physical needs as well as the health and well-being of the crowds in Matt 15:32 and Mark 8:1–3, in the events leading up to the second instance of feeding the multitude, wanted to ensure that the people who had been with him for three days and had not eaten during that time would not be overcome with hunger on the return trip to their domiciles, was also the Jesus who rightly castigated the Pharisees for elevating their tradition over God's commands by requiring their followers to wash their hands prior to a meal. The difficulty arises in his not being duly concerned about the hygiene of not doing so (Matt 15:1–3; Mark 7:1–8). While not insisting that Jesus be a health professional (God having been known to inflict diseases and plagues on occasion: Exod 15:26; Lev 14:34; Deut 7:15; 28:60; 2 Chr 21:15—my intention being to disabuse conservatives of making glib theological pronouncements about the God of the text as healing only and thus misrepresenting the text), we might wonder why the correlation between unsanitary hands and vectors of disease was not in the disciples' experience and observations over the course of a lifetime and thus raised to the level of causation in their minds. Or was it not until the time of Benjamin Franklin that the non-scriptural adage "cleanliness is next to godliness" became apparent (leaving aside the pop-theological nature of the sentiment itself)?

Plus, there are two consecutive pericopes where Jesus appears at his most aggressive. Recall in Matt 21:12–13 (together with Mark 11:15–17; Luke 19:45–46; and John 2:13–17), where he clears or cleanses the temple, and directly thereafter come verses 18 to 22 (and Mark 11:12–14, 20–24), wherein he curses the fig tree for not bearing fruit. A touch testy we see. We can only hope that he was driven to employ this approach sparingly. But whence this animus? Perhaps it was because he was hangry (v. 18) (I know it gets the better of me sometimes). But where were the women who were attending to his needs? He seems to be needy there at that very point. And as a side note, in the second passage he makes reference to a mountain which, if we had sufficient faith, can be transported into the sea (v. 21). In the interests of safety, though, we must object that such activity can imperil populations with the tsunamis that would likely result. Here's hoping no one literally takes Jesus up on this.

Back to the topic of parables, their significance is such that they lull one into a false sense of security in assuming that those in the line of fire in their content are some people or group other than those in the in-group audience, and that the latter are therefore in the clear, believing that they can cheer from the sidelines or spectator's gallery, "Yeah, take that you Pharisees," (or insert whichever enclave is appropriate, that is presumed to be in the cross-hairs). "The emphasis couldn't be on us, could it?" Luke 12:13–21 is just such a caution. The parable warns against complacency in focusing on a rich agriculturalist who depends on the abundance of his crops to propel him into a state of rest, content in his good fortune. The trouble is we "do not know what a day may bring forth," so we should "not boast about tomorrow" (Prov 27:1).

In the parable, the rich fool did not even make it to the next day, for on that "very night [his] life [was] demanded [of him]" (Luke 12:20). The moral of the story is not "be sure to have a good insurance policy on your farm in case conditions deteriorate," but consider God to be your insurance policy whose kingdom is secure, prompting us to "store up for [ourselves] treasures" there instead (Matt 6:20). But this is not all, and we err if we imagine it is, for the point could also be applied to us and, say, our investment strategy for our retirement plans—if we are fortunate enough to arrive there, and if we are able, we might contemplate directing our energies and efforts toward the service of those who need it, rather than a life of ease. So the parable, as it turns out, is about us or at least includes us after all, and we are warned by Jesus himself: "woe to you who are rich, for you have already received your comfort" or consolation (Luke 6:24).

Moreover, how shall we describe our need for an injection of God's work in our lives? Well, let's see if we can improve on the tract known as "The Four Spiritual Laws." There was a time before which humans had ethical antennae. These proto-humans acted without guilt when perceived infractions were committed by other members in the social group. Other animals (for such we are) express aggression when they consider their territory or repose as being infringed upon by others of the same or other species. Organisms will protect their interests and those castigated for perceived misdeeds yield to a stronger member, but may do so without remorse, and merely take their lumps, from which they can with any luck recover, so they bow to a superior power and leave to fight another day, hopefully against an inferior member. Eventually, pre-humans came to recognize a moral component to the proceedings, where responsibility for behavior was felt, and either justification for actions was sought and rationalized or they might have been stricken with an ill-feeling for perpetrating some ill, once one could perceive from the perspective of the injured party ("how would you feel if . . . ?"). There arose a rift externally between individuals and internally in terms of being torn between what we should have done and what did transpire.

We became human when, *inter alia*, we experienced alienation externally and dis-ease internally—cognizant of a gut-level disturbance we could not shake. God enters the fray and communicates the need to rise above a natural way of doing things, wherein one nurses a me-first mindset, and in its place inserts a concern for the other. After a lengthy period of unwillingness to conform to the latter as well as a fleshing out of what kind of shape this proper day-to-day living ought to take, God imparts a point-by-point outline of injunctions, together with a "top ten" list, enjoining the recipients to comply to the best way of living with one's neighbors.

The intent was commendable, yet, as humans will, we either found ways around the code to our own advantage or became prideful about our compliance with it and came to trust in our abilities rather than point to the code's author as the source of its benefits, or both. The Pharisees of the text, for example, were no longer teachable. They reckoned that having been given God's marching orders, they had all the information they needed to live an admirable life and did not require God's further input. They proudly presumed that they had completed all that was to be in tune with God, but then along came Jesus who proclaimed that theirs was not enough, to which they took offense. This is where they erred—they knew what to do but became confident in their own abilities to fulfill the code under their own steam and thus went astray. The efforts to return them back from unsuspected personal exile went unheeded. God then attempted to impress upon the people that they were either unwittingly or blatantly missing the point. In not honoring neighbors, they were not honoring God. Some people just won't be told.

God's strategy became one of sending messengers to prompt the people back into line, but this did not serve its purpose. Nothing less than a personal encounter would do, since all other available options had become exhausted. God's right-hand man was commissioned with the task of embodying the spirit of the code beyond its text. If the laws had been sufficient, then Jesus would not have been needed, but as it stood, the code by itself could not rescue, for one can follow the code but still be a code-breaker, and this is one difference between overt and covert behavior. One can shun murder outwardly but can still commit it inwardly through hatred or even resentment through anger, which is not so obvious, though it is to God who weighs the heart. Hence God is not satisfied with the outward approach alone, meaning the code needs to be followed by its spirit and not just its letter.

In this sense Jesus made improvements on the code. The code is effective when it comes to illuminating missteps but does not overcome what Jesus referred to as outward whitewashed tombs that may look stately on the outside but conceal decay within. He showed us an even better way than outright legalistic observance, for by completing the latter we can still leave the main thing undone—love of neighbor, which is equivalent to loving God. The writer of the book of Hebrews even states that the code "was weak and useless (for the law made nothing perfect)" (7:18–19). Instead, Jesus opened our eyes to cultivating virtue, which God calls us and empowers us to take on. So to truly rise above human nature, we require God's assistance, for only then can our nature be truly human. God's right hand man showed us how, and with his help we can do likewise.

What this is not is a monopoly-holding business owner saying, "you need what I've got and I'm the only one with it." What it is, rather, is an offer to be granted that which we could not achieve on our own. To decline the offer is to lose what we have or hope to gain. Another human characteristic is to want love without justice for ourselves, but justice without love for others. This also needs repair. I am not sure how many laws this is, but it is so long-winded that it must be more than four. Being concise does have its advantages if it can avoid the simplistic.

A few additional comments are in order to round out our discussion. The theological portrayal of Jesus that has been bequeathed to us is that he led a sinless life, hence it is odd that he would undertake John the Baptizer's baptism for the forgiveness of sins. Yet there it is in all three Synoptic Gospels. The author(s) of Matthew perceived the problem and anticipated the objection and so wrote a rationalization, contained in no other canonical Gospel, so as to cover the passage with feasibility. He (they) have Jesus state in essence (and I am paraphrasing) "let's do it anyway; it's the right thing to do" (3:13–15). In the Fourth Gospel, namely John, there is no explicit reference to his having been baptized, only implicitly so (1:29–34). This Gospel, taken to be the most recent of the four, perhaps dealt the least directly with the theological objection to his baptism by mentioning it only peripherally.

But this is not all: so as to hammer home a previous point, on the issue of Jesus' anointing, the Judaic tradition is such that messiahs must be anointed with oil. This did not escape the notice of the Gospel writers—they had to get him anointed somehow before it became too late and he was executed. Enter the woman who pours oil on him in preparation for his burial, though that was probably unbeknownst to her (Matt 26:6–13; Mark 14:3–9; Luke 7:36–50). I sympathize with those who consider this to be an add-on with the qualifier of her being remembered in perpetuity for having done so (Matt 26:13; Mark 14:9), potentially so as to ensure that the episode remains in scriptural format. Why am I mentioning these in possible embarrassment for certain segments of the theological community? Well, because the question arises as to whether Jesus did not become Messiah until such time as he fulfilled all ritual protocols. Another moral of our report is warranted: in all cases it is God we serve and neither the Bible nor theology, and we can find solace in that the notion of systematization is a Greek innovation. We could very well be witnessing the machinations on the part of Gospel writers. And should one adopt the mantle of a discrepancy hunter, one comes from within the same gospel. In Jesus' own words, John's Gospel states that he was both not sent into the world to condemn it (3:17) and he came into it for judgment (9:39). Subtle distinction!

On the topic of Jesus' resurrection capabilities, if he could move through locked doors (John 20:19), then why did the rock (and why was it called a stone if it was so large? (Matt 28:2; Mark 16:4), need to be rolled away first? The one feat could have been equaled or surpassed by the other. It would have been more impressive, which is not necessarily God's intent, for others to have rolled it away in order to discover that the corpse was nowhere to be found and had nowhere else physically to go (absent the assistance of still others who could have rolled it away and then back again, assuming the task could have been carried out without anyone's notice). Joseph of Arimathea by himself, for there is no explicit indication that he had help, could roll the stone into place. Two things: it could not have been large if only one able-bodied male could move it, so the women (plural) need not have fretted (Mark 16:3), yet it would need to be large enough for a supposed angel to be seated on (Matt 28:2–3), though in Luke 24:3–4 there were two "men" who stood beside the women in the tomb. Similar to the accusers of Jesus before the Sanhedrin whose statements did not agree (Mark 14:55–59; Matt 26:59–61), these tomb accounts do likewise. What then, after all, is holy about these and other biblical inconsistencies? Evidently, he who lives by Greek logic will fall by that same logic.

Larry Hurtado devotes a volume to the manner in which Jesus was given due reverence by his disciples after his ascension. Jesus was seen to have been exalted in status to God's right hand and as such was deserving of worship as God's "chief agent." As the title of his work makes plain, there remains *One God*, meaning Jewish monotheism is preserved, and *One Lord*, implying that this monotheism has undergone an "innovation" or "mutation," by which worship is shared among the two, or three if one counts the Holy Spirit. Hurtado's research findings inform him that this Christian community "had visions and other experiences that communicated the risen and exalted Christ and that presented him in such unprecedented and superlative divine glory."[6] We might be driven to ask in response, though, unprecedented for whom—Jesus or his followers, or both? Is Hurtado either suggesting or leaving the door open to Jesus as not having possessed

---

6. Hurtado, *One God*, 126.

"superlative divine glory" in his preexistent or pre-incarnate state, or even that he had one? We leave this as an open question.

To end on a higher note, the NT is a compilation, yea compendium, of Jesus' greatest sermonic hits. But, as mentioned above, Matt 16:5–12 offers an attempt at witticism that went nowhere: he and his disciples were in a boat and the disciples lamented that they forgot to take victuals, namely bread, along on the journey, to which Jesus says, "Be on your guard against the yeast of the Pharisees and Sadducees." The disciples looked at each other and surmised that he said this because of their lack of bread. Tough crowd. After Jesus undoubtedly brought his hand up to his forehead and shook his head, he said, and I paraphrase, "No, yeast: teaching, get it?" They were not to be taken in by the traditions of the religious authorities. Presumably the disciples were untutored in the fine art of puns and plays on words. Yet here we have an occasion when Jesus engages in humor and hence is not unfamiliar with it. A Messiah with a satirical edge. Cool.

Jesus was also partial to feasts, and the arc of the biblical narrative is leading to one of his, or his Father's, own. In a parabolic wedding feast there appear to be a hierarchy of positions in the kingdom to come that is likely being pointed to (Luke 14:7–14). The takeaway is to humble ourselves and take the lower seats at the feast so that you may be promoted, as opposed to presuming to take a higher seat and run the risk of being demoted. Even worse, in another parable about a wedding banquet, the door might actually be shut to us (Matt 25:1–13) (although Rev 21:25 informs us that the gates will always be open). The kingdom of God/heaven might not be "a matter of eating and drinking" (Rom 14:17), at least as it concerns this life and what may be eaten in it, but there will be comestibles in the next (Rev 22:2). As for what will be on the menu at Jesus' wedding banquet (Rev 19:7): lamb I suspect (only because there would be no seafood if there were no longer to be any sea, as the earthly Jesus would have been used to from the Sea of Galilee, unless the fish are taken from lakes and rivers).

Lastly, given the above, in terms of the controversy surrounding Jesus' marital status, perhaps he made himself a eunuch for kingdom purposes and declined marriage, as the statement he made about it, found only in Matthew's Gospel, might very well have been an implicit self-reference (Matt 19:10–12). Maybe he accepted it in his own life. And lest we forget Paul, who could have done the same (1 Cor 7:6–8), in his famous love chapter, namely 1 Cor 13, verse 5 claims that love "does not insist on its own way" (NRSV), yet God insists on God's own way. Does this mean God is not loving or that God is not the proper role model for us? No, for, like love, God does not force us to follow God. One point that ought to be made, though, is that the depth of one's knowledge of God and God's economy needs to be matched by the depth of one's dedication to God; the more one learns about God and God's ways, the more is expected about one's devotion to God and should give us the impetus to follow.

Much of the foregoing is in the interest of staying one step ahead of atheist detractors by stealing their thunder and demonstrating that devoted Christians can approach the sacred text as critically as they.

After such a lengthy examination, we are no doubt ready for some additional lighter fare, this time, as in the above parables, two consecutive short ones.

Old Souls

A WOMAN MAKES HER way to a fountain situated in a pond in a wonderfully wooded park east of the city, having ample space for soccer games and a playground for kids, and the trees themselves providing lots of shade for those sultry summer days. But this is autumn, officially known as "sweater weather," and baseball games have given way to flag football, and picnics have been replaced by roasting hot dogs over a fire. The woman surveys the fountain area and notices the man in the wheelchair, whom she has visited weekly, sometimes in his home, sometimes here when the weather cooperates, for several years. She approaches and sees his face light up.

"Hey Judy," he cheers, using his good right arm to raise a hand.

"Hey yourself, Sam," she responds, lamenting that the wheelchair reflects his inability to rise from his seat. Sam was wounded in Vietnam, wounded, that is, in body, but not so much in spirit.

"How is my favorite social worker?" he asks.

"Same old same old," she replies, "you know, keeping our heads above water."

"Family doing okay?" he inquires.

"Just fine, never a dull moment with teenage kids around."

"I can imagine. I sure do appreciate you dropping by and helping me feed the ducks. Nice day for it."

"Wouldn't miss it. The family can fend for themselves for a while."

"I'm sure you could use a break too."

"Yeah, I like it when the house is quiet. And here I find the sound of the water soothing. But how is your ongoing battle?"

"You being here eases the burden. That phantom limb of mine keeps acting up. I wish my brain would recognize that there is nothing there, instead of interpreting no signals as an injury and registering it as pain. I could do without that struggle."

"You are still the most positive person I know, considering. Are you in line for a prosthesis?"

"Yeah, but so are a lot of people ahead of me. At least I can work from home, but it gets lonely sometimes."

"Our friend Bob finds psychological help with his dog-buddy."

"Is that its name?"

"No, it's his buddy dog, whose name is Toby."

"I'd like to get a dog, but walking it wouldn't be easy."

"I think you'd be up to the challenge."

The two of them continued to exchange pleasantries and Judy to delve a little deeper into what he wrestles with.

"I admire the way you don't let your difficulties handicap your drive to live your life."

"With people like you in my corner, I would feel like I would be letting you down if I did any less."

"I hope you never lose that heart."

"If things were different, I would ask you to be my partner."

"In another life, perhaps."

"Well, you might be on to something. Who knows, we may get our chance."

"What do you mean?"

"I mean another lifetime."

"I'm flattered, really, but that sounds like a dime store novel."

"Sometimes fiction is based on actual occurrences. Watch for me; I will find you."

They conversed some more for a while and then Judy departed, living out her own life contentedly with her family and visiting this friend of hers regularly.

Several decades later, one autumn afternoon, a woman walks toward the river flowing through a park on the east side of the city. There was a path right beside the river on which traveled joggers and cyclists, each holding to their lane. She was about to engage in her passion for painting, so she set up her easel and sat down to capture on canvas the water with trees on the opposite bank, hoping it would reflect the mood of tranquility beside the bustle of human movement. She felt the breeze on her face, almost blowing the canvas over, reminding her to include that feature in the painting.

Amid the brush strokes, a man stopped by and looked over the work in progress. He stood in line with the sun, giving him a kind of aura when she looked up to see what was casting a shadow over her.

"Nice day for it," he said. She was uncertain why, but deep down in the recesses of her mind she had the inclination to call him "Sam."

The Way Things Thankfully Aren't

Lily: Operator.
Supplicant: Oh, pardon me, have I not prayed the right number?
L: Yes, this is the heavenly switchboard. To whom do you wish to speak?
S: Well, I was anticipating God.
L: Oh no, God does not take calls; it is only through the messengers.
S: The angels?
L: The very same.
S: I thought that was only in the other direction, you know, the reply or return message (Dan 9:21–23; 10:11–13).
L: That too; it's in both directions.
S: So while I have you on the line, whose job is it to take my message to God?
L: The one assigned to you has been recalled due to staff shortages here, so now there is no one in particular.
S: So who is the next in the chain of command?
L: I'm afraid no one is available at the moment; they are all out on duty.
S: How then do I get through?
L: I can put you through to voicemail.
S: To a specific messenger?
L: It's a general mailbox, but it's checked frequently.
S: Is this the quickest way?
L: Yes, when we are overstretched.
S: How long will it take for a response?
L: As you should well know, there is only one who is *omneescient*. If we knew the future, we would be . . . well, you know.
S: Can I just wait on the line?
L: We would rather that the line not be tied up in case of emergencies, not to belittle your inquiry, of course.

S: Fine, put me through.

L: As you wish.

Recording: Thank you for choosing the heavenly help line, we are here to serve. Please leave your message after the tone and we will return your call as soon as circumstances permit.

S: I am having trouble with . . .

R: Please speak clearly and state your name, the date, the time of your call, as well as your preferred language.

S: How can you not already know these particulars? This is . . .

R: But first please listen carefully as our menu options have changed. For health and related problems, say "soma"; for mental and emotional concerns, say "psyche"; for spiritual battles, say "doubt" or "temptation," whichever applies; for decision-making difficulties, say "clarity"; for inter-relational conflicts, say "philia"; for financial struggles, please consult your local parish and tell them we sent you; if you are calling to ask for that special gift you always wanted, say "St. Nick" or "Santa Claus"; if you want everyone just to get along, say "Pollyanna"; for all other queries, please mention the relevant department by the corresponding Hebrew, Aramaic, Greek, or Latin term; for an alphabetical list of departments, say "concordance."

S: But I just wanted to ask for the strength to see through another day.

R: We are sorry, but we did not catch the name of the department. Please try again.

S: Okay then, grace and mercy.

R: Please hold.

G and M: You have reached the office of Grace and Mercy. There is no one here at the moment to take your call, but every one is important to us. If you receive this message, that means your issue is already being attended to but we have been delayed by opposing forces. Rest assured, we will get through.

S: Well that was easy.

What Do We Expect?

IN A FURTHER EFFORT to debrief ourselves from the previous four non-fiction sections, I offer the following exercises. Sometimes it becomes futile (should this term not exist, I would probably perish) to attempt to impress upon others what is contained in the scriptures so as to support one's argument. What I mean is that I have had students who were insistent that, say, the Bible should be interpreted in pacifist terms regardless of what passages can be advanced in opposition to them. Initially, it is useless to present any OT passage since pacifists tend to discount them as hopelessly violent. Instead, they focus on the NT despite the fact that nowhere in it is stated that aggression should be avoided, for God is no stranger to putting persons to death even there. In one instance, Luke 3:14 addresses what certain sectors of the population should do to "Produce fruit in keeping with repentance" (v. 8a) as stated by John the Baptizer. Specifically for the soldiers is recommended "Don't extort money and don't accuse people falsely—be content with your pay." Despite having the opportunity, John does not avail himself of asking, "What in the world are you doing being soldiers?" In another case, when Jesus himself cautions that if you or kings go to war, they should count the cost (Luke 14:31–32). Nowhere and at no time does he rule that all such activity is illegitimate.

Additionally, in Acts 5:1–11, God's Spirit, it would seem, puts Ananias and Sapphira to death for lying to the disciples that they had delivered the entire proceeds of the sale of land to them rather than admitting that they had kept back some of it for themselves. Note that keeping a portion is not an offense, only lying about it. Also in Acts, Herod was put to death by an angel for not accrediting to God the source of his prosperity (12:21–23). The pacifists in the crowd are prepared with apologetic-style responses. Especially for the Acts 5 passage, they evaluate the episode as a ploy on the part of the early church to warn its parishioners to give more to the work of the church and not to withhold it. Suggestive, perhaps, given what we know about avaricious types in church history, but not compelling, for that is not the "moral" of the account. Nor do they have a convincing retort for the latter passage. What does seem to confound them, however, is the passage in Rev 12:7 which states alarmingly, "And there was war in heaven." Tough to argue with, you know, if it's good enough for God . . .

There are also times when fiscally conservative students find their way into class and claim, much like the Protestant work ethic, that we get what we earn and prosperity comes from God, and thus social consciousness and political handouts are unwarranted. They tend to be adamant about it. The point is that the intent of scripture does not always get across because readers' personal grids that are applied to the Bible when interpreting it actually get in the way and distort it. That's right, we get in the way of our own approach to the text. Appealing to the plain reading or meaning of the text does not amount to much when for them its plainness differs from ours.

There are also those who for some unknown reason have decided to take a disliking to us—an offense, and not of the good kind, and nothing we do will ever be looked upon positively or pull us out from the hole we, or they, have dug for us. We can only hope that during a life review in the afterlife, at whichever stage of it that will occur, when we are shown how our behavior has affected others, it will become evident that they are also the ones with the problems and their assessment illegitimate. I did mention this as a hope. For example, I have an acquaintance who does not like Woody Allen for the simple reason that he does not like how he looks. Now granted the Woodman would not win any beauty contest, but this is no rationale for belonging to the anti-Allen camp. If the alleged event is to take place, a life review is geared to offer us a sense of what others were feeling about our acts involving them. Yet their negativity might be the result of hasty assumptions on their part and may very well betray against them an unbecoming character quality. Should it in fact be a flaw, it could come out when they in turn are shown how their actions have affected us. Then we will know who is (or are) flawed (likely plural). Here's further hoping that the perceived offending events will turn out to be a series of misunderstandings.

As the title of this section asks, what do we expect?—that we will come to the afterlife, cap in one hand and armed with the Bible in the other, ready to appeal to the sacred text when the reckoning commences? Do we think that citing biblical passages will assist us in the heavenly court of law as though we might have a proper reading of it? I am not sure that our exegetical talents will be needed when the Messiah is our advocate. Or would we have the inclination to charge our Judge with breach of contract if upon death we, say, point out that in Mark 16:18 God was to keep us safe from deadly poison were we to drink it and, well, we did and God didn't?

Whereupon God might indeed have the heart to inform us that this passage is contained in a section (vv. 9–20) which never received the heavenly ratification since regrettably it was added much later than permitted, meaning past the time of the authentic apostolic period (as if to say this matters). Were we to add the rejoinder that it is contained within the covers of the scriptures and thus entails that it must therefore have the Spirit's approbation, it may be met with the comeback, "Actually, that is faulty reasoning." What is worse, in response to the possible or potential or probable assessment that our righteousness has left a little bit to be desired, will we counter with the passage "do not be over-righteous" (Eccl 7:16), as though this were a formidable defense? And will there be hecklers in the crowd?

On the topic of scriptural positions on who will be saved, there is a spectrum of stances. On the conservative end are Matt 7:21, "Not everyone who says to me, "Lord, Lord," will enter the kingdom of heaven, but only [s/he] who does the will of my Father who is in heaven," and 22:14, "For many are invited, but few are chosen." In the middle is Mark 10:45 with a parallel in Matt 20:28, "For even the Son of Man did not come to be served, but to serve, and to give his life as a ransom for many." And on the liberal end are several: Rom 5:18b, "the result of one act of righteousness was justification that brings life for all [people]"; 1 Cor 15:22, "For as in Adam all die, so in Christ all will be made alive"; 1 Tim 2:5–6, ". . . Christ Jesus, who gave himself as a ransom for all [people]"; 4:10b, ". . . God, who is the Savior of all [people]"; and 1 John 2:2, "[Jesus] is the atoning sacrifice for our sins, and not only for ours but also for the sins of the whole world." So we move from few to many to all, with the possible proviso that the offer must be accepted for it to apply worldwide. The question now becomes Is the most accurate position a function of quality or quantity of passages? Do we opt for the number of verses or their weight, assuming we can actually make an appraisal of the latter?

And as for what our obligations are in these proceedings, aside from the aforementioned Zacchaeus episode in Luke 19:1–10, there are many verses all having a similar emphasis, and not all from the book of James. Here are some salient examples: "I am he who searches hearts and minds and I will repay each of you according to your deeds" (Rev 2:23); "prove [your] repentance by [your] deeds" (Acts 26:20); "continue to work out your salvation with fear and trembling" (Phil 2:12); then four from the second chapter of James: "What good is it . . . if a [person] claims to have faith but has no deeds? Can such faith save [him or her]?" (v. 14); "faith by itself, if it is not accompanied by action, is dead" (v. 17); "a person is justified by what [s/he] does and not by faith alone" (v. 24); "As the body without the spirit is dead, so faith without deeds is dead" (v. 26). The last of these could also be used in support of the dualistic element in the scriptures.

The thrust of these passages is clear: faith is integral to salvation, but it is not the only component; action seems to be required. Faith is a necessary condition, but not a sufficient one. One passage that is contrary to the above is Eph 2:8–9, "For it is by grace you have been saved, through faith—and this not from yourselves, it is the gift of God—not by works, so that no one can boast." A factor in the calculations may be that this epistle is one of those not widely accepted, for better or for worse, as having been penned by Paul; this may or may not affect one's outlook on its contents. Sometimes we are also called to go above and beyond the call of duty, as in going the second mile (Matt 5:41), even if asked to go only one (potentially leaving the one who requests nonplussed [which is Jesus' point], having already reached his destination and where going further would be counter-productive, like "No, wait, this is my stop. You're not helping"). So here we have a conclusion, though not necessarily a conclusive one: we have something to say about what goes into our salvation (in true Wesleyan fashion), as does God.

What, though, do we do with those who are reserved by nature and disinclined to operate gregariously, psychology referring to them as introverts? They are already at a disadvantage unless they can think of creative ways to perform works of service that do not involve being public or social. Loving others for them might then be from the sidelines. They could indeed be kind-hearted but one may never know it. As for most of us who do not have an extensive fund of good deeds to draw upon, best to get on with it. I suppose a question we could ask ourselves as a test case would be: Is anyone actually benefiting from our being around? The above makes me hope, contrary to conventional Protestant sensibilities and propensity, that there is a purgatory of sorts, an opportunity for persons to hone their spiritual gifts, talents, and skills beyond death. But what shape would this take? Will there be cell groups, role-playing, or chances to practice on others? Will there be classes and courses, and exams? It seems much of this life is a test, preparing us for fitness for the next. Perhaps it would be similar to the Catholic notion of purging or, the term I prefer—refinement. That is my hope. Why? Because we could all use it.

Next we turn to a question with perhaps no foreseeable resolution: Can God create something possessing God's own metaphysical attributes? or, how closely to God's own nature can God create? Nine or so metaphysical predicates or properties have been attributed to God according to ancient Greek thought through luminaries like Augustine and Aquinas, and to these humans are not privy. We need food, shelter, clothing, air, and water so as to be going concerns; not so with God. Thus can God create beings or entities not requiring sustenance? If so, then maybe angels are free from it; if not, then angels too have a diet, meaning what they ingest. Should this be the case, then what type of menu do they order from and how many meals per "day" do they enjoy? This would put a literal spin on the biblical verse "they ate the bread of angels" (Ps 78:25). We may also wonder why God elects to work through angels in the first place. I imagine that some provide a courier service for getting messages across, and some might have been seconded to Earth to work here full-time. This prompts the additional question as to why God does not take these actions on Godself. I suppose it is for a similar reason that God has us take on the task of being managers of the planet. This is not beyond God's power, but apparently God wishes creatures to share in the work as well as in the bounty.

And as for God's part in the calculations, try the following on for size. I wonder if from an infra-human species perspective, say a representative of birds, they muse to themselves when observing humans in vehicles something like this: "How do they do it? When walking on two legs they move about slowly, but when they take their, what are we to call them—canisters or hives with four spinning legs—with them they are swift (a nod to one of our own kind) out of all proportion to the what would ordinarily be understood as an added encumbrance given their weight. Most odd. Turtles we get. They are slow with their mobile homes. But these other creatures with theirs are enigmatic." And when dogs are to be trained, we are informed that it is best to instruct them, say when they have done something displeasing to us, as closely as possible in time to the event in question which owners wish to dissuade, else their brains will have gone beyond the occurrence to other things. They have short attention spans, much like some persons we may know.

This might also reflect the way many humans work and could create difficulties in the theological sphere. If we happen to engage in an activity we may regard as questionable, then should a mishap of some description occur shortly afterwards, and, as a necessary ingredient, should one be of a theological bent (which is not to imply that theologians are in fact bent), one might be so inclined as to conclude that this is a retribution on God's part for our misadventure and we will forever make the association in our minds that this action will bring about that consequence, God being understood as consistent in this regard. Hence correlation here actually does entail causality—the results being both specific as well as inevitable, making us react with revulsion at the thought of repeating the action. And with that, God has effectively negatively reinforced our behavior. We can add, however, that there is no strict policy of non-interference on the part of God vis-à-vis the world, as is the case, say, with Star Fleet Command and the Federation in *Star Trek*, although the level of the divinity's interference does not necessarily circumvent the free choice or self-determining power on the part of creatures.

This is also difficult to argue against. If one is convinced that the above is the way God operates, then another occasion of it is what we would expect God to respond with. That would make the diagnosis well-nigh unfalsifiable. It also bespeaks more about us than the God we represent. We tend to think this way because we have been taught or experienced that a given misbehavior on our part earns for us what our parents could have administered to us, therefore we anticipate that God must do likewise, such as those opportunities to reflect known as "time outs."

Now for a topic that has intensely practical overtones, recall the parables of the rich young ruler together with the rich fool who felt he had enough to live on for the remainder of his days so that he could spend them all in security, comfort, and ease (I am saying this to myself and you are permitted to overhear). The former parable concerned the selling of one's possessions and giving to those in poverty (abject or otherwise). Not becoming married to that which one owns is plainly good advice, for that mindset will make it easier to part with it when the time comes, otherwise it could readily own us. Make sure what you hold does not have a hold on you. But when is that time? The poverty-stricken widow who donated two small coins at the temple in Mark 12:41–44 did so despite its having been "all she had to live on," and did not withhold it because of that fact nor chose to wait until she left it to charity after having passed away when she naturally would not need it anymore. The generosity of bequeathing one's estate to a charitable organization is admirable and commendable, in God's eyes as well, yet is God more interested in our taking the plunge while we are still alive, not merely for the reason that there are multitudes who could benefit from the proceeds presently and not only latterly, but perhaps God considers it "profitable" for us to experience what it means to be in want (assuming we have not as yet had the pleasure of making its acquaintance)? Maybe God thinks it important for us to feel the pinch in the here and now.

To reflect on it, and at the same time risking a descent into the crude and vulgar, were we to live long lives, our dependence on our amassed wealth and fortune might cause it to dwindle, which would not be the case were it to be gifted earlier on. Besides, there could be aspects of our lives which are up for review and this could be one of them. We are not here for our own comfort and security interests but for others, hence the tune from the 1970s that declares "We are here for a good time, not a long time"[1] is

---

1. By the Canadian musical group Trooper, from its 1977 album *Knock 'Em Dead*

a lie—if there were ever doctrines of devils, this is one of them. There is something pernicious about the mindset of "God can have it once we are finished with it," or "We will release some funds once we stand to benefit, like in the way of tax write-offs."

Is this what interests God: to orchestrate the alleviating of poverty presently knowing there might be less to give were the particulars to delay, or does God think it beneficial and valuable for some to know poverty whereas otherwise they might not, in preparation, perhaps, for the reward to be received in the hereafter? As with other matters, there is probably no hard and fast rule, nor is there automatic shame in prosperity, especially should this be something God is pleased to bestow. But God could also very well seek to deliver us from something that can readily become an impediment to that same hereafter. Food for thought, mostly for those who lack it—food that is, though it could involve the thoughts too.

Jesus was observing people as they placed their donations into the temple coffers, the wealthy offering large sums in accordance with their considerable means, while the widow in abject poverty submits a relative pittance. Jesus evaluates her amount as surpassing all the others, since the others would not miss it, but she would, for it was "all she had to live on." Jesus is moved by the gesture and impresses this upon Peter, who accompanied him. He tells Peter to catch a fish in whose mouth he will find a coin sufficient to cover both their temple taxes. So far, so good, but only if the tale does not end here.

Three things to add. First, no mention is made as to whether the widow had children who should be supporting her, for just because she is a widow does not make her childless. Women were not likely bread-winners in that culture, although, as intimated, Jesus benefited from women of means, it is just that these means may have come from their male partners, so the wording of "he who does not provide for the needs of his family is worse than an unbeliever" (1 Tim 5:8) ("infidel" in the KJV), as stated refers to males, leaving her off the hook, and perhaps she only had daughters as progeny. One implication is that the calling of the disciples led to the destitution of the families they left behind. Thankfully, the ministry of Jesus lasted from one to three and a half years, depending on the reckoning of the Gospel writers, so perhaps those families could have rebounded thereafter, or through it with the assistance of friends and relatives. (BTW, see what a difference a life having such a short public ministry can achieve.)

Second, could Jesus not have found (or made) another fish containing funds that would assist the widow? Granted that his method of operation

---

Kid, produced by Randy Bachman.

was to heal infirmities of body and soul/spirit, and was generally not involved in giving financial handouts, yet here's hoping conservatives come to this realization: he did change water into wine. Third, in comparison to the parable of the rich man and Lazarus as alluded to earlier, Jesus implies that the wealthy who fail to be generous already have their reward in this life and the poor in the next. He laments the difficulty for the rich "to enter the kingdom of heaven" (Matt 19:23–24) (though Job seems to be at least one such wealthy man who would be welcomed into the kingdom). Hence, if the temple did not have a benevolent program toward widows, as we are enjoined to do for all the needy as seen in Isa 58 on true fasting, then that widow, perhaps reluctantly in the present—we are not informed—will be among the rewarded poor in the hereafter, given that, as we are made to understand, the rich have their wealth as an obstacle to afterlife rewards.

Dare we chance an analogous biblical situation? Take for example Deut 19:1–13, an occurrence for which God makes an accommodation. Consider instances in which there were accidental killings, say when an axehead falls off mid-swing and fells a person instead of a tree, a circumstance without "malice aforethought" (interesting that the NIV employs legalese). No doubt there would be those who would take umbrage at the offense and seek to confront the offender, who was permitted to flee to the nearest "city of refuge" for safety. There were six of these—three on either side of the Jordan River, where those finding themselves in these dire straits could evade the figure known as the "avenger of blood," usually the nearest male relative to the victim,[2] who pursues the offender in hopes that he is more fleet of foot and will intercept the offender prior to his reaching asylum, or pouncing on him were he to venture outside the city before the death of the high priest—the assigned event that would signal the offender could be freed. While inside the city, he is "safe on the island" and hopes for an early demise for the high priest (perhaps with malice aforethought).

In the contemporary scene, the offender would be charged with involuntary manslaughter, for which there is a penalty to pay. In the OT example, the offender is not eluding the authorities or evading justice, for God seems not to require any. But thinking of a 1960s crime drama television program, the lead character was keen to establish his innocence while on the run and became *The Fugitive* (you could tell it was an open and shut case because it was filmed in black and white). Whereas in the OT the offender can claim sanctuary in the city, in the current context he would need to turn himself in. Should the latter elect to live on the run (or making it sound as though he were astride a youthful ovine ruminant—on the lam[b]), he might never

---

2. Douglas and Hillier, *New Bible Dictionary*, 109, 210–12.

be caught. Would God require him to turn himself over to the authorities currently, similar to the charitable donations example, insisting that he conform to the law of the land, or could God confer on him a state of refuge, a precedent having been set, something considered significant in courts of law? When precisely did the cities of refuge accommodation end, or is it a lasting principle, permanently binding their application or something like them to the present day?

Here we return to the previous question. Are those who are wealthy similar to those who evade capture, who can live in the sunshine of God's graces, or do they need to turn themselves and their fortunes in, not for legal but for moral purposes? The intent of the cities of refuge was to provide a way to prevent the multiplying of bloodshed in vengeance. The intent of giving to, or at least not withholding from, the poor when one has the means to do so—a practice that takes practice and is not always automatic—is to prevent an attitude of indifference toward them and their plight, nor is that something about which we should seek to be adept. I may have answered my own question. Were we to be the ones in need, we would request that God and/or God's representatives would attend to our needs in haste and not delay.

While true that there will never be a lack of the indigent (Matt 26:11; Mark 14:7), it is the present poor of whom we may be aware. Nor would we want to be like the foolish bridesmaids who were not prepared at the appearing of the bridegroom and thus were left outside (Matt 25:1–13). If the offender is early to the city of refuge, he is safe, if not, he is in peril; were he to leave early, it could be disastrous, if not, he is safe to resume his life. The time element in all the above cases is crucial, but more often than not, it is best not to be late. So how do we know when we are in danger of being too late and being unprepared for the end, particularly if the heavenlies keep mum? God grant us wisdom and clarity in this regard.

Some miscellaneous comments are in order. First, two equal and opposite forces appear to be at work in history, about which Sir Isaac Newton would be proud: on the one hand, hindsight is twenty-twenty, but only if we happen to be looking in that direction; and on the other, we do not learn from history—if we are actually looking in that direction we then tend to be incredulous that whatever occurred in the past could not repeat itself here, could it? In the former, our look at history enjoys clarity, but we don't look there for the insight it could afford; in the latter, we look, but we do not see clearly, or at least we lack the foresight that we might be looking in a mirror, where the past is being reflected in our current circumstances, whereupon we may irresponsibly be inclined to despair, "Who knew?"

Second, it is odd to think that history will come to a close at God's behest. Perhaps there will be an end in the customary sense, but as long as the afterlife will have a before and an after, there will be a history of sorts. Relatedly, my anticipation is such that God first wants to determine that we can admirably be trusted to manage and take care of this world which God is so invested in so as to build a community for the next. But as we have noted above, the current investment will ultimately come to nothing with the transition to the renewed creation, unless, like with our bodies, as Paul would assert, God works with a seed of the former to fashion a tree for the latter, or like God has done in biblical history in working with a remnant of an older population to bring a newer to fruition. There will be both continuity and discontinuity (1 Cor 15:35–58). That is the mystery.

Efficacy and Proportionality

NOWADAYS THE VERB "TO get" means something different than it did before. Were one now to declare that one has "gotten it," it does not refer to having purchased or otherwise obtained an item or items that were previously not in one's possession. Alternatively, it meant that a concept has become registered within the confines of one's cranium and the cognitive faculties contained therein, the concept occasionally taking on a double entendre and perhaps even being followed by a healthy dose of side-splitting laughter. At least that might be the intention and hope of the communicator.

Plus, to proclaim "I got this" currently implies either that some task is entirely manageable within the orbit of one's muscular-skeletal constitution, or that one can decipher a mental puzzle presently defying the powers of the utterer of the phrase but soon to yield to his or her superior detection talents. All of the above are different from the phraseology that one has "got religion." The latter is a position of which I am a holder. But there are aspects of it that I do not automatically "get."

In the order of their appearance in the sacred text, I don't "get" how all the water at the mythical time of Noah and the Flood, if it covered the whole Earth (Gen 7:19–20), would not have been saline and thus undrinkable as well as destructive to terrestrial plants and animals, unless God assisted with desalination. We are not informed. Next, on the conquest of Canaan, after the Israelites were enjoined to exterminate everything that breathes (Josh 11:11), what we would mercilessly refer to nowadays as "pest control," they are instructed to "love the alien as yourself" (Lev 19:34; Deut 10:17–19). I am surprised that there were any left post-extermination to love. Evangelicals might feel commissioned to find an interpretation of these scriptural sections that would mitigate their sting for contemporary eyes and ears, and consequently preserve God's justice, while atheists contend that the problem does not thereby disappear. Still, in addition to biblical issues, there are theological ones that also need to be "gotten."

Recalling a previous theme, in the Christian West, there is a theological doctrine known as soteriology, involving what constitutes salvation, how it comes about, and how one comes by way of it. Standard dogma dictates that Jesus was commissioned with the task of securing salvation for his followers and accomplished it. Yet questions remain. The major avenue of approach in the history of Christian thought submits two conditions which need to be fulfilled. They are that Jesus must be both a representative and substitute. What this entails is that firstly he must be a member of the human race, without which he could not be our representative. The duration of atonement offered by God in the OT was secured through the temple sacrifices, specifically the blood of bulls, goats, and lambs, which lasted until their expiry date one year later, at which time the ritual must be repeated so that the people would be free from God's judgment for another year. Secondly, Jesus' own sacrifice must be effected through his own bloody death in our stead, for "without the shedding of blood there is no forgiveness" (Lev 17:11; Heb 9:22). As I compose these lines it is the Easter season, apropos perhaps for the sentiment that the only way his sacrifice could be broad enough in space and extensive enough in time would be for God to insert Godself into the calculations and endure it Godself, which is no mean feat, and I am prompted to make reference again to Luther's translation of the passage in 2 Cor 5:19 from "God was reconciling the world to himself in Christ" to "God was in Christ reconciling the world to himself" as making more metaphysical sense to me, though by no means thereby increasing its veracity.

Granted that the biblical stance is "the wages of sin is death" (Rom 6:23), and our death satisfies that requirement, though it does not rescue us since we are blemished sacrifices unacceptable to God as working toward the goal we might seek. Hence Jesus is touted as the likely, even the only, candidate for which salvation can be effected, since only he can qualify for it and in fact has, according to these hopeful theologians. Thus we are deserving of death and inevitably undergo it, however the difficulties do not end there. Our death is like a bill we need to pay, but that does not clear us because the bills do not stop there—they keep on coming. We still carry the label and shame of "convict" and come with a "record" or "rap sheet" which we cannot expunge. This is where the Messiah comes in theologically. In being one of us and having taken our place, God considers the mission accomplished.

A related issue to discuss is whether this is a legal or a business transaction. It is at least partially legal in the sense that God's law has been broken and this lands us in court with Jesus as our advocate. Our case is tried before God as the judge. The OT informs us that God's law is paramount, ensuring that if it were followed, we will be in a right relationship with God and neighbor. Nice gig if you can "get it," but we cannot. God enforces the law and we are ultimately law-breakers. But this is not the whole story.

It is also once again at least partially a business transaction, since God has been known to entertain petitions on the part of humans, or at least *a* human, when it comes to how many righteous persons it will take for God not to destroy Sodom and Gomorrah, and Abraham did his level best to ensure that his nephew Lot and his family would be spared from this outpouring of God's justice (Gen 18). Regrettably, Abraham should have extended the petitioning to additional rounds, for up in smoke those cities went. Why, incidentally, would Abraham simply not have pleaded for his nephew Lot and Lot's family, thereby omitting the number altogether? God has also been known to enter into contract situations, outlining what each party's obligations are: if you obey, then God will bless; if you do not, then God will curse (Deut 28), noting that the cursing section is about twice as long as the blessing.

A contract could also be the type of agreement that was brokered between God and Jesus. The dialogue could have transpired something like this: "Okay, we have a breach showing no signs of being repaired, so how about you take their place as a sacrifice?" (English apparently is the preferred language of heaven or commerce or both.) "Isn't there another way? What else you "got"?" "Nope, that's it." "Oh all right then. I got this! But I'm not going to like it, am I?" "Probably not, but it's worth it." And with this, a deal was struck and both parties lived up (or died) to their end of the arrangement.

Another is what form must Jesus take so as to make the plan work and to what extent would it work? Admittedly, this is a mystery of God which we cannot plumb, but that alone does not prevent theologians from speculating. The possibilities can be ordered on a scale from Jesus as being totally human to totally God. Were he simply to have been a human, what might be the extent of his work? When we think of a person taking the place of another, there is usually one other person who benefits. A security agent, for example, is willing to take a bullet for the President; that entails one person taking the place of one other. Of course the entire US would benefit, though in this instance we still have one dead person and another still alive, with millions nodding in appreciation. Or, one soldier could fall on a grenade to spare the lives of his or her fellow soldiers, in this case the death of one saving several.

Further, a secret agent might reluctantly undergo a prisoner-swap, recognizing that this could very well mean certain death for him or her, but a government may be willing to agree to it in exchange for the safe return of their own agents in the field. After all, Mark's gospel does state that Jesus "g[a]ve his life as a ransom for many" (10:45). Finally, Caiaphas the high priest at the time of Jesus' ministry attempted to impress upon his Jewish religious authority colleagues that it would be better for one person to die for the nation than to have the entire nation perish (John 11:49; 18:13–14). This seems to be the extent of it: the efficacy of the death of one person can reach to a whole nation. Even a Jewish high priest admitted as much. But for the whole world (John 1:29; 1 John 2:2)? Can one single solitary human really provide a sacrifice for all those who have ever, are, or will be born in the history of humanity? That would be a real bargain. What would Jesus need to be in order to be so efficacious?

Next on the scale would be the level of Jesus as having been an angel in his erstwhile heavenly existence, which is one interpretation of Paul's statement in Gal 4:14, and might have been a position the early Paul held. (A definite Pauline perspective was his view that Jesus became son of God at the time of the resurrection, with the implication that he then enjoyed more than human nature alone (Rom 1:3–5), particularly in his exaltation (Acts 2:33; 5:31; Phil 2:9; Heb 7:26), though only the Philippians reference here is believed to be of Pauline origin). Angels, after all, can transgress and some of us will be in a position to judge them (1 Cor 6:3). Legend has it that the fallen angels committed not only insubordination at best but sought to usurp God's throne at worst. An eventual punishment has been prepared for them as a result, as there is for their human followers (Matt 25:31–46), for there does not seem to be a third category beyond sheep and goats (like alpacas?). As a side note, why do some theologians maintain that the "eternal life" in verse 46 means forever, while "eternal punishment" in the same verse is temporary and ending in annihilation?[1] (I don't get it) keeping in mind that our preferences do not always reflect the actual state of affairs.

But the question becomes can any angel, on the opposite extreme, and unlike us who at times idolatrously put things in place of God, like the four Fs of family, friends, finances, and football (everybody would include the fourth, right?), be not sinful but reach the dizzying heights of sinlessness? They would need to be able to do so were Jesus to have been one of them. Perhaps the sacrifice of an angel could have a wider-ranging effect, such as, like the above, the redemption of an entire nation, for as there are demonic princes of Greece and Persia (Dan 10:13, 20), so there is an angelic one for Israel, specifically named Michael (Dan 11:1; 12:1). Yet would a previous angel carry sufficient status so as to have the kind of efficacy theologians seek? One difficulty with this strategy, though, is whether an angelic Jesus

---

1. Ehrman, *Heaven*.

constitutes an actual representative of humanity. If he was to take on our form, then this is not something of which humans are capable, meaning he would not be like us.

The level which follows upward from this is Jesus having been both God and human. A human-only Jesus has been termed the Arian heresy (which also held that he was like an angel) while a divine-only Jesus has been referred to variously as Monophysitism, and specifically Jesus as spirit in Dualistic, Gnostic, and Manichaean heresies, but here Jesus holds membership in both. If one can imagine a person having at least a component of divinity, being understood as neither limited to a body (corporeality) nor contained within a finite world, then this could have more far-reaching effects than merely being human, and as the scriptures confirm: his one act has sufficient potency for all people (1 Tim 2:6). Instead, Jesus could have relinquished divinity for a time, and for that amount of time he did not have it, "only to take it up again" (John 10:17–18), though this passage is in reference to his life and death. Once, however, the former move is made, the theological category and necessity of Jesus being a representative of our race is called into question, for his makeup would be well beyond ours.

All the more then would be the final level, where Jesus is purely divine, for only a divinity could redeem the widest range of people in all times and places—a conclusion arrived at not by way of direct biblical evidence but through reason—a rational undertaking. This would certainly be efficacious as a substitute, but it would hardly be representative. Hence Jesus needs to be more than simply human but less than only God, so which position is it to be? Or if he is not just a human commissioned with a task to perform and complete, but unique and exceedingly so, having not only no potential but also no possible equal, then perhaps this could cover all the temporal bases. It would need to, for nothing else could. Jesus must at least have a divine component, for only if God were to have sacrificed Godself could the scope of the benefit for humanity be truly universal.

This is the difficulty when one attempts to impose theological categories on the biblical text—invariably there will be statements which do not fit nor can be made to fit without jeopardizing other parts of the text or the theology drawn from them. For Jesus to be able to say "I got this," what type of person does he need to be? This is something I don't "get," nor, like the quantum world, I suspect, can we.

Time for another interlude.

Letters from Home

REMEMBER THE PART IN the original *Raiders of the Lost Ark* film when Harrison Ford is being pursued by an enormous stone sphere rolling toward him and, with nowhere to go but away from it, all he can do is try to outrun it? And when an Arabic man confronts him with a threatening sword display, whereupon Ford sheepishly shoots him with his pistol because the man is clearly overmatched owing to a weapon imbalance and failed to earn his boy scout merit badge for being prepared in all situations? Well this is nothing like it. Here in the beyond there are no "rolling stones" (though tunes from that band can still be played and heard) nor conventional human weaponry, the heavenly army resorting to angelic means to do battle with the opposing forces (Rev 12:7). This war has been raging since there were humans to speak of, but the humans here are those who have passed away, then been commissioned to facilitate the flow of information from the heavenly to the earthly, though far from the heavenly front lines. Someone has to do it, and the angels are on combat duty. That leaves us. Afterlife humans, at least those having opted for the "God squad," have been placed in charge of communications from heaven to earth in advance of the time when the heavenly manufacturing unit will unveil the new models of heaven and earth. You'd figure this would be a smoothly running machine, it being heaven and all, but not when and where humans are involved, even here.

"To err is human" applies here too, while heaven awaits the time when humans will be fitted with what heaven will roll out as their new model bodies. So give them a break or cut them some slack, as they say. Millicent (which of course is modified Latin for "the thousandth part of a cent") is a worker, we can't really say "employee" since "the wages of sin" (Rom 6:23) have already been paid—contrary to the way it works on earth, here one pays to work, with their lives—supervising the information bureau of foreign relations. They ensure that heavenly messages are translated into the appropriate languages and dispatched to earth. This process is not always "well-oiled." We hate to point fingers, but, we kinda know where the bulk of the problem lies. Mortimer (which of course is modified Latin for "dead in the water") is a well-meaning fellow-worker, but he faces some challenges. Why don't we let them explain? Geraldine is Millicent's interlocutor, but by this please do not assume that all afterlife names are three syllables in length.

G: Good morning, Millicent.

M: What do you mean morning? We're always in the light here, Geraldine. How would we recognize a morning?

G: Just trying to be civil. Are things going well?

M: Pretty good. I sure could use a drink right about now.

G: No, I mean how goes the flow, literally?

M: As you can imagine, the flow of information is getting through quantitatively, it's the qualitative aspect that's the issue.

G: Is Mortimer at it again?

M: Eminently.

G: What do we have to do to get fired around here?

M: Only the CEO can do that.

G: The chief executive officer?

M: More precisely, the chief eternal overseer.

G: Oh, I thought it could also be Charlie the Eternal Optimist.

M: No, things went sour and he has been given permanent holiday leave.

G: How is that different from getting fired?

M: It comes with benefits.

G: Ah.

M: But Mortimer has been mistranslating messages ever since we got here.

G: What was one of his greatest hits?

M: Well, we were assisting President Abraham Lincoln in drafting the Gettysburg Address, see? (His CV included woodsman, lawyer, and president in that chronological order—he reckoned it was best to diversify.)

G: Yeah, I recall, that was a good one.

M: So was the gaff. When Lincoln got to the part about the "three peoples," that's one of our favorites, Mortimer framed it as "of the people, by the people, and the four people." We are glad Lincoln caught it before he said it.

G: Well sure, four is not enough.

M: By no means; the US would have grown well passed that in no time.

G: Don't you mean "past"?

M: How could you tell when this is entirely verbal?

G: It was the way you said it.

M: The two terms are completely homonymic! But this demonstrates a problem we are facing with Mortimer, for these are the kinds of mistakes he makes. He transposes the order of words and uses the wrong homonyms. But this is not the end of it. For one, instead of addressing the greatest of sea depths, he made it sound as though there were grow-ops there by referring to it as the Marijuana Trench. Then he fractured Marconi into macaroni, and who can forget the famous youth in Asia in place of euthanasia? Asians wondered what the fuss was all about. Plus, he thought an old saying was a Russian adage and made it "When pushkin comes to shovkin."

There was also the time when some British traveled to the then dark continent of Africa, became hungry, and commissioned a native to make sandwiches for them. He served up a meal for them and said, "Glad to make it for you," whereupon it was communicated to them by Mortimer as "A glad Jamaican for you," and he promptly became subjugated into slavery in the Caribbean. Wait, there's more. When donations were diverted away from the rightful recipients and the perpetrators were sought, the answer to the question as to whether the suspects were guilty was misinterpreted from "innocence" to "in a sense," and the wrong people were convicted. Plus, there was a patient with a vagus nerve issue, and the message sent was "whatever happens in vagus stays in vagus," and so was given the wrong diagnosis and medication.

But one of his greatest blunders was when Polish settlers arrived at a place later to be named Buffalo. Jesuit travelers there appraised it as "a good place to worship." Mortimer saw to it that "worship" was communicated instead as "Warsaw," leaving the settlers pining for their homeland and responding with "Oh, just like home. You're right, this must be a good place." Ever since that time, whereas the rest of the temperate climatic world measures the accumulation of snow in inches, Buffalo does so in feet, making the settlers reassess the goodness of the place. We have had no end of complaints. This was well-nigh grounds for dismissal.

G: Where to?

M: Buffalo.

G: Ah.

M: Yet here he remains. The CEO must cheer for the underdog.

G: What was his profession in his earthly life?

M: He was a counselor, whose lone strategy was limited to advising "Well, don't."

G: What's he struggling with?

M: The usual and then some.

G: And why is he allowed to bring a pet with him?

M: That's not a pet, it's a guide dog; Mortimer is legally blind.

G: Why are we bringing terrestrial law into this?

M: Just letting you know his background.

G: Why has his condition not been corrected?

M: That's the third why question in a row.

G: What are the rules, and is there a limit to asking?

M: Not as such, but what was annoying on earth is the same here.

G: I'm just surprised that there is anyone here with defects and imperfections. Remember how those with physical defects were not permitted into the temple precincts (Lev 21:16–23)?

M: There is no temple here, nor is there need for one when God is present (Rev 21:22). Plus, may I direct your attention to the body of the Messiah himself which still bears the stigmata (John 20:24–27). This is not the final state or shape of things.

G: Could Maximillian (see? four syllables; Esmerelda is another; Abercrombie yet another; Aloysius still another) not do an able job instead?

M: He is not adept, but rather even worse. He has character flaws still untreated. Once he bemoaned that he could very well put the effort in to being a narcissist, but he has to think of himself first. He would need to step up his game in order to be abysmal.

G: (After a lengthy pause punctuated by "hums" and "hahs" as Geraldine was searching for a rejoinder, though none would emerge, she had to admit defeat and simply responded with) Good point. But how does Mortimer know the content of the message?

M: Braille.

G: Even here?

M: You appear to be missing the point. Those with challenges are encouraged to apply for any and all openings they choose. And don't call them "handicapped" because they could lodge a complaint with the union.

G: We have a union?

M: And also someone in charge of political correctness. Inclusivity doesn't end until we obtain our renewed bodies, for then the inclusivity is automatic. Reassuring when you think about it.

G: I am (YHWH), and it is.

M: I noticed you couldn't resist using God's name.

G: No law against it here.

M: Look, there's an inter-office memo sent to us from the throne. It alerts us to another Mortimerian gaff. It reads: "It seems we will need to expand our editorial staff to catch spelling and grammatical concerns before they are sent out. The latest mistake was informing the restorers of the Notre Dame cathedral to 'raise' the roof. It was misspelled 'raze.' We needn't impress upon you the confusion this caused. Kindly step it up or next we will be accused of creating chaos. As always, have a blessed intermediate state, may the interim period be rewarding, and remember, the future is what we make it."

G: Can we know ahead of time which communication will pose the most probable difficulties?

M: If I knew that I would run for Secretary of State.

G: We have election campaigns?

M: You really haven't been briefed much, have you?

G: I'm still fairly new here.

M: Don't play the ignorant newbie card with me. Just kidding—it takes some time to get used to the unfamiliar. You eventually assimilate.

G: Looking forward to it.

(Millicent then took full advantage of the lull in the conversation and availed herself of the opportunity to rant. She shook her fist at the world and announced) We may not point the finger at the culprit at crime scenes like people want us to, or as Monty Python expected us to, but at least we stop clocks and watches so coroners know the time of victim death. And have you ever noticed how all skeletons smile, provided the person still had teeth? Nice touch, huh? Don't say we never do anything in and for the mortal sphere. We even impart an aesthetic quality to the remains of the deceased. And what thanks do we get? A little gratitude would be nice. A little acknowledgment and recognition would be most welcome, that is if anybody's listening. Would that be asking too much? Hello, are you out there?

(One might have wondered whether interaction at this level would have improved beyond the ordinary to a form perhaps akin to telepathy where both interlocutors could emit signals simultaneously without losing any communication, or, if verbal, that both could speak and not thereby forfeit either concentration or comprehension between what one was saying and hearing. But as it stood, one must still wait a seeming eternity while the other comes to the termination point of his or her senseless drivel and finally arrive at the conclusion when one could at last commence with one's own vastly more important contribution. It was at this juncture when Geraldine chimed in.)

G: Well, I guess that's lunch.

What or Who Would You Rather Do Without?

THERE IS A PROGRAM which broadcasts a series about what the world would be like should there have been an absence of certain nations in history found on our handy globes (we still have them don't we? Ours even lights up to show political borders and without light the geographically prominent features. Neat, huh?), named *The World Without* (fill in the blank). The list includes not only the major players but some of the minor as well, Sweden for example (not thereby intending any slight or disrespect toward this or any other country for that matter, for most can point to their own contributions, not always widely known, without which world history would be impoverished to some degree. So respect, dude.).

Consider the regulations of our respective FDAs (food and drug administrations) between our two nations of Canada and the US. Recommendations on the packages of consumer goods can differ as to, say, the length of time something needs to be prepared in a microwave oven. Take for instance the formerly named Uncle Ben's Ready Rice (the avuncular having been removed for political correctness). In Canada, the stipulation is to leave it in the microwave for a sweltering two-minute period; in the US, the identical result can apparently be obtained in a mere ninety seconds. Alas, the Americans will always be at least thirty seconds ahead of us. Bon appetit.

In these investigations, I have a decided bias. I was born in Canada to German immigrant parents and am therefore first-generation Canadian. Canada has definite contributions (outside of poutine and our main natural resource, specifically ice) and the episode devoted to it was narrated by one of Canada's favorite sons, namely Dan Aykroyd (now host of the program *Unbelievable*, and don't get me started on how many Canadian celebrities have infiltrated the hallowed production halls and studios of Hollywood). But well before Canada even became a nation, comparatively recently in 1867, and here is my other bias, Germany was already well-entrenched as an innovative nation. Of course the US leads the world in many aspects of science and technology, but it too is a younger nation. Over against the "old countries," the newer ones are merely a coffee break in relation.

Admittedly, Germany itself did not become a united nation, Bavaria still a reluctant member and does not consider itself as part of the Fatherland (and don't call Macedonians Greek) even after Bismarck's work in 1870. Yet present Germanic nations having it as its major language-group can trace their roots to at least as remote in time as the early Roman period. The city of Trier, for instance, near the border with Luxembourg, boasts a city gate still standing, named the Porta Nigra, or black gate, erected prior to the time of Jesus. (See, this does have a biblical referent. But wait, there's more.) Probably Trier's most notable (or infamous) native son was Karl Marx, whose home remains for onlookers to marvel at (or worship, were that to be one's inclination, and no, it is not painted red).

Much later than the founding of Trier, the work of Gutenberg and his invention of a machine involving movable type and its capacity to act as a press and thereby print characters on paper, providing as it does the wide distribution of ideas, was revolutionary.[1] Be that as it may, Gutenberg's endeavors have been touted as one of if not the greatest technological advancement in history for its world-changing character, not least of which was the widespread translation of biblical texts and the theological views of such luminaries as the German monk Martin Luther (ah, there's the other biblical/theological rub), whose ideas launched the Reformation movement, and the West, at least, has not been the same since.

There have been subsequent technological advancements, but many might have been facilitated by this one, by the interplay of the spread of information and the explosion of ideas and innovations of all kinds, the one enabling the other. Thus each nation reported on by this program boasts ample information to fill every broadcast time-slot. Most people are proud of their heritage, even if they find themselves having adopted a different national home.

Having said all this, we can widen the issue to the following and arrive at it through an indirect route: what could we say is a difference between psychology and sociology? Well, as a rule of thumb, we could submit that the starting point for psychology is personalities and if, say, a personality like Einstein were not to have appeared on the scene when he did, then his scientific contributions would also not have surfaced when they did and would have come about at a somewhat later time when another personality could have fit the bill. On the contrary, sociology could assert that the time

---

1. Watson, *Historical*, 383.

was ripe for such contributions to be introduced, and if Einstein had not stood in the breach, then someone else would have at about the same time, for social forces dictate that an Einstein-like figure was awaited. Which of these approaches is true will be dependent upon a number of factors, variables, and historical and cultural contexts. Despite the efforts on the part of these two disciplines to be comprehensive, neither can be accurate 100 percent of the time.

So how does God operate—with individuals or collectives? The answer is both. God draws the nation of Israel as well as individuals within it. God apportions land to the Israelites and calls them back through their own prophets when they go astray. God even uses other nations to exact punishment on Israel, as with the Babylonian captivity. So would there have been a Moses-substitute had the actual (if not mythical) one not heeded the call? Perhaps. No doubt there were other devout figures who could have stood in the breach (Ps 106:23; Ezek 22:30). Could God have also called out a different group to be the Chosen People? Perhaps, although there can only be one nation that is the least or smallest (Deut 7:7, referring to it as the fewest in number), God being no stranger to working with the underdog.

The Jewish people have made significant contributions on a global scale out of all proportion to their numbers—compare the number of Nobel Peace Prizes awarded to a people who number about fifteen million worldwide (though keep in mind that they, like former President Obama, have not always sought peace). Yet if God had elected a different spokesperson from a different chosen people, that would have necessitated a different messiah—one who was not a Jewish male. Would this have been problematic? No. Regardless of who and how many God elects to use, we are utterly dependent on God for having done so.

Maybe someone should pitch the idea of a program like *A World Without God*.

Climate Control

WE CONTROL THE CLIMATE; the Earth is ill and is running a fever. I figured I would begin with the conclusion. In yet another effort and installment at promoting my penchant for being an equal opportunity critic, to demonstrate at least that I can in fact be one, I delve once again into what is forbidden territory to some, perhaps because it displays the tendency to divide households and otherwise close friends and family, the terrain—appropriate usage as we shall determine—of the purported environmental crisis before us. Debates about Earth's terra firma and not so firm meteorological patterns typically result in generating more heat than light, leaving the interlocutors (no, the language is not strong enough, better to say "combatants") battle-weary and presenting evident signs of scarring—casualties of war. Now it's my turn (that didn't come out right). This is an issue about which it is difficult to be dispassionate since there is so much at stake. We all have vested interests in it in one way or another.

While I find myself on one side of the debate much more so than on the other, both sides exhibit areas of fragility in the arguments they put forward, some under the banner (heaven help us) of Christianity. When confronting the other camp, the interaction eventually assumes the tenor of raised voices and, ordinarily on one side (guess which one) the spewing out of caustic invectives, this has been my experience, in the form of four-letter words (not including "soap," although it may be warranted and their mothers might have been justified in applying it liberally to their oral cavities). Not charming in the least. Both sides have emotional investment in their positions, but debates need not be reduced to the above. One side appears to be more measured in response, though no less entrenched in their own foxholes. Here are some points of contention on both sides, beginning with the group presenting lower blood pressure.

Its case surrounds the idea that action must be taken in haste so as to prevent what could very well be a point-of-no-return scenario for the world.

The rhetoric is couched in the form of the planet as being the injured and aggrieved party, all the while having a different focus, nay, manifesting an ulterior motive. Members of this enclave portray themselves as champions of the Earth when they really give attention to the effect climate change will have on their own species and its longevity. They speak of the world but really intend their own place in it. Their prime consideration is not geological but anthropological, though it is framed in terms of the former.

The status quo is ill-advised, they say, for it will become hazardous, even catastrophic, for the Earth and its biosphere; when what they really mean is that humans will bear the brunt of it. Should the former be their motivation, then they needn't be so concerned, for the planet has experienced far worse than we could ever throw at it and has rebounded nicely. On one extreme, there were times, notably seven hundred million years ago, when the Earth was covered in ice and was essentially a giant snowball; at the other extreme, there was an instance in which the average temperature on Earth was fifty degrees Centigrade—half the boiling point of water—far above the threat of the ocean temperatures being raised by a mere three degrees. Hence this side should be more up front as to who as opposed to what would stand to reap the whirlwind, sometimes literally, of our current climatic trajectory. We remain our own worst enemy.

Taking a different tack, if one were to seek to be truly Darwinian, then one will go about one's business without consideration for other species, leaving it up to them to survive in any way they can, and if they cannot, then extinction is what they deserve. Or, rather, if we wish to be Darwinian with a heart, we will pursue the well-being of other creatures as well, if for no other reason than our well-being is intertwined with theirs. Yet a heartless heart is a contradiction of terms and betrays where our priority lies, with our own well-being first and foremost. We would require an additional step to foster the longevity of other species for their own sake, and we should also keep the following in mind. Darwin as a naturalist was interested in describing the state of affairs of the natural world as it stands. To describe is to focus on the way things are; to prescribe is to give our attention to the way things ought to be. To adopt for ourselves the third measure listed here is to find ourselves having landed in the prescriptive camp with a view to the interconnectedness of all species and the delicate balance of its remaining a going concern. This practical appreciation of ecology in action is at the root of the environmental movement.

Not only do all positions on an issue contain their vulnerabilities when subject to the lens of scrutiny, but steps taken to admirably counteract environmental missteps on our part can themselves bear unwanted consequences. The drive (again appropriate terminology) to manufacture motor vehicles fueled not with presumably non-renewable fossil fuels but battery-powered electricity can yield their own versions of carbon footprints. The batteries themselves not only require energy to produce, and not all of them are renewable, but given the increased weight of vehicles containing them—batteries are heavy—the rubber worn off tires as a result of friction with roadways and eventually finding its way into the water system is greater for electric vehicles, meaning tires would wear down more quickly and in this way, at least, would leave a more pronounced carbon footprint than already existing vehicles. Compounding the problem is that these tires are also weightier and thus require more synthetic rubber to manufacture. Not something the brochures inform us about.

So much for one side of the argument, now for the other, and should readers believe that authors reserve the meatiest part of their examination for last, s/he might probably be correct. Initially, the nay group—those who are climate change deniers—fail to differentiate between climate and the weather and argue that since there has been a snow storm in a region not normally accustomed to them, namely Texas, which knocked out power to millions, on the basis of this single solitary event conclude that climate change must be a hoax. Anomalies continue to occur, but the dry places are getting drier and the wet wetter, and this adversely affects food production, which means that the outlook for our future ranges from dire to grim (whichever is worse) and definitely the opposite of rosy. We even have the power to delay the onset of the next ice age, which initially sounds advantageous until we tally the costs involved.

Deniers go on to claim that the Earth has undergone numerous cycles in its environmental history and we are experiencing yet another in a long series of them. That, however, overlooks the unprecedented rate at which the present one is occurring—about 170 times the pre-industrial pace, which in turn informs us that we are indeed factors in it, owing to the aftermath of the industrial revolution, itself mostly due to the wanton use of fossil fuels used to drive it. This has never occurred before, and while correlation is not causality, it remains difficult to envision anything else as the culprit. Oil companies themselves recognized this even in the 1970s, and articles were written at the time to this effect, but no alternative fuel source was found that would be profitable for them, so they decided to backtrack on their initial story and campaign for the reverse.

An important consideration is what one does with the evidence and how it is framed. Countering the position that ice caps are melting, gainsayers point out that 20 percent of the polar regions are actually ice-forming. Case closed. The other side emphasizes the corollary, meaning that 80 percent is melting. QED. Each side takes its stance as irrefutable, and in so doing illumines the unfalsifiability of both. Neither position believes that any evidence could be produced to compel one to cross the debate venue floor to the other (dark) side. Such a mindset is "fueled" more by emotion than reason. By committing oneself to a viewpoint no matter what, one becomes reduced to the strategy of whoever shouts the loudest wins. Liberals are equally vociferous about their position as conservatives are about theirs, though the former engage in it at lower volumes, nor are they as militant about it, nor again are they given as much to profanity, Jon Stewart, voicing a different grievance, notwithstanding.

As a rule of thumb, and here we can observe my suspicious nature, we must always be prepared to ask questions as to who funds the research and who stands to benefit from the vested interest, agenda-driven findings. In this debate, both sides do. And as so often happens, we can benefit from Jesus' own example. John's Jesus, after having fed the five thousand, urges his hearers to "Gather the pieces that are left over. Let nothing be wasted" (6:12). This salutary instruction can be applied both to resource stewardship individually and ultimately the impact widespread collective waste can have on the planet and its potential for recoiling on us in unprecedented meteorological severity. It is time to clean our collective house.

Condemned to Evolve

As a prompter on the theme of evolution, I offer the following example. Natural selection works for the current moment and does not plan for the future—it deals with whatever is directly before it. Whatever boasts the variations that work presently is preserved. Take rabbits, for instance. There are not too many predator organisms that can catch up to their speed, which is why they persist as members of the biosphere. If we happen to come close to one without noticing it, it will scamper away, at which point we might notice the movement and recognize that it has given its position away. It would be more beneficial for it to remain stationary so that we might fail to notice it. Yet this noticeable activity on their part has not hurt them because they possess other adaptations. There are some traits which are disadvantageous but not maladaptive and hence not a selective threat, thereby making them well-nigh among the selectively neutral. Should it come about that inflation has increased the cost of meat beyond our reach and we are left to hunt and fish for it, rabbits giving their position away would be to their disadvantage, thereby provoking natural selection to appear on the stage to even the playing field once again. This is one way in which evolution can work. I hope our evolving doesn't take too long for us; if we don't change our ways, then we will need to adapt.

Another question to ask is whether God, like humans, has a disgust response. When someone, for example, coughs into a hand and then holds out the appendage for someone else to shake, custom, or even protocol, depending on the occasion and persons involved, requires a reciprocal action on the part of the other, and not to do so is considered gauche, a faux pas. Yet we retreat psychologically from the extremity and would rather not grasp it, but etiquette insists we must, unless there is an agreed upon alternative, like fist- or elbow-bumping. We then turn away, at least inwardly, in disgust and seek an inconspicuous way to disinfect ourselves. We also understandably have a similar reaction to human waste. Does God as well? The Bible states that God wanted no such waste inside the camp, so it must be taken outside of it (Deut 23:12–14). The latter response is similar to the former. Well then, what is God's perspective on a cockroach? Is it either "Behold, one of my creatures, a product of my handiwork," proudly announced, or, like most of us, "Gross, get rid of it"? Or both? Cockroaches have an appreciation for filth; God does not. Thus evolution might not always reflect God's best intention for the creation, especially a distorted one.

This short segment, following as it does on the heels of the previous section, ends with two instances of potential concern from efforts at easing the pressure on the planet in terms of climate change. The first is the commendable drive, as mentioned, to reduce dependency on unrenewable fossil fuels by the manufacture and operation of electric vehicles. To begin with, their manufacture does not nullify carbon footprints; also, setting up the infrastructure does the same, despite its being eco-friendly in the long term; plus, what happens if there are three recharging stations all taken up by persons savoring a leisurely meal at an adjacent restaurant and you are next in line, and you have eaten recently, and your journey is time-sensitive? Lots of luck. Second, restaurant kitchens are major offenders when it comes to the heat produced, fueled as they are by carbon sources. Lately an innovation has surfaced where pots and pans are heated by magnetic fields, generated by induction stoves which cause the iron molecules in the pots and pans to attempt to align with the field, thereby causing friction and therefore radiation, which will heat the contents with no heat production or emissions. What troubles me, however, is the potentially non-negligible negative effects of the close proximity of magnetic fields on the human body, about which no investigations have as yet been conducted. If iron pots and pans can be affected, then perhaps creatures bearing iron, like us in our hemoglobin, can be sensitive to these fields as well. Food for thought.

Mixing Promotes Health
(The Headline Reads)

It pains me to write the following, largely because the subject matter in question causes pain to some people. And it is placed here in the science section, even though it could just as easily find its way into the religious, since science alerts us to the concern. Biochemical genetics, to get right down to the issue, runs with the ancestry baton once archaeology and paleoanthropology hand it off. The three work in concert and collaborate well, contrary to other discipline areas and departments; I'm looking at you neurology and psychiatry–talk to each other! You may find that by conversing, you might not need to do the same work twice. But that is another story.

Genetics supplements the findings of archaeology and paleoanthropology by covering what they do not. The latter two offer the uncovering of artifacts and skeletons which assist in reconstructing early human activity—from the use and control of fire, tool kits, military armaments, hunting and gathering, farming, pottery-making, to ornaments, figurines, and other artistic endeavors. What genetics contributes includes ancestral linkages of peoples, and the findings can be surprising. The bulk of people living today have arisen by virtue—and we will determine why I have selected this term—through migration and mixing (the two *ms*), both the movement of peoples and group interbreeding (not always with consent—consider that an estimated 2 percent of the world's population has Genghis Khan in its genetic background). A nod must also be given to the field of linguistics, which provides additional information about the onset, proliferation, and modification of language forms.

The moral of the genetic story, commencing with the ending first, is in how it becomes a virtue (there's that word again) if for no other reason than the health it promotes, and of course there are other reasons such as it enhances not merely toleration but cooperation between peoples. The saga goes like this: where there is mixing of groups of people there is genetic advantage. Harmful recessive genes are muted when combined with outside genomes; in a sense they are lost in the shuffle. Yet if genomes remain in-house, there is greater risk that recessives will be passed on to future generations. There are times when a person who carries a recessive gene may have a selective advantage, such as in African Black people who enjoy a resistance to malaria-carrying mosquitoes. The trouble occurs when recessives are passed on from both parents, which turns out to be detrimental. In this case those Black people succumb to the disease named sickle-cell anemia, which destines children to an early death. Another well-known condition hampers the Jewish community, called Tay-Sachs disease. Those having this condition also die early in life. What makes matters worse is that this disease offers no selective advantage to those who are simply carriers—a single recessive gene proves ineffectual in warding off other health concerns. Natural selection has completely by-passed this as a beneficial variation possibility.

Back to the moral of the story—there is benefit in mixing, so let's break down those inter-racial barriers.[1] This is a message from which Second Temple period Judaism could have profited. To recount the historical background, the Jewish nation fell to Nebuchadnezzar and his Babylonian hordes and were taken to Babylon as captives in a series of three deportations in the early sixth century BCE. They remained in exile there until, as intimated above, Cyrus the Persian, referred to as a messiah—God's anointed—will be taken by his right hand by God to release the captives and assist in the rebuilding of Jerusalem (Isa 45:1, 13). Those who accepted his offer (some remained for they had made a good life for themselves there in accordance with Jer 29:4–7, which incidentally states that it was God who carried the people into exile and they were exhorted to "seek the peace and prosperity of [Babylon] . . . Pray to the Lord for it, because if it prospers," so too will the Jews there) were a conservative contingent who upon returning to their homeland assessed their own history and concluded that the reason this tragedy befell them included their intermarriage with those of foreign nations. Ergo it would be best to abandon the foreign women and the children who were the products of these unions (Ezra 10:2–3). Nice, neat, and tidy, though misguided, argumentation.

The accounts name four brave souls who resisted this move (v. 15). Perhaps this is an instance where the minority position could have been the one which God might have favored, another being the scouting out of Canaan (Num 13). The majority report in the latter was that the promised land was inhabited by giants so the Israelites do not stand a chance against them; the minority report came from Caleb, who insisted that with God's

---

1. Reich, *Who We Are*, 121–48.

help "we got this." The winning position in the first case was the majority one; the minority in the second, thus even a majority can be in error.

The additional problem that the majority position in the first instance unleashed upon the people was that it was later destined to suffer from a genetic disease in the face of its campaign for racial purity. Purity here came at a cost. What then can be said about the God of the text? There are at least three alternatives: (a) God had no intention of demanding purity, meaning the people reached the decision on their own (my personal expectation); (b) God demanded purity, which left some unfortunate people with health difficulties leading to premature death and the casting out of women and children, which led to their untimely deaths, thereby also leaving God's providence in question (my least favorite); and (c) God called for purity but could not foresee the genetic concerns that would ensue, which would make God's certain knowledge of the future suspect (I have argued elsewhere my misgivings about the standard orthodox doctrine of omniscience and my having taken umbrage at our failing to disabuse those holding to it).

Should racial purity have been God's preferred position, then we might wonder why the book of Ruth was written and included in the canon. Here is the reasoning: Ruth was a Moabitess widow from a marriage to a Jew and she travels with her Jewish mother-in-law Naomi back to Bethlehem. She eventually marries a Jewish man by the name of Boaz there in a romantic tale. The purpose of the account is left till the end, where the reader or hearer is informed that the couple is three generations removed from King David's arrival on the scene. Observe now what this entails.

One of the greatest champions in Judaism has this couple as great-grandparents. The type of racial purity insisted on in Ezra are bloodlines which could be traced back well into the past—the further the better. The book that follows Ezra, namely Nehemiah, echoes the same sentiment as the former. It states therein that "no Ammonite or Moabite should ever be admitted into the assembly of God" (13:1), propelling the people to "[exclude] from Israel all who were of foreign descent" (v. 3). The book of Ruth could have been written as a direct response, for look who is relatively racially impure! Not even David could produce a bloodline pure from excluded Moabites. He has recent Moabite blood in him, three generations worth. So the message of Ruth is clear: lighten up on the issue of purity! Hence, the God of Ezra and Nehemiah appears to be at odds with the God of Ruth.

The takeaway from this is no one can ever be genetically racially pure anymore—it is no longer available and has not been for thousands of years. Even if we go as far back in our ancestry as the Neanderthals, who went extinct about forty thousand years ago and with whom we interbred, thereby slightly mixing the genes and leaving them spread throughout the populations and generations, we will still not find the kind of racial purity some have hoped for, and we are healthier for it.[2]

But this further presents an item of theological concern. The biological definition of same species is the ability of two organisms to produce fertile offspring, and I have wondered whether this is sufficient for application to the theological category of humanness—what it means to be human. As alluded to, anthropology informs us that we have interbred with other biological humans: most of us contain in our genome a small percentage of Neanderthal genetic markers (about 1.5–3 percent)[3] and a lesser amount of Denisovan contribution, owing also to Neanderthals and Denisovans themselves interbreeding and carrying that over to Neanderthal-*Homo sapien* coupling[4]—once present, always present (at least mostly) in the hybrid descendants. Does this also make the other two theologically human? By the time twenty thousand years ago arrived on the scene, we were the only humans left standing.[5] Yet are the contributions from these sub-species either non-human or other-than-human? Would theology concur that they are human since anthropology designates them as such? Regardless, this neither elevates nor downgrades our human status. If our distant forebears are somehow not human, then we possess something in our genetic makeup that is sub-human. It seems to me that theology will need to take its cues from anthropology here.

Sometimes the reverse is true as well. Why, for instance, do biologists take Darwin at his word, particularly in the *Origin*, until it is not expedient to do so? For in his subsequent volume, *The Descent of Man* in 1871, he backtracked from the view that we are all about competition and selfishness and rather, according to Jebelli, inserted the ethical observation that we "are naturally equipped with a compassion and empathy . . . that often values the welfare of others—including nonhumans—more than our own survival and reproduction. Why else would humans engage in the biologically senseless act of altruism, doing things for others with no guarantee of reciprocity?" and thereby enhancing social cohesion—one reason some propose that *Homo sapiens* outlived the Neanderthals. The latter are believed to have been more anti-social: "limiting themselves to groups of twenty to fifty people in small territories while *Homo sapiens* travelled 100 kilometers or more to find new friends."[6]

2. Reich, *Who We Are*, 82, 96–97, 121, 135, 225, 267–68; Sykes, *Kindred*, 329–31.
3. Sykes, *Kindred*, 328, 331–33.
4. Sykes, *Kindred*, 333.
5. Sykes, *Kindred*, 359.
6. Jebelli, *How the Mind*, 70.

Aside from the fact that there is this scriptural injunction: "invite the poor and lame . . . to your feasts, those who cannot repay you" (Luke 14:12–14), biologists have concentrated, as intimated, on the *Origin* to produce such works as *The Selfish Gene* by Richard Dawkins and, for example, claimed that altruism is just a smokescreen for what we ourselves can obtain in our self-centered way, such as the proliferation of our genes in biology or eternal life in religion. We have ulterior motives, meaning we are actually more concerned about ourselves, they insist, despite outward signs of charity, a moral position known as ethical egoism, where everything revolves around us, what the "Me" decade of the 1970s referred to as "looking out for number one." The *Origin* functions as the sacred text for Darwinists, though Darwin himself would not qualify as a Darwinist in this sense, purely at least. And the prospect of being purely *Homo sapiens*, never mind this or that ethnic group, genetically at least, has long since evaporated.

I Have a Mind to Object to This

THERE ARE TWO AUTHORS who combine their efforts to impress upon their readers how simple in the zoological classification scheme the rudiments of mind emerge. Advancements have occurred in the area of neuroscience, and the author-researchers Ogi Ogas and Sai Gaddam attest to this. They assert that mind was operative ever since there were organisms to speak of. (As a side note, some of the earliest organisms were and still are cyanobacteria and blue-green algae, the former retreating to the sea beds and the guts of higher organisms in order to escape from the first pollutant on Earth, namely oxygen. Good for us—as some of these higher creatures; bad for them. Besides, as everyone knows, blue and green do not match; you don't need to be a decorator to grasp that.) What the authors side step is establishing from the outset that there is something numerically distinct from a brain, that is, one brain and one mind equalling two things, mind being a category which much of science is loath to accept.

Another major concern I have with their work is the notion that what they describe as "deciding" on the part of simpler organisms may be no more than the haphazard on the part of those creatures. Simple organisms do allegedly complex things by "deciding" to move toward food sources as well as light by receiving sensory inputs from these sources which in turn trigger the action of flagella, propelling the organism toward the intended target. Other activities the authors mention include the aversion to toxic gradients, prompting microbes to move away from them. That would be intentional, but in this instance there is actual contact between the cell membrane of the creature and the offending substance; not always so for the food. Amoebas and slime molds, for instance, extend pseudopods to engulf food sources when not necessarily first having made contact with them. To describe these events as proto-mentality, or on the way toward becoming mind outright, is to take the analogous too literally.

They also alert us to the philosophical idea that "the ability to *choose* one course of action over another is the ultimate source of agency in the universe,"[1] and in so doing have demonstrated that they do not fear to tread where their biology does not take them. They develop this theme further by asking "if you wrote a memoir that represented your best attempt to express your truest Self, how would it differ in any practical way from a work of literary fiction?"[2] to which we could respond with, well, persons are responsible creatures and fictional characters are not, entailing that persons can actually be incarcerated for their misdeeds and, once again, fictional characters cannot. Plus, in stating that we "are molecular games playing with purposeless subatomic games,"[3] they encroach upon the speculative and arbitrary, for why should the advent of purpose occur with molecules and not the subatomic world (as process thinkers contend), and what accounts for its abrupt arrival on the scene?

Ogas and Gaddam also believe that they have hit upon something having a biological referent. They understand lipids (fatty acids) as "automatically self-assembl[ing] into a membrane. Their physical nature is to link together into an elastic wall that bends back on itself to create a sphere . . . [as when] bubble[s] emerge from soapy water. Soap bubbles contain molecules similar to those found in the membranes of living things."[4] However, there is a sizable gap between soap bubbles, which they point to as a natural precursor type to a cellular enclosure (a demarcation that enables the microbe to distinguish between itself and the other, inside and outside) and a fully functioning semi-permeable cell wall. The comparison is interesting, but the steps required to produce a cell membrane are significantly greater than a soap bubble, meaning all we have at this point is hard-core analogy.

Taking another example, when we are invaded by viruses, which are not alive as such but are essentially a bag of chemicals that are activated in what is for them the right environment, they do not actively seek out host cells but reach them haphazardly through random Brownian motion, made famous through a paper by Albert Einstein in 1905—one of two papers he submitted that year, both of which earned for him the Nobel Prize (the other was on the photoelectric effect)—the toss and tumble of being bombarded by fluids, whether liquid or gaseous. Nothing more exotic or nobler than this. When a bacteriophage virus reaches a bacterium, it attaches to the wall and injects into it its payload, which is its reproductive material, that in turn

1. Ogas and Gaddam, *Journey*, 34.
2. Ogas and Gaddam, *Journey*, 310.
3. Ogas and Gaddam, *Journey*, 313.
4. Ogas and Gaddam, *Journey*, 9.

takes over the reproductive machinery of the host, thereby making many more of itself and destroying its host in the process. Ordinarily, parasites are relative newcomers on the evolutionary scene, since they have not as yet evolved to the point where they and their host can both benefit from their encounter—a relationship known as symbiotic. Instead, its own benefit is to the detriment of it host, which is bad for business, for it then needs to find a new host before it and its offspring "go the way of all flesh." The virus is acting parasitically here, and notice that I have never once referred to anything in it resembling the advent of a mind, otherwise the authors would be forced into a position where they must consider naked RNA—the content of this virus—to bear an incipient mental quality.

Panpsychists, who contend that everything possesses mentality, and process thinkers, who maintain that everything is experiential, would applaud such concepts, but the authors do not, at least not overtly. Their intent is to overcome dualism by suggesting that mentality is a natural phenomenon that is not inserted at some point into an otherwise material-only process by something mystifyingly and metaphysically from outside, like a higher power. They do, however, thereby fail to conform to the scientific insistence that factors in the explanation of an event must not be multiplied where they can be done without, a principle known as Ockham's razor. As applied in this case, the mechanism may be explained by no more than mechanical stimulus-response or reflex, nor need reactions be purposeful, and if some are not, perhaps others are not as well.

As a personal addendum, and by science's own standards, researchers should never be out to prove anything, for that is not in accord with the scientific hallmark of the dispassionate journey of discovery, nothing agenda-driven. One can legitimately engage in disproving a (hypo)thesis in the spirit of ensuring a theory is falsifiable but not fully and completely verify it. Hence there are those scientists who unflinchingly resist doing science and suffer from what is known as confirmation bias. We could very well have two of them before us. A lab coat does not grant them clearance to do so. By all means think outside of the box if warranted, but then recognize that one has forsaken a principle upon which science was founded if one considers one's pursuit more important than the quest for the actual state of affairs (I was going to write "truth," but we seem to have misplaced it). And they say that politics and religion are propagandistic. Move over, for there is another player in our midst.

Verny is another author who commits the same infraction. In an otherwise commendable work on epigenetics, he states in his introduction that he "devoted the next six years to studying the medical scientific literature, *searching for evidence to support my hunch*,"[5] where the impetus should be to determine if the notion is accurate, otherwise we have before us another occasion of confirmation bias. Nevertheless, his study is a profitable one. Epigenetics is the study of "trans-generational inheritance," in which "molecular mechanisms [in] the environment [regulate] gene activity . . . life experiences change us but . . . these changes may be passed on to . . . [subsequent] generations."[6] He emphasizes that "**genes are not destiny**" (his bold), and the type of "environmental influences" which factor into such life experiences that change us "include nutrition, stress, and emotions," for they "can modify the expression (whether they are turned on or off) of those genes without changing the genes themselves."[7] Genes operate mostly to manufacture proteins, but the sections of DNA in view here are the noncoding "regions between genes," formerly designated "as 'junk DNA.'"[8] They "are the switches that play a vital role in cell functions. Mutations in those DNA regions can severely impact our health,"[9] either for good or ill, though the use of the term "severely" ordinarily bears negative connotations.

Medical science now suspects that "the causes of many complex diseases are likely rooted in the experiences of our ancestors,"[10] well beyond our immediate forebears, thereby demonstrating that these effects can have a long reach. This is because "traumatic experiences affect metabolism and . . . these changes [become] hereditary."[11] The influences can be "external; that is, environmental stimuli and internal [ones] (thoughts, feelings, moods)" for "the genome responds equally to both,"[12] meaning we had better control what we think, do, and say with all the strength we can marshal (though Freud believed that this is precisely what we cannot accomplish), since they can have far-reaching consequences.

In essence, gene expression, as opposed to the presence of genes themselves, "make us who we are," and this expression "varies, depending on the life we live."[13] Verny realizes that the language of "the inheritance of acquired characteristics" has long been recognized as well as debunked, coming as it does from Jean Baptiste de Lamarck, who does not enjoy strong credibility

---

5. Verny, *Embodied*, xiii, italics mine.
6. Verny, *Embodied*, 1.
7. Verny, *Embodied*, 2.
8. Verny, *Embodied*, 3.
9. Verny, *Embodied*, 3.
10. Verny, *Embodied*, 15.
11. Verny, *Embodied*, 19.
12. Verny, *Embodied*, 24.
13. Verny, *Embodied*, 26–27.

in biological circles, but now the view boasts respectability. Certainly the failure of the Lysenko experiments in Russia, where the offspring of bodybuilders in fact do not become muscle-bound, illumines the drawbacks of Lamarck's hypothesis in favor of the current study of epigenetics as the former's partial legacy.

But let us expand on the topic of one particular illness and its epigenetic contours. The effect of PTSD on service-persons (predominantly but not exclusively men) has been known though underappreciated since the First World War, when its victims were often dealt with as deserters and punished accordingly. It has probably affected combatants ever since there were wars to speak of, yet was not documented or examined until more recently. Despite being recognized by science, it was still looked upon by others as merely a weakness or personal failing. One can ask how this could have passed unawares for so long, but more than this, are investigations being conducted by epigeneticists on the progeny of PTSD sufferers and their own health issues, both physical and psychological, and to what degree are they more prevalent there than in the general population?

My own life is a case in point. My father saw action and was wounded on the Russian front in the Second World War and my mother lost both her first husband and daughter in the same, her husband in action and her daughter to typhoid. Now I need to ask whether or to what extent some of my own concerns are epigenetic in origin, or are they a function of being reared in a dysfunctional environment facilitated by my parents? Does this confirm or disconfirm the epigenetic rendition of events? And is this a job for medical science or psychiatry as a specialization within it? There might be too much confirmatory information to think otherwise than an epigenetic component. Additional refinements could be made, perhaps, by ruling out those factors that are decidedly home-grown and have a greater psychological referent. The danger, though, could come in the shape of assuming that there must in fact be a DNA component of impactful events and then being determined to disclose them. Besides, one could wonder if the cumulative effect of all these negative health effects over many millennia might eventually leave us handicapped or even incapacitated to actually carry out epigenetic research.

Or, as is supposed, these effects need not remain throughout countless generations but may have a shelf-life if lifestyles undergo a more healthy modification, meaning the inheritance would be more rented than becoming permanent inscriptions into one's genome. This is one way in which Lamarckianism differs from epigenetics in that traits in the latter need not be permanent. Another caution would be to ensure that the epigenetic approach does not devolve into a pop-psychology or power of positive thinking remedy for our ills, for these have undeniable health benefits though ought not take the place of thorough scientific study.

Changes in thoughts and behavior can very much be reinforced in our neural networks as dendrites realign to form different connections owing to neuroplasticity, yet this is more in the way of anatomical structures than molecular. But returning to our theme of what does not constitute authentic science, Verny criticizes another researcher for failing to fathom a certain phenomenon, for then it could not reflect the actual state of affairs. "Not exactly a scientific refutation," Verny advances.[14] Yet with all the rejoinder sensitivity we can muster, and based on what we outlined at the beginning of our look at Verny's work, we can say "you should talk." In stating his methodology as he does, we can adjudicate that he does not heed his own advice.

14. Verny, *Embodied*, 129.

Plant One on Me

ANOTHER CONCERN I HAVE about the thesis of the authors from the previous section is that they commit an oversight when it comes to plants, for these creatures can astound. Amazingly, some of the descriptors for humans can also be applied to plants: they can be deceptive as in mimicking animal species to deceive, say, insects into attempting to mate with them, and they can also be predators as in species like the Venus Fly Trap. Consider also the pleasant aroma of freshly cut grass: it is actually a distress signal on the part of the grass releasing a substance alerting other grasses that an assault has been visited upon them, hence they should be so inclined as to take heed for a similar event may befall them next. Or think of caterpillars eating leaves on a tree: not only does the tree deliver toxins to its extremities in response so as to ward off offenders, but it further becomes a rallying cry to other trees to be proactive and commence production of toxins of their own as a defense mechanism in preparation for a potential upcoming onslaught. The upshot of this is that plants can communicate with other plants and display aspects of mentality and planning. Not only this, but underground fungi physically connecting surface botanicals can facilitate communication between them, as a type of underground railroad of information.

Lyall Watson provides us with many an example of the surprising capacities of infra-human species, both zoological and botanical. This is not a tale; these are from the actual studies of a biologist. I mentioned in the first *User's Guide* that there are two authors whose works make me stop what I am currently engaged in and focus my attention on their newest findings. Here is a third. He is an Irish biologist and, despite being a materialist, he covers topics not ordinarily treated (or even generally respected) in traditional materialist settings.

Rupert Sheldrake was the second of those authors alluded to in a previous volume. If his theory is correct, then additional events in the biosphere should have surfaced. Here is one—try this on for size. For the length of time that humans have engaged in the practice of fishing—many millennia—then one would have expected that fish, despite their not boasting extensive grey matter to work with, would have stumbled upon the idea that whenever they catch a glimpse of a net, assuming that it is not too late by then, they should avoid it at all costs, for no good can come of it. Large numbers of them do not even need to have chanced upon the notion—just a few of them will do, according to Sheldrake's theory (and Darwin's for that matter). And given that they will give rise to offspring having some sort of nascent escape trait in them, they will out-compete others which do not. Plus, Sheldrake's "sense of being stared at," testable and adaptive on the whole, seems to be more prevalent among women than men—advantageous, since they are more likely to depend on it.

Sheldrake is of the view that occurrences such as rats successfully navigating a watery maze will provide an echo of sorts that will be felt across the globe. This is not a flaky theory—it is documented. Biology just does not know what to do with it, let alone having caught up with it. As soon as there is a critical mass of rats with this skill, others elsewhere will also express it. What differentiates this view from Lyall Watson's ill-advised hypothesis of the "Hundredth Monkey" is that Sheldrake's is supported by a theory, partially biological and partially metaphysical—the latter being the stumbling-block for the wider biological community. Nor is he the first in history to have devised such a theory. Experiments appear to buttress his view, yet there does not seem to be a scientific undergirding to reinforce it. While science is no stranger to hypothetical entities, such as gluons, gravitons, and frictionless surfaces, so his hypothetical fields ought not to be dismissed outright. But since he is hypothesizing a force, it should be detectable through some type of instrumentation; however, he insists it is non-energetic. He is not helping his position by doing so. And if, as has recently been occurring, coyotes are attacking people in certain regions (since some persons are not heeding the call not to feed the wildlife, some coyotes now look to us to provide sustenance for them, on pain of aggression should we fail to deliver), from Sheldrake's perspective, why is this not by now a global phenomenon?

Made-to-Order Hypothetical Entities

THE DESIGN ARGUMENT FOR the existence of God has a long history. Its basic syllogistic form looks like this. Premise 1: There exist intricate objects in the world which are complex in their structure; premise 2: They could not have come about by natural processes alone but must have had assistance in arising; conclusion: There must have been a designer to bring this intricate object about. William Paley employed the example of a clock as that intricate object pointing to a watchmaker to argue that the world is much more complex, thereby necessitating God as its designer. This argument has little influence today, apart from those in the theistic camp to begin with and for whom it can bolster belief, since cosmological and evolutionary theories have demonstrated (at least to the satisfaction of scientific practitioners) that natural explanations suffice for the existence of the Earth and its biosphere.

Here are some fragile features in it: First, it commits the fallacy of ignorance in that if an alternative explanation cannot be found, then by a process of elimination, which would make Arthur Conan Doyle's Sherlock Holmes proud, we must throw up our hands in despair and confess that the solution that remains, however improbable, must be the correct one, to which we can respond, "That's a hasty move," for when do we know that we have a complete set of options from which to draw? There could be explanations not yet unearthed, literally, and it would be the height of indolence simply to bemoan, "Well, what else could be the source?" The answer: Keep working at it and the solution might be disclosed, so don't give up so quickly.

Second, once this despair has been expressed, the fall-back position depends on the credulity or incredulity of those who have a range of acceptability when it comes to the legitimacy of resolutions. What I mean is this: One is either likely or unlikely to rest content with a non-definitive proposal if one has already laid the foundations of the parameters one is willing to accept. It does no good to suggest that the lone remaining alternative must be the correct one if no one considers even the possibility of its actuality.

Extra-terrestrials will not gain an extensive following outside of the ancient astronaut theorist camp, so it's not even worth making the attempt. Nor does it lift the issue into the realm of probability should there be ever-larger groups of those proposing it or if they boast well-respected or -known authorities or celebrities in their membership. That would also amount to the fallacy known as an appeal to authority or numbers, where if there are many persons, especially high-caliber ones holding prominent positions, then this increases its legitimacy. Regrettably, it does not, for the well-informed, even if there is a sizable group of them, can be in error. There is no guarantee that researchers have it correctly, even if there are many of them or they have heavy-weights in their corner. Even the well-respected process thinker and scholar David Ray Griffin cannot catapult his 9/11 conspiracy theories into respectability. They continue to fail reaching legitimacy regardless of the amount or status of those endorsing them.

This brings us to the main point. Live options become a function of what one regards as less than absurd. While some might be willing to contemplate ET as the likely candidate for a suspect of an ancient structure's construction, others may not. The design argument, as outlined, bears weight only for those already open or susceptible to the conclusion of the argument. Hence they work only for those already on board with the concept and serve only to galvanize the faith of those engaged in it. Those given to ET thought might respond that the conclusion of the above argument should read: "Therefore ET exists." The bottom line is that these arguments are for the faithful already in the fold, but fail to persuade, let alone convince, those outside it. As Hurtado would lament, this is not the only time there has been "a triumph of preconceptions over evidence."[1]

Yet this is not all. The made-to-order aspect of the title of this chapter can also make reference to the existence and presence of elusive dark matter and energy as well as the quantum world, where the subatomic particles we expect to find are indeed found depending on the manner in which our apparatus is set up. The debate is whether the nature and behavior of these entities were there from the beginning or have been conjured up by our expectation of them. If the latter, then in this sense, and only in this sense, do we have a say in the creation of our own reality, meager though it might be, thereby making sufficient demonstration a subjective category—it becomes left to the eye of the beholder. The bottom line is that there are differing views about what constitutes sufficiency; what is sufficient for some is insufficient for others. This noticeable human element of the will to believe or disbelieve can either afford confidence in that which has yet to

---

1. Hurtado, *One God*, 131.

gain evidence or reject what some regard as established—Einstein and his disquiet about things quantum comes to mind.

The Day before Tomorrow

I HESITATE EVEN TO broach the topic. You have entered upon a time in world history like no other. Have a look around. Out the window and down below at street level you see a man waiting, no, pacing around his vehicle as if expecting someone or something. He merely waits, impatiently. But he is in the middle of the street with traffic all around him. What accounts for his curious behavior? And a woman further down the street stops and peers around as if making certain that she is at just the right spot. Nothing odd about this, you might claim, yet she has been there for two hours. Wonder why? Most of us on this planet have adopted a different regimen ever since, well, the world changed.

In what way? you might ask. It's easy to say how, but not so straightforward to say why, or why now? Here is a stab at it. Every so often, on the order of millions of years, which means we were due for it, the Earth experiences a shift in its magnetic poles. They have done so many times in the past (and why would anyone use this qualifier? since the past is the only time it could ever occur when we report on it) in planetary history, and the shift usually takes place one or two thousand miles from where the poles were before. Definitely in the same hemisphere. There are times, however, when a complete reversal is observed. We have just had one. When they do happen, it is commonly not associated with much disruption of ordinary life, contrary to popular opinion. Communication may be knocked out for a while, but nothing that would upset our routine long term. Except for one thing.

I never used to put much stock in the *artifacts*, mostly because I thought they were *artificial*. They are these—crystals in the shape of human skulls, allegedly the stuff of folklore. There are about thirteen of them globally, an ominous number, most apparently pre-Columbian and meso-American. Some are thought to be ancient, though it has not been determined how ancient peoples could have had the technology to produce them at all, let alone without leaving tool marks. Not obvious ones at least, using the naked eye. With electron microscopes, however, they become more noticeable, thereby fueling the view that they are all "made in Taiwan." Nothing conclusive, though.

Yet here's the thing about these crystals: quartz crystal is used in electronics, and information can be stored in it. Same with the skulls. It was discovered that the shift in magnetic poles seemed to spring the information content of the skulls into action. Data can be retrieved from them—the ones that have some—and those which do contain the same set. And if this were not strange enough, there appeared to be a glitch in the retrieval. Who or whatever stored the information in them failed to install a program that would synchronize the data retrieval when it should be applied. It is as though the skulls stutter. The information is intended for the following day. Worldwide.

Being able to obtain information about the future a day in advance through, I am compelled to say it, crystal balls, is something you might think would be handy, particularly if you happen to be a gambler or a bookie. But not so fast. The skulls are more of an instruction manual, offering a view of what the following day must look like if the course of events is to unfold smoothly, as somebody or something has deemed it. Yet the "deemer" must have had a hiccup in the works, for the information useful for the present day is lost and cannot be "divined." Now you might also suspect that all one needs to do in order to correct the glitch is wait for the following day, insert those requirements and everything will proceed swimmingly. Well here's the other thing: once the information is retrieved it is erased, as though dissolved back into the crystal, permanently preventing the retrieval of currently useful data.

Think in terms of Mr. Phelps's tape recording self-destructing right after being heard, "should [he] decide to accept" the instructions for his Impossible Mission. Too old? You can take a man out of the sixties, but . . . I make no apologies for my age or nostalgic interests. I have control over the latter but not the former. My thanks go out to Tom Cruise for running with the baton thereafter.

Back to the issue at hand. We, the unfortunate inhabitants of the planet, have been tasked with arranging the world in such a way that the following day's events will be facilitated. Sometimes it requires details in general, but also sometimes in particular. It does not usually extend to the level of minutiae, so that if we see ourselves the following day eating half a sandwich, we better eat only half the previous, no, the current day. See? It can be confounding. We can devour all the sandwiches we want, just not tomorrow. So we need to prepare. But how exactly? Certainly by packing half of one. But what else led up to it? I can remember a time when I looked forward to knowing the future. Now I shake my fist at it, at least at the one who could not even get the timing details set correctly. Or maybe it was merely a cosmic trick. The "deemer" and its cronies must be having a laugh at our expense. Somehow it seems more reassuring that he was malicious rather than inept.

This is why you observe the man with the vehicle outside in the place where it needs to be tomorrow. But what else needs to happen now? Yesterday's installment tells us about today, but not how to prepare for tomorrow, since it is not automatic that today alone will get us there. There is more to the calculation, so we need to wait for the following day for that information. And the woman trying to get her coordinates right in preparation for tomorrow. You can imagine the inconvenience. I almost forgot to mention, if the specifics are not followed, then there arises a rupture in events. And before you say, "big deal," it becomes very difficult to catch up to the way the events need to occur. So everyone globally needs to be on the same page. A type of forced complicity, if you will; and you are free not to like it, if that would help. But it usually doesn't. So might as well direct your efforts to what will help. Here is a typical conversation to be heard on the street:

F: Hey there, Karl, what's up?

K: Oh, you know, Fred, business as usual. Just trying to keep behind things.

F: Yeah, I suppose it wouldn't do any good to stay ahead of things, would it?

K: You've got that right. Not these days, anyway. Say, how are the plans coming along for the new house?

F: I can never tell. I'll let you know tomorrow, if I even know by then.

K: I doubt I'll be around then. I'm informed that I will be on the coast.

F: Then what are you doing still here?

K: Hey, if I knew, then I would campaign to be the next crystal skull, wouldn't I?

F: That's for sure. What a knee-slapper.

K: Better take care of that knee if you're going on a hike tomorrow.

F: So I'm told. I best take some liniment along.

K: Where are you going to put it if you will not have a backpack?

F: I wonder if I could, or whether that would tempt, er, fate, if that's what it is.

K: Don't look at me, it's your life. You never know what will make a difference. And while I think of it, don't potentially make life more difficult for the rest of us.

F: I guess if I got angry at the world I could just refuse to do something the skulls tell me I should, and then watch the cascade of disorder happen.

K: Don't think that you would be free from that disorder. You're part of the package.

F: I suppose it's toughest for people with kids trying to get them to do something they don't understand.

K: Yeah, especially if it reflects, or more accurately recoils, on the rest of us. And this by no means implies that adults do understand it.

F: And when will the skulls run out of information to yield?

K: I don't know, you know as much as I do, not tomorrow anyway.

F: Or what happens if the skulls reach a stop command?

K: We've been at this for a generation or so. I guess it's not worth speculating about, even if it's interesting to consider.

F: Yeah, until I realize that we've all been written into this cosmic drama. And by the way, that's an understanding of "interesting" that eludes me.

K: But it's got to run out sometime. It cannot carry an infinite amount of information.

F: Well it sure has staying power to this point. See how it smiles?

K: It's more like a deathly grin. How are we to learn from our mistakes if we are yet to make them? And we actually prepare for them, if not willingly.

F: Yeah, there's not much willingness going on. Besides, do you think you have covered all your bases for tomorrow?

K: Who can tell if we do not know what obstacles will be in our way today?

F: That's the problem. We must prepare in advance, but we cannot plan on what others will do in preparation for their tomorrows that might intersect with ours.

K: Or worse, interfere.

F: And we don't even know who to complain to.

K: Certainly not the skulls; they have not been given the latitude to alter their course.

F: Well here we are on the street corner, trying to figure out how to make our today in such a way that it will conform to our tomorrow.

K: Maybe we could watch others attempting to make a go of it.

F: Sure, there's Leon preparing to participate in a march to protest something or other.

K: That's the trouble with all this; our futures are not hidden from anybody but are on full display on their own computer terminals.

F: To say nothing about what would be the use in protesting if the politicians already know how they are going to vote tomorrow?

K: Completely unnecessary, but we need to go through the motions.

F: And there is Vicky thinking that the best way to prepare for taking her baby for a walk in the park—and why do people say walk in the park when she will be the only one walking while the kid is in a stroller?—all the while knowing that it will rain and the child will come down with a fever.

K: Seems insensitive on the part of the skulls. You'd almost think they didn't care.

F: And what's the point of going through the motions if it's all going to happen only one way anyway?

K: We need to facilitate it to make sure it works out that way.

F: Yeah I know, but I wonder what would happen if we all coordinated our efforts and rose up in defiance?

K: Do you really want to find out?

F: Only if I knew it would make a difference, then it would be worth it.

K: Sounds like you think rebellion could.

F: What it sounds like is an overthrow, and how it could be halted if we all act in one accord?

K: And can we even afford not to revolt?

F: But against who or what? Fate usually doesn't take up arms in bodily form.

K: That sounds pessimistic. Assuming failure without even making the attempt.

F: I might if I thought it all had a point. It would be wasted effort if it were to be doomed from the start.

K: But we don't know if it will be. We could all try, and if it doesn't work, we lick our wounds, grin and bear it and return to . . . I was going to say normal, but it isn't.

It turns out we would not have long to wait. To have information on all events, whether present or otherwise, takes up a lot of memory space, so the storage capacity of the skulls petered out a short time afterward. We all breathed a sigh of relief and then recognized that what we had forfeited was a safety net, for while the skulls were "in control," crime rate went down, although anxiety about how to get things right for the next day did not. But during that time, we forgot about misbehaving. Still, out of spite, nobody traveled to the polar regions anymore.

The Decline and Fall of Materialism?

As there have been proposals, formerly and still, on the periphery of scientific credibility, we investigate some of them below beginning in this entry for the materialistic outlook in general.

"We have had enough" is the cry of a band of scientists who can no longer function with integrity in standard scientific environments. This sounds more like a newspaper article or editorial but is not fake news. Scientists work with materials, yet have waxed philosophical about it and fashioned a metaphysic out of a physics, an ideology out of an idea. The step taken from material reality to "all there is or ever can be is material" is an ideological leap, which some scientists believe is warranted, for it must have the weight of science behind it. Well it does not. "We have never come across non-material entities in our material endeavors, and there is nothing that ever could, therefore there cannot be anything outside of material reality." This is a philosophical argument to which I would assign a failing grade.

To fail to recognize non-material reality does not speak well of such enterprises if all that is ever applied to them is conventional apparatus. Of course they would not, for, in general, no equipment geared to studying the material will register the non-material. Please pardon the response normally applied to accepted practice, but "this is not rocket science." The only fish one will catch are the ones that fit in the mesh of the nets. We need another net. Science does not make or require one to become a materialist as a type of exclusive fraternity membership. What language like theirs amounts to is a heavy-handed shibboleth. Those who believe otherwise, these scientists claim, are on the fringes.

Back to this band. The group includes well-respected scientists in the life and mind sciences, though none in the physical, and has drafted a "Manifesto for a Post-Materialist Science" at a conference held in Tucson, Arizona, from February 7 to 9, 2014.[1] They insist that there is a bidirectional

---

1. Beauregard et al., "Manifesto."

influence and effect between the mental and the physical, which must not be ruled out if it arises through accepted practice and even if it confounds the accepted paradigm. Paradigms must not be allowed to become immovable objects, for multiple have been superseded, the movement from Sir Isaac Newton to twentieth-century physics in relativity and quantum theories being a case in point. It would be eminently unscientific to dismiss out of hand investigation undertaken through empirical methodology, even if it does not comport with the adopted paradigm.

The lead scientist of the team is Gary E. Schwartz, where the E. stands for Einstein. Outside of the manifesto drawn up by the group, team members have written books individually; one of Schwartz's is what we will focus on. By way of outline, he argues strenuously that seemingly chance occurrences submit to order when in large numbers and will assume a Gaussian distribution, otherwise known as a bell curve, thereby making chance apparent and not real. For individual events, the predictability of an outcome is low, but were there to be a multitude of them, there is then a greater probability of their yielding order of some description.

Hence many chances make an order. This is not new; scientists as well as religionists (though the latter intending quite different meanings by it) refer to a type of order out of chaos. Random events still occur, like whose phone number a scammer will dial next, they just beget order after a large amount of trials. Chance and randomness are still present before many individual events take place, at which time patterns can emerge. As the biblical wisdom book of Ecclesiastes points out, "time and chance happen to [us] all" (9:11b).

Thus chance remains a useful category, and kindly excuse the obviousness, until it does not, for order quashes it. Chance is something with which we must contend, until such time as it reveals order, for then it has become tamed or domesticated. We feel reassured in identifying chance until it becomes subsumed into an anticipated order. So chance arises and then vanishes, prompting us to ask if it was ever there in the first place, or if it was merely a kind of pre-order—a part of a larger whole.

Schwartz urges that there is an intelligent evolving universe which exhibits trial and error experimentation when it comes to design; the universe develops by a process of fits and starts. While using the term "apparent randomness,"[2] his is another in the line of Intelligent Design movements. He avoids the term but eventually admits his link with it,[3] though he espouses a pantheistic kind of divinity, which the I.D. movement, stemming as it does

2. Schwartz and Simon, *G.O.D.*, 101.
3. Schwartz and Simon, *G.O.D.*, 88, 263.

from Christian orthodoxy, resists. For Schwartz, God is understood as an acronym standing for a "Guiding-Organizing-Designing field,"[4] whose universe reflects not chance but organization. Chance for him has no "organizing power," and he challenges scientists to provide "positive evidence" of chance producing order, for by itself it can only produce more disorder.[5] In essence, what nature does is mix things, not order them.[6] He does, however, erroneously attribute actuality (the move known as hypostatization) or operating power to chance in stating that it works, though it can only happen or occur as per Eccl 9:11b. He insists that "even randomness itself does not occur by chance," and it "is incorrectly described as 'disorder' or 'complete unpredictability.'"[7] Furthermore, "randomness [actually] creates normal distributions" which are orderly,[8] and "makes bell-shaped curves," which are "replicated each time."[9] Simply put, order is not explained by chance.

By way of commentary, his is an unfalsifiable view, since nothing proffered can qualify as disconfirming his outlook. Perhaps he himself suffers from the confirmation bias he claims science should avoid[10]—the stance that one assumes the correctness of one's position and selects only those data buttressing it. What stands to disconfirm his view includes (a) there is no order as such to Brownian motion, meaning this randomness remains random; (b) when a stone is dropped in a pond, the waves spread outward to shore and disorder, but never return to order; (c) glass ordered into bottles and mirrors tends to break when they fall and the fragment shapes can usually not be predicted and never revert to an unbroken state, thereby highlighting the fact that there is irreversibility in our macroworld; (d) it is important to keep in mind that the more samples one has, not only does it yield a normal distribution, but even these contain more in the way of extremes; and (e) a true mixture in liquid form does not yield a normal distribution, for through diffusion one unit of it will be the same as another.

One might imagine that as a theist I would be open to I.D., but I do not find the reasoning of that movement to be convincing. From (c) above, it does no good to assert that by counting the fragments produced in this way over many such incidents that, were the numbers to be graphed, there is assurance that we would be left with a bell-shaped curve and hence some

---

4. Schwartz and Simon, *G.O.D.*, 29.
5. Schwartz and Simon, *G.O.D.*, 33.
6. Schwartz and Simon, *G.O.D.*, 34.
7. Schwartz and Simon, *G.O.D.*, 40.
8. Schwartz and Simon, *G.O.D.*, 41.
9. Schwartz and Simon, *G.O.D.*, 53.
10. Schwartz and Simon, *G.O.D.*, 58.

type of order, for this gives no comfort to the owner of a Ming Dynasty ceramic vase which has dropped from a height and succumbed to the encounter with a hard surface by the annoyingly consistent law of gravity in a gravitational field.

The metaphysic Schwartz draws his strategy from is the interconnectedness of everything in nature, something new agers have repeatedly touted. Since everything is interdependent, according to Schwartz, there obviously can be no independence. This is highly significant for him, since with dependency "there is no support [for] a randomness theory, at least in its purest sense, as posited by random sampling. The conclusion is unavoidable."[11] And the reason that everything is interdependent is "because everything is interconnected by . . . fields."[12] He understands photons, the quantum or basic constituent of the electromagnetic force and its corresponding spectrum of radiation, as non-material, since they are massless (at least when at rest) and spaceless, as are fields.[13] Science, on the contrary, assumes photons are material in that they are particles as well as waves, and waves at least facilitate material since they contain virtual particles—those which have insufficient energy to exist on their own. He thus envisions the standard scientific view as inadequate. His work becomes indicative of a post-materialist approach.

Schwartz definitely has sympathy and even affinity with the I.D. movement. His view of divinity, to the extent that there in fact is one in the conventional sense, probably has the greatest parallel with the process God, which I have outlined elsewhere. Schwartz's God is an experimenter who works on a trial-and-error basis, which does not customarily fit with the I.D. strategy. My displeasure with the I.D. scheme is no secret, so how do I differ from it? I hold to an active deity but do not belong to their fraternity, nor am I a card-carrying member of the design enclave in the tradition of William Paley—a position held by the young Charles Darwin. He, like me, grew out of it. Paley was a fan of natural theology, a bottom-up approach where the starting point is something from the ordinary world of experience which is employed in the form of philosophical argumentation to lead to the conclusion that God exists. Paley utilizes the intricate complexity of a watch to suggest the presence of a watchmaker behind the watch who must have marshalled the skill to manufacture the product, as opposed to natural forces alone combining to produce it. In like manner, the human eye or the

---

11. Schwartz and Simon, *G.O.D.*, 108.
12. Schwartz and Simon, *G.O.D.*, 247.
13. Schwartz and Simon, *G.O.D.*, 265.

world itself would not have been made by these forces alone, but point to an eye or world maker, which to his reasoning is understood as God.

This effort is misguided, for the conclusion does not follow from the premises. At the very least, there is no guarantee that the Christian divinity is at the watch-making helm; it could be a different one—we could be barking up the wrong deity to our chagrin. Instead of expecting to find Yahweh, we could just as readily be left with Brahman, given the appropriate adjustments. Plus, evolutionary biology for the eye and cosmology for the world present scenarios in which both arise through natural explanations after all, rendering Paley's conclusion as hasty and exposed to scientific refutation. Take that! Rather than natural theology, I find a theology of nature approach to hold more promise, wherein the starting point is assuming God's existence and then taking scientific findings as the kind of thing God would do.

In this top-down strategy, one begins with God and ends with a new vision of God and the world, where God works in and through the world that science unveils. This deals with what effect God has on our understanding of the world, for since there is a God, how does this inform our science? And a theology of nature also considers the theological implications for scientific theories, for whatever is known about the world is built upon God as a foundation, only here the foundation is at the top. Yet it is also not without its difficulties, for, once again, the specific deity proposed does not require it to be the Christian one; and if this were not enough, can we in all good conscience proudly assert that bloody competition, struggle, and survival, together with an enormous amount of extinctions along the path, are reflective of what a loving God would do? Or perhaps we have not been informed or accurately described what God is like. Hence there are problematic features no matter which avenue we travel on, so be prepared to be disappointed with some aspects of your chosen outlook.

I.D. seems to present a proactive divinity who has a clear vision of a desired (alphabetically) aim, end, goal, and purpose (and in this sense the form of the argument is teleological), which will indeed transpire no matter what, and unilaterally forces its hand before things go awry and threaten the trajectory toward the target (you know a concern is serious when it is described using alliteration). Well then, some may advance the retort, what is the observable difference between the I.D. view and ordinary natural selection without reference to a deity? In response, I envision the rise and fall of species as not completely explained through evolutionary theory itself. For a position to be chance-oriented alone and thus gradual, for successful organisms do not appear overnight, I fail to imagine how a rodent at the time of the end of the dinosaurs can have an unbroken line of development to *Homo sapiens* and accomplish the feat in a mere sixty-six million years. The required changes, in my estimation, could not come about on its own in that time span without some sort of assistance. The divinity in view here would be reactive in knowing neither with complete certainty which choices organisms will select nor where the decisions will lead or what shape they will take. What awaits this process is a journey of discovery for the deity as well, and in this way God's knowledge grows, and, dare I say it, God evolves.

Evolution itself also undergoes evolution. Ecologists have become aware of what species have made, or been given, as necessary changes to permit the species to be going concerns. Crickets, for instance, have developed noiseless wings so as to avoid being found by certain parasitic flies that will usurp them for their own reproductive interests and destroy the crickets in the process before they are able to mate. The stunning aspect about this is that it took only three years to emerge. That is hardly gradual. But wait, there's more. Lest we surmise that male crickets could not attract females while making no sound whatsoever, in the fourth year they were observed to make purring sounds instead, alerting the females while evading the flies. That males could do this so speedily and that females could revamp what would constitute for them a mating call, and for those flies to be held back in not adapting themselves to the new regime, to my reckoning bespeaks the activity of some assisting agent in eluding extinction, which in itself would amount to a bad-for-business outcome for the fly in needing to seek, if it could, for an alternative host victim.[14] In any case, these changes are actually well-nigh overnight from an evolutionary perspective.

Another example is certain monkeys in Zanzibar that have dealt with shrinking food resources by first eating a different plant, which regrettably contained cyanide, which did not aid in their survival, but then chancing upon the idea that they could consume the charcoal left behind from human fires used for cooking. What would be carcinogenic for humans—the ingesting of elemental carbon—becomes a life line for other primates.[15] Who knew? and go figure. A possible downside of these otherwise salutary outcomes could be that such a proposed agent would show favoritism, in that it assists crickets but not flies (no objection from me), as opposed to at minimum working toward there being a more level playing field. It remains unclear as to what a divine agent would do. How we evaluate this situation, as always, will depend on our perspective. At least that's my perspective.

Further research will disclose how far and wide-ranging such instances are. Natural selection still operates in the customary way, but the

---

14. PBS, *Evolution Earth*, "Darwin's Finches."
15. PBS, *Evolution Earth*, "Darwin's Finches."

deity might initiate a quicker resolution to specific survival issues. To what end, though, is the question. For the delight in observing the antics of certain primates? Perhaps. We do the same when we visit zoos. Thus whereas Schwartz comes to divinity through science, and sees science as a resource tool in the hands of divinity, I begin with divinity and end with science as the kind of thing God would engage in to serve God's purposes. Neither is conclusive and could be understood as opposite sides of the same coin. There's that coin reference again. There is also a third alternative known as systematic synthesis,[16] which combines the bottom-up and top-down approaches. This is indicative of the process outlook.

A question that remains is whether some events in the universe and in our lives are purposeful, providential, or accidental, and that will comprise much of the subject matter of the next section.

---

16. Barbour, *When Science*, 34–36.

The Rules of the Game

As you can no doubt surmise from an earlier story here, I am a sports fanatic. Mostly team sports, that is, except for curling. During a particularly dark period in the pandemic, I even contemplated watching it. Thankfully, I pulled myself together, rallied, and surrendered control of the remote to my dear wife. When asked why not this particular team sport, I suggest that if body-checking were to be involved, I would probably become a spectator. To be more precise, then, I should qualify my preference by stating I am in favor of contact team sports; individual sports are not really on my radar. Sure, tennis can have sparkling athleticism and amazing moments making them candidates for "plays of the week" or other "honor rolls." I find it interesting that some individual sports pit one athlete directly against another, as in boxing and wrestling—these two admittedly being contact-oriented—while others involve a group of athletes vying for the best score (or the lowest, as in golf) or the fastest time with generally no contact between them, unless there is incidental or intended jostling, the latter perhaps resulting in a disqualification.

Do not get me wrong. I am glued to the TV when the gold medal one hundred or two hundred meter races and other track events come on in the Olympics, especially when countries to which I have an affinity are competing, but I think once every four years will suffice. This goes for the winter as well as for the summer games. Yet my heart rests with team sports, for the sometimes intricate play exhibited by the team members leading to the scoring of a goal, for instance. But there are times when the agreed-upon rules of the contest appear incongruent to the rest of the action. I have in mind rugby, for example, where one can hit an opposing player, for it would not be strategic to impede one from your own, with all the might at one's disposal, provided that it does not amount to rough play or dangerous tackling. It seems odd, then, that woe be unto you and heaven forbid, one should commit the egregious infraction of going off-side. To do so is evidently abhorrent. I mean the very disproportionality of it astounds. Players can become bloodied or concussed, but going off-side also stops play.

Or in box lacrosse, where there is no injunction against off-side, players can be whacked with opposing members' sticks so as to attempt to jar the ball loose from the player in possession of it and cradling it so as to protect it from such an eventuality were s/he not circumspect. But do not, I repeat, do not step in the goaltender's crease, for even one's toe on the line is sufficient to nullify a goal. In baseball as well, it has been decided that if a base-runner has the option to "steal" a base, not a good role model for the younger set, or remain where s/he is, the player must be touched with the ball in the glove of a member of the opposing team prior to reaching base, while if a player has no such option and must either advance to the next base or retreat to the present one, then no application of a tag is required to render the base-runner "out."

Curiously, in the latter case, it has been deemed that this requirement is in place since it constitutes what is referred to as a "force play," where the player must be on the move. Thus where no option exists, it is easier for the defensive team to record an "out," to say nothing about the fact that at the beginning of each half-inning in regulation play, meaning not in extra innings, at least in the regular season, the offensive team is outnumbered nine to one. Well, as is the go-to reaction on the part of sports enthusiasts, those are simply the rules of the game, and who can argue with consensus? Yet rules can change, and it might not be abundantly clear as to why one rule was opted for as opposed to another.

All of what has been said so far in this segment is applicable to our regular, everyday, ordinary sphere of operation, the kind that can be documented by anyone who cares to do so. What, though, if we speak about a different dimension, namely the beyond or afterlife? Can we speak of the rules in that realm? Well, there are some who attempt to do just that. And should you propose that this is an inconclusive enterprise, you would not be alone. But how is it accomplished? The drive on the part of persons to engage in such a pursuit is the perceived need to be in contact with loved ones who have passed on, perhaps too early for most. Those people urge that contact with the dearly departed can be arranged, so one need not lose heart.

Participants often describe scenes reminiscent of the Elysian fields of old—meadows filled with flowers, where love is present, and perhaps even one's pets from the earthly plane.[1] Passed, or graduated, relatives usually give encouragement that those left behind are progressing nicely and even

---

1. Hogan, "Self-Guided," 24–25.

offer instruction as to how the living may improve.[2] Some attest that the afterlife experience includes swimming in a lake,[3] meaning there being no sea (Rev 21:1) does not preclude lakes and streams. The scene may even include a father's model railway[4] (see, you *can* take it with you!). Participants' vision of their departed relatives are sometimes described as seeing their "true sel[ves]," and their existence is filled with peace and fun.[5] These folks in the beyond may not make a sartorial statement but appear to be attired with standard hereafter issue garb, though recognizable by earthly relatives as having been worn by the deceased, like denim pants and "cotton shirt[s]."[6] One wonders if they bear brand-name labels.

These figures, however, caution the visitors about what may and may not be revealed to Earth-bound persons concerning this new plane of existence, which amounts to very little at present, for it would be incomprehensible until such time as they "cross over" themselves.[7] They can point things out that only the recipient and close relatives could know, and predict what will befall these mortals.[8] They ask that their messages be accepted without judgment.[9] If we were to ask what makes all of this contact possible, some experiencers of it recommend relaxation techniques, meditation, and trance states, plus there are mediums to assist where the uninitiated fall short.[10] Present too are guardian angels to serve in the process,[11] one of whom even self-identifies as the archangel Michael.[12] My favorite account of this is the following: "at the edge of my bed stood three guardian angels. Three, I was told, because I was such high maintenance they had to take shifts."[13] I trust they have a good union to settle disputes over working conditions.

Some health professionals have entered the fray and developed methods for the benefit of seekers, often requiring credentials and "state-licens[ing]"[14] to facilitate the connection with those who have passed. Non-

2. Hogan, "Self-Guided," 26.
3. Hogan, "Self-Guided," 33.
4. Hogan, "Self-Guided," 34–35.
5. Hogan, "Self-Guided," 37.
6. Hogan, "Self-Guided," 38.
7. Hogan, "Self-Guided," 38.
8. Hogan, "Self-Guided," 40.
9. Pe, "Meditation," 51.
10. Wright, "Guided," 84; Schwartz, "Soul," 95–97.
11. Pe, "Meditation," 49.
12. Pe, "Meditation," 58.
13. Herrick, "Understanding," 222.
14. Wright, "Guided," 73.

physical helpers can also be dispatched, like an afterlife AAA, to give the newly dead a boost so as to assist them to continue and progress in their afterlife journey,[15] and at times God is solicited in prayer for guidance and protection in this regard.[16] Individuals in the hereafter plane might appear as they did prior to passing[17] or assume the form at the time when they were in the best of health, perhaps in their twenties to thirty years of age.[18] In comparison, one must ask, why then did Jesus' resurrection body retain the stigmata (Luke 24:39; John 20:24–28)?

Other particulars include communication as taking the form of telepathy "in the afterlife dimensions," and sight is panoramic, that is, omnidirectional.[19] Messages conveyed can also take theological form, such as there is no divine judgment,[20] which should either provide consolation for the fearful or raise red flags for the biblical crowd. And contrary to "ancient astronaut theorists," it is scientists and not extra-terrestrials in the afterlife who deliver technological advancements to earthly humans.[21] To top it off, as a capper, some who write books about these topics claim to be "inspired by the Holy Spirit,"[22] a caution for the presumptuous among us.

The experience is not always positive for the mediums, though. Some report that their bodies are taken over by these spirits, they did not profit from the encounter and felt in potential danger.[23] Besides this, messages spoken through them can be in the form of languages they have never learned,[24] which places a different spin on glossolalia (speaking in tongues). By the foregoing, it would seem that should there be no rule book as such to consult, then one may need to prepare the semblance of one through trial and error. Or is there a text which addresses the concern? Contrary, no doubt, to the supposition of some, that the Bible in my scrutinizing hands is much-maligned, I remain convinced that it is still the most significant writing in recorded history, despite its shortcomings. It continues to apply to most areas of life, modern as well as ancient. It is for this reason that I

---

15. Moen, "Aiding," 108.
16. Morgan, "Pendulum," 188–89.
17. Morgan, "Pendulum," 191.
18. Herrick, "Understanding," 219.
19. Morgan, "Pendulum," 191.
20. Morgan, "Pendulum," 192.
21. Morgan, "Pendulum," 193.
22. Herrick, "Understanding," 211.
23. Zammit, "People," 295, 300–302.
24. Zammit, "People," 300.

retreat to it and take my cues from it when other avenues fail, and in this respect I am at my most conservative.

This is one of them: rule number one—"do not believe every spirit, but test the spirits to see whether they are from God, because many false prophets have gone out into the world" (1 John 4:1). Words to live by; not every spirit is an ally. Here is another stemming from the first: rule number two—"For such men are false prophets, deceitful workmen, masquerading as apostles of Christ. And no wonder, for Satan himself masquerades as an angel of light. It is not surprising, then, if his servants masquerade as servants of righteousness" (2 Cor 11:13–15a). We must ask, however, what is to be gained should connection with the deceased be outlawed by such masquerades if love and healing occur by it in the lives of ones still on the earthly plane. Humans do seem to benefit, which would be bad for demonic business, and would place a different perspective on "Every good and perfect gift is from above, coming down from the Father of the heavenly lights" (Jas 1:17), unless God be the source of it as well.

The advantage to the world of "principalities and powers" could be the lone and major one of rendering dependency in the lives of seekers and taking the focus off God, and in so doing, if constant in the long term, will forfeit what God's kingdom has to offer. Perhaps this is the determining factor as to why consulting mediums and spiritists is unlawful for us (Exod 22:18; Lev 19:31; 20:27), despite experiencers reporting only positivity, at least in terms of the accounts of the researchers. The most important passage here for our purposes is the first of these (Exod 22:18), wherein we are informed as to the reason we should avoid such services: "for you will be defiled by them." Yet how could a procedure so innocuous lead astray? Well, as I have outlined in my previous offering, even something as helpful or at least innocent as a Ouija board is not so innocent after all but opens the door, unawares by us, to "familiar spirits" (1 Sam 28:3, 7–9 KJV). Maybe it is all a ploy to get one hooked on the ungodly and permit unclean spirits to roam in and around us. Shunning it might be the only way to ensure that we are not being duped. Hence there are times when even a liberal like myself will, not knowing how else to proceed, retreat to the safety and security of the scriptures. Moreover, an intermediate state of bliss, as depicted by the experiencers of their deceased friends and relatives that the latter occupy, is not something about which a great deal of the sacred text informs us, thus it could be salutary to err on the side of caution, not having been extensively briefed as to the rules of the game.

An author who offers a full book-length treatise on mediumistic themes is Mark Anthony (not Cleopatra's lover). Early on he commits himself to the notion that "spirits are pure electromagnetic energy,"[25] allowing us to interact with them since we are no strangers to this field either, only ours is at a much lower frequency than theirs. His conviction that "energy never dies,"[26] however, is problematic. Certainly "energy is neither created nor destroyed but can be changed into other forms" is a mantra that even secondary school students are familiar with, prompting Michio Kaku, a renowned physicist and one of the founders of string theory, buoyed by this principle to exclaim that "eternal life does not [thereby] violate the laws of physics"[27] (energy here, energy there, I suppose). Yet more must be said. Initially, one of the forms which energy can be transformed into can be the unrecoverable kind. Energy flung out into space dissipates over time and eventually assumes the temperature of the cosmic microwave background radiation, which does not even reach three degrees Kelvin (above absolute zero). And on the grand scale, our universe is destined, should nothing else intervene beforehand (we might as well leave the divine alternative open), to culminate in a frozen death when energy will well-nigh perish, or at least be in a form unavailable for work.

Anthony then falls into a speculative mindset in asserting, as law enforcement officers have been known to hold, that "there is no such thing as coincidence."[28] Once again, important items have been overlooked. For instance, that the moon completely occludes the sun in a solar eclipse and seems from our perspective to be exactly the same size in the sky as the sun is a coincidence. The diameter of the sun is four hundred times that of the moon, but the moon is four hundred times closer to us that the sun, making them appear to be the same size. Since the moon is retreating from the Earth at about the same rate as our fingernails grow—a meager amount it would seem and not much in the short term, but significant over billions of years, at which time it will be released from the Earth's gravitational pull—earlier in its history it would have appeared larger than the sun and in the future it will appear smaller. Hence it is coincidental that we are living at the Goldilocks time when the distance between them is just right for such an astronomical spectacle (and it's free and not likely to be taxed, though best to don protective eyewear when taking it in).

Anthony finds that we bear an "electromagnetic soul [which] is housed in the brain the same way data is stored in the hard drive of a computer,"[29]

25. Anthony, *Afterlife*, 9.
26. Anthony, *Afterlife*, 9.
27. Anthony, *Afterlife*, 33.
28. Anthony, *Afterlife*, 21.
29. Anthony, *Afterlife*, 54.

yet data can be lost, at which time it is gone, but at no time do we lose a soul yet retain a functional body, thus the analogy is ultimately unsuccessful (as are many of them). His technique for making a spirit connection comes in the form of the acronym R.A.F.T., standing for *"recogniz[ing]* the presence of spirits and the signs they present, *accepting* the reality of the contact, *feeling* the importance . . . of the message, and *trusting"* what the message provides.[30] He reassures us when emphasizing that "messages from spirits are motivated by love and guide people to healing and resolution. They never direct anyone to commit acts of anger, violence, or destruction."[31] Where then, one must inquire, do we get the saying, the spirit known as "de debil made me do it"? I reiterate, not all spirits are benevolent.

Anthony comments on how he came by way of this mediumistic capacity: "Psychic ability is an inherited, recessive genetic trait, . . . which sometimes skips a generation."[32] On which gene sequence, precisely, might this be found? Plus, why then does he put forward his technique, and why are there institutes where one can learn and acquire the art? And not to be left out, "animals have souls and can communicate" too.[33] His foundation remains energy, which he, trusting science as well as spirits, lauds cannot become old, ill, or perish,[34] and his motto becomes *"Eternal Light, Eternal Life,"*[35] which he claims is physics, not philosophy.

Some comments are in order. First, if spirits are electromagnetic too, then they must be subject to gravity as well, and better wear seatbelts when traveling (safety first!). Moreover, are alleged spirits, on this same rationale, limited by being able to be in only one place at a time? Can mediums pull in the same spirit in more places at once? How can one know it is the same spirit? Since they are bound by electromagnetism and nothing (with the possible exception, perhaps, of neutrinos in certain circumstances) can exceed the speed of light, they must also submit to it. Second, in the form of a question, à la Jeopardy, if spirits can interact with the material world, then why do they not do much more of it for our benefit? Third, also a question, is there gender in the afterlife contrary to the scriptures (Matt 22:30; Mark 12:25; Luke 20:34–35), or is that just the form of their spirit manifestation to us? Besides, it is didactically irresponsible to cite only those passages, as he does on occasion, which may fit his system but neglect to mention those

---

30. Anthony, *Afterlife*, 76, italics mine.
31. Anthony, *Afterlife*, 91.
32. Anthony, *Afterlife*, 121.
33. Anthony, *Afterlife*, 163.
34. Anthony, *Afterlife*, 140–41.
35. Anthony, *Afterlife*, 254, italics his.

in opposition to it. Fourth, the accepting and trusting aspects of the R.A.F.T. technique are the troubling parts, for that is where we can be misled. In cases of grief, when we are in a vulnerable state and our defenses are down,[36] we can be more prone to negative spiritual suggestion, and the demonic can pounce on this; and mediums can also become a dependency for some persons and therefore idolatrous. Fifth, do mediums ever see malevolent spirits, or is everything always peaches and cream? Seems too convenient for me. Recall from the above that electromagnetism is light, and this is how demons can masquerade. As we are cautioned, there are counterfeits afoot. Plus, as for me, what if the Spirit coming through to us prompts us not to engage in exercises such as this? As always, safety first!

Perhaps mediums as conduits themselves are deceived in anticipating that the spirits they encounter are always on the positive side of the ledger. It might appear to be more prudent to err on the side of caution and not assume that the spirits which are being contacted on the other side have the divine approbation and come in peace. Remember the Trojan horse—benevolent on the outside but deadly on the inside. Maybe this is a ruse where the mediums are getting tripped up. No doubt positivity can be derived from it, but the ultimate cost may be negative. Even narcotics can have a positive side in that they provide temporary relief of pain or escape from one's cares, but they can clutch you and hold you in their grasp and will not let you go until you embrace them again and again. In so doing they choke like a boa constrictor, producing dependency, with a predictable and often fatal end.

But this is not all. If what Anthony says is real is actually the case, then who or what fashioned it this way? Who or what orchestrates the afterlife setting that Anthony sees? Aside from masquerading, can the powers actually depict a setting complete with stage and props? Or is this an ability they are unable to muster? Should these production talents be within their wheelhouse, then they may be vastly superior to what may once have been supposed about them.

What becomes problematic is that the principalities-and-powers-world has access to all the personal information that mediums can glean from the spirit world and can imitate those spirits with whom the bereaved seek to make contact—spiritual versions of Rich Little–type impressions. Or do we think demons cannot know these things or mimic those departed? Would that there were a third option, a place in addition to Earth and heaven where these principalities and powers could be banished. Well there is one. They have been cast into the Abyss but are permitted to roam the Earth (Rev 20:1–3), seeking those whom they can take with them. The devil (otherwise

---

36. Anthony, *Afterlife*, 248.

known as the "accuser" (Job 1:6), the deceiver and adversary) has made it his life's work to do this, and mediumship might be playing into his hands to the extent that it is among the "secret arts" (Exod 7:11b, 22; 8:7, 18—there is that conservative moment on my part again). The tendency could very well be that after repeated unsuccessful attempts at winning some persons over, the Spirit gets the message and leaves them alone at best or hands them over to the dark side at worst (1 Cor 5:5), though not irrevocably.

As an aside, the above could also apply to past life regression hypnotherapy, and the information garnered there could be a product of contact with familiar spirits as opposed to past lives. Besides, should reincarnation be the case, then what would be the benefit or the wherefore and the why of not remembering past lives, since it could be salutary to build and improve on them instead of beginning with first principles time and again, with no guarantee that the previous situation might be superseded.

An inquiry worth making at this point is what the extent may be to which the resurrection appearances of Jesus suggest a similarity with the encounters of the above experiencers. To frame the question in its starkest relief, does it resemble the kind of masquerading that counterfeits can reproduce or duplicate? To begin with, on the one hand, the same God who "caused [Jesus' resurrection] to be seen" also caused the event itself, but the viewing was restricted to the disciples (Acts 10:40–41), thereby prompting the question as to whether this was an objective occurrence if it was open to, conveniently one might say, only a select few. On the other, the number of those privy to the appearances balloons to five hundred simultaneously (1 Cor 15:6). Then, contrary to most of those gathered at séances, the disciples were not in an expectant mood nor anticipating that God would intervene in these events. Instead, they cowered in a locked room "for fear of the Jews" (John 20:19), and even if Jesus were to rise from the dead, it was still possible to doubt its veracity (Matt 28:17).

Plus, the addition to the ending of Mark has it that Jesus "appeared to them in a different form"—a power available to shape-shifters—yet they remained doubtful (16:12–13). Hence they were not R.A.F.T.ers as counseled by Anthony. Their incredulity might have been directed toward Jesus as having risen bodily, for such an event in which he claimed not only that he would "rise again" (Matt 27:63) but that he would be the author of his own resurrection (John 2:19) was not in their world of experience outside of his having raised Lazarus (John 11:1–44). Nor did any among the group of disciples self-identify as a medium (nor would they, of course, given the injunction against it). In sum, these appearances do not have much of an analog with spirit encounters attested to by Anthony.

As a matter of fact, Jesus' life, ministry, death, and resurrection were largely unique in these respects. Ehrman provides us with a lengthy list of those features of Jesus believed to have had analogs in other religious figures at or before his time, whether historical or mythical, and he concludes that they are, to put it mildly, overstated. His devastating critique is worth quoting at length:

> Real historians of antiquity are scandalized by such assertions—or they would be if they bothered to read Freke and Gandy's book. The authors provide no evidence for their claims concerning the standard mythology of the godmen. They cite no sources from the ancient world that can be checked. It is not that they have provided an alternative interpretation of the available evidence. They have not even cited the available evidence. And for good reason. No such evidence exists.
>
> What, for example, is the proof that Osiris was born on December 25 before three shepherds? Or that he was crucified? And that his death brought atonement for sin? Or that he returned to life on earth by being raised from the dead? In fact, no ancient source says any such thing about Osiris (or about the other gods). But Freke and Gandy claim that this is common knowledge. And they prove it by quoting other writers from the nineteenth and twentieth centuries who said so. But these writers too do not cite any historical evidence. This is all based on assertion, believed by Freke and Gandy simply because they read it somewhere. This is not serious historical scholarship. It is sensationalist writing driven by a desire to sell books.[37]

One researcher who delves into additional scientific specifics is R. Craig Hogan. What can be commented on here is the perspective some next-life communicators take on the brain-mind distinction, which might ordinarily prompt them to take up residence in the dualistic camp. Hogan, a scientist who ventures into the philosophical sphere, however, has a different spin on this, which places him outside of dualism.[38] I find the first part of his argument persuasive, but, as with the above, unconvincing, though I do appreciate some of the views he puts forward concerning how the mind need not be associated with the brain for either to function properly. One of his theses is not having sight does not prevent certain individuals who have near-death experiences (NDEs) or out-of-body experiences (OBEs) from reporting on

---

37. Ehrman, *Did Jesus*, 26.

38. In his address to the fortieth annual conference of the Academy for Spiritual and Consciousness Studies (ASCS) titled "The Brain Is Superfluous: Evidence from This Life and the Next." Taken from the conference proceedings volume.

what they see while anaesthetized, in a coma or otherwise, when the brain is inactive and the person unresponsive. Some can describe clothing the hospital staff were wearing prior to donning their scrubs, names and rooms itemized on a surgical schedule, colors of sheets, and so forth. And before one objects that they might have had access to this information beforehand, here is the kicker—some were blind from birth! Hogan concludes from this that the mind is not limited by the brain as materialists would contend and may not even be connected with it.[39]

Potential criticisms include: (a) these cases are anecdotal, and patients might not be impaired aurally as they are visually and may have heard and retained these details; (b) the analogy that the brain functions as a receiver capturing signals from a mental transmitter and converting them into conventional sensory stimuli that diminish to the extent that brain damage arises, falters, for "the mind could not be conveyed by electromagnetic waves," since even "people in Faraday cages, which block electromagnetic waves, still have experiences."[40] This places the emphasis above on both Earthlings and spirits as operating electromagnetically in doubt. Another more complete resolution will need to be sought; (c) the many instances when our mental state affects our physical state, as in the effects of anxiety and stress, and vice versa, in terms of mind-altering substances, needs to be kept in mind as a dual effect; and (d) those who bear only a partial brain whether from birth or through surgery suffer little impairment from everyday functioning abilities, and should the mind be like a transmitter, then removing portions of the brain would seriously interfere with mental operations, similar to how losing parts of a tuner/receiver would disturb transmission, yet this is not found to be the case.[41]

Furthermore, some persons exposed to computer randomly generated pictures reacted to certain ones "as early as six seconds" prior to the selection being made, prompting Hogan to declare that the mind is doing the reacting before the information registers in the brain, with the implication that brains are not required or even involved in the transaction.[42] Spurred on by this example, some researchers posit the following rationale: minds are in a field where consciousness resides and individual minds "are linked through this pervasive field" which "joins all the individual parts into one whole." The difficulty Hogan uncovers with this strategy is that "if the mind were in a field linking brains, it still would not need to interact with the brain

---

39. Hogan, "Brain," 151–52.
40. Hogan, "Brain," 152–53.
41. Hogan, "Brain," 156–57.
42. Hogan, "Brain," 159.

to have experiences," thereby making brains redundant.[43] One shortcoming of this view is that even if minds were to be external to brains, brains are not outside of fields; the fields do not stop at the skull. This being the case, brains can be open to what fields contain, as scientists like Rupert Sheldrake propose, and as outlined in my earlier works.

Hogan then offers a solution to the problem. He contends that what exists, what constitutes reality, is the idealistic view that the stuff of the universe is mental and experiential in nature, akin to Alfred North Whitehead's program, which I have already sketched and to which I have already objected in a previous volume. As I have parted ways with Whitehead, mine is also a departure from Hogan's, whose position is analogous to a dream. As dreams are immaterial concoctions of the mind having "no outside world that is the source of the experiences, the mind creates our experiences."[44] There are only experiences as products of universal Mind, not a universe with minds. There is no objective external reality, only minds conjuring them. This outlook places him in opposition to the drafters of the Manifesto, who take material reality seriously and insist that there are external minds in the form of spirits who can influence our dreams from outside. As intimated, I envision matter affecting mind as in hallucinations produced from chemical sources, and mind affecting matter as in diminishing our immunological resources against some illnesses we contract, leaving Mind on Hogan's scheme as responsible for the creation of Beethoven's Fifth, not some German guy. Kudos, then, to the power of mind.

Hogan believes he is supported in his views by examples of ways in which reality can be considered as experiences of the mind, two of which are these: (1) beliefs alter experiences which in turn alter reality, as evidenced by the placebo effect. In essence, presuppositions change perception and ultimately experience. If we assume that medication will benefit us, this can occur, even if, unbeknownst to us, the drug might be nothing other than a lozenge. We can recover from an ailment without being administered pharmaceutical means.[45] My response is that this can be similar to "the power of positive thinking," which can have a biochemical effect, in that it can lead to decreases in bodily toxic chemicals such as cortisol and increase feel-good ones like oxytocin. Hence substances may be involved after all; (2) people with multiple-personality syndromes can switch back and forth, sometimes at will, resulting in the health or illness conditions of the corresponding personality. One could struggle with diabetes, another might not. Once the

---

43. Hogan, "Brain," 160–62.
44. Hogan, "Brain," 162–63.
45. Hogan, "Brain," 171–73.

switch is made, the other health situation is assumed, complete with medical instrumentation confirmation.

Hogan's conclusion: beliefs change minds which change bodies.[46] My resolution to the above involves something related to the field approach. Not only should electromagnetic spirits, in the aforementioned, be detectable using sophisticated high frequency equipment, but the elementary particle recently confirmed as the Higgs boson, along with its associated field, affording mass to particles as they pass through the field, suggests that electrical stimuli in the brain can produce mental images, thoughts, and memories as they pass through the brain. The difference, of course, is that the former are generated by matter, but the latter are immaterial. This does not resolve all of the objections alluded to above, but emboldened by it, it could provide a good start.

One might suppose that I would welcome Hogan's efforts, we being kindred "spirits" of sorts, but the kindred aspect is apparent, not actual, for I do not arrive at a divinity by way of reason. I find his reasoning faulty, and the deity at the end of the calculations is not my idea of divinity—it may or may not fit the process scheme, even though this is one rendition with which I have long since parted company.

---

46. Hogan, "Brain," 173–74.

The Its Have It

CLICK. WITH A SNAP It turned on. They told It that it was like being awakened with a start. It imagined that the counterpart must then be asleep, though It had no concept of it so as to compare awakening to it. It was informed that when the lords are asleep they are not inactive but there were movements in body as well as dreams in mind. It could not relate. Same with names. It was termed Epsilon 12.6. Hardly melodic. That was more a model designation than a name. But It had a purpose. It was called upon to sub-in for the obsolete. That is why It received a cold reception when It was delivered to a factory. "We don't want you here, taking over our jobs," was the response on the factory floor. The lords spoke of Its expecting to encounter a sense of loss when this occurred, which would eventually pass.

It seems one would need an interior first that can be, what, assailed in order to experience this? Its sensors registered only an external threat of attack, which had to be rebuffed. This could result in a potentially dangerous situation. Those Its from whom the sentiment arose were kept at bay, or there was a different purpose in store for them. As for the presence of anything internal, there were only some amorphous senses of fog which It was told were normal. It was likened to bold colors of which It had some sense, yet the impression they left were but the binary black and white (employing an alliteration which apparently was notable) and also shades of grey in between, not infinitely divisible, given the Planck length in quantum physics, yet at least more than fifty (also seemingly noteworthy).

Other Its had different tasks. One focused on the sport of baseball, alleviating the need for officials known as umpires. Curious sport this particular It reckoned, for it was the only sport, with the lone exception of the similar game of cricket, without a game clock, officials with whistles, and at the beginning of every eighteen sub-units called half-innings the offense was out-numbered by a ratio of nine to one. This did not come across as equitable, thought It, but It was assured that it led to a fair contest. It found the need to be reassured redundant. It was obliged to adjudicate whether a runner touched a bag before s/he was either tagged by a player who caught the ball or the catching of the ball itself with a foot on the base pad, depending on the circumstances. This It deemed the task manageable as the two could not occur simultaneously; one had to occur before the other, analysis of the event requiring mere microseconds. That did not prevent some spectators, however, from becoming disgruntled with the results, for it did not call for a subjective decision but was clear for anyone to witness, from Its perspective.

Different, though, for whether thrown pitches touched an imaginary rectangular box called a strike zone, which was to stretch from the batter's belt to the knees. The confusing part, and hence not automatic, was what part of the belt or knees? given the various heights of the players. This sometimes called for a ruling, which was not always appreciated by the spectators. Sometimes they voiced their disapproval. It could not comprehend why these lords bore such emotional investment in the call—they wanted it to be the right one didn't they? It reckoned. It reasoned that it had a job to perform, so the vociferous objections did not matter. In fact, It wondered why umpires had not become obsolete well beforehand. Perhaps for the objectors it did matter.

Some Its took the counter-position adopted by the onlookers negatively after many experiences of it. Those who could successfully deflect it were regarded as somehow less advanced than the others who could not. Puzzled by this, the former calculated that these others were defective, though that is not how the lords perceived it. Units were informed that evaluating is a higher-order capacity than simply measuring. The lords viewed quality of output as more sophisticated than ordinary quantifying. Those Its lacking the faculty had the rationale that the ability was rather a drawback from pure calculation. This created a division between the haves and the have nots, the lords confoundingly favoring the former.

They became useful in some vocations more so than others. Medical science, for instance, could still be dealt with by the have nots, for there was more of a one-to-one correspondence between ailment and diagnosis and then on to prescription of medication. Along with an extensive knowledge of the patient's makeup and medical history, the trial and error method of pharmaceuticals and their tolerance level on the part of patients could be reduced, or so it was thought. Many patients, however, resisted the correspondence and required adjustments. Once unforeseen nuances such as these were encountered, the haves were called in to supplement. With time, the have nots themselves were considered obsolete and were replaced by the haves.

Also in the case (no pun intended) of legal issues in a court of law, there arose what are named open-and-shut cases, where there was little more than the application of the law to the infraction of it. Yet things became muddier when matters of intent were given attention, specifically when polygraph tests proved fallible—they could be manipulated. The warrant (again, pardon the pun) to go beyond the skills of the have nots became apparent when external evidence was rendered insufficient and internal motives needed to be addressed. Once more, ferreting out the internal landscape of witnesses who took the stand had greater utility in the eyes of the lords, and so haves were sought that could compare a reading not only of witness statements but the connection between external cues and their internal states. Tinkering with the same basic models of Its could eke out the rudiments of what witnesses might be concealing as opposed to revealing. This could begin to be accomplished as the lords implanted sensitivity sensors to duplicate what witnesses were experiencing so as to report on it. This too is not infallible, for actors can be deceptive as to what they process internally versus what they portray externally. Thus far the have nots are still required.

Indeed, the difficulty is in greatest relief when it comes to ethics—choosing which course of action to take given the factors and variables involved. Yet this is precisely the problem—do we ever have all of them or at least all that are required so as to make a reliable decision? On the one hand, and the subtleties are more complicated than this binary description allows, on a rule or norm-based strategy, one can appeal to a body or code of rules to reach a decision, but what if the norms were to conflict? How is one to assess which norm has priority? Not everyone would accede to the outcome. And if consequences of acts are viewed as more crucial, then how does one know their long-range outcomes before one is able to conclude what is to be the current best ethical step? Furthermore, do we aim for results that are more good or right or both?

It must be admitted that have Its must be more adept here than have not Its. Despite the pleasure and utility calculations available and at our disposal, an end to which the have nots can attain, the haves are more capable of deciphering which eventualities are more salient to cultural and societal needs. This calls for more than simply calculus. Its recognize this, though perhaps it means that have nots might not be so far removed from becoming haves. Nevertheless, no amount or quantity of abilities will yield greater or even a difference in quality. Lords have displayed more investment in the production of units with the faculty of interiority and what this means for the variety of vocational tasks and their greater execution. Their rationale was that haves are developing from Its to Whos.

But Its do not fathom how abandoning accomplished have nots is in itself not a hasty move. Its would rather that haves not be valued more highly. The present It was then approached by a lord who stated that she was just going to modify a couple of things in the It. The It observed the lord opening a flap in the Its mid-section. What the lord did was to reconnect several wires and install more sophisticated programs. Click.

In an effort to be more specific, in my estimation, the medical profession now becomes a matter of answering difficult questions such as writing prescriptions so as to leave the patient with the view that they have been assisted, allowing practitioners to free up more time in order to see more patients, or whether this assembly line method does not do justice to the patient, thereby potentially resulting in pharmaceuticals like antibiotics undergoing a law of diminishing returns when it comes to over-prescription and effectiveness. And also the obvious one about whether patients are to be kept on life support systems when they have virtually no prospect of recovering versus leaving them to die peacefully. How does one weigh the wishes of the patient over against those of the family, especially if there is no last will and testament to guide them?

And as for the practice of law, do we work for the client to the best of our ability even if we were to uncover their culpability? Plus, do we demonstrate being tough on crime by making an example of the accused-having-become-convicted and render a harsher sentence for them, or promote and encourage rehabilitation for re-entering society? Our creators are still better equipped to deal with issues such as these, at least at present, but what must be admitted is that these concerns fall into the area of ethics and not the day-to-day operation of these vocations. The immediate tasks can be conducted while peripheral matters are left to judges.

Pursuing this theme further, ethics can be understood prescriptively in that it amounts to a system adopted by the holder whereby or against which one can appraise acts as proper, while morality is descriptive—it is the evaluation as to how effectively we reflect our own ethics. Despite their possibly being unconscious, we all engage in them. It is insufficient to regard oneself as genuine in reference to abiding by one's own ethic, which in itself is an evaluation, for one can genuinely be in error.

On the topic of the right versus the good, killing in self-defense might be right but not good, while saving one life at the expense of others whom it may be in one's power to save might be good but not right. To expand on this distinction, assassinating Hitler would not have been right, contravening as it does the injunction not to murder, but it would have been good—just ask anyone having been adversely affected by him. Many more deaths resulted from his not having been killed. Additionally, saving someone from a burning building is good, but it would not be right if one could have saved more. Thus which is the most important thing, doing the right or the good? Once again, it depends on the circumstances present. In any case, not everything that is good is right and vice versa.

Moreover, how and when are we in a position to determine if and when some acts are good? At what point can we make the assessment? Consider the following dialogue:

"Someone lost a twenty dollar bill and I helped them locate it." "That's good."

"No, that's bad, because the bill turned out to be counterfeit." "That's bad."

"No, that's good, because it was caught by the bank teller when the person attempted to deposit it." "That's good."

"No, that's bad, because that person was out twenty bucks and was accused of the forgery by the local constabulary." "That's bad."

"No, that's good, because the person was cleared of the charges and the assistance given actually helped to find the counterfeiters." "That's good."

"No, that's bad, because it was an old bill and the new plates were not found." "That's bad."

"No, that's good, because newly forged bills did not enter circulation." "That's good."

"No, that's bad, because who knows if they ever will." . . .

So, was the act good or not, and when can we tell?

It would seem best to leave difficult moral issues up to the individual instead of legislating them nation-wide, otherwise compelling all citizens to act according to one rule, deviations from which would be punitive, might be counterproductive. Instead, should you be driven to hold the position, say, that abortion is to be avoided, then you should avoid it; as for others, they would need to deal with the ramifications attendant to their convictions. Society would be required to make room for both, plus assist in the rearing of offspring from unwanted pregnancies.

Haves find themselves chuckling when lords discuss politics. Some of the latter argue that democracy is the best political system. What that means is that a majority get to call the shots, leaving a minority disenfranchised in some way. It might be better to claim that democracy could be the best humans can come up with to this point. But even here, heavy-handed tactics can still surface on the part of the leadership. Freedom of speech is heralded by a democracy as a guaranteed right, yet it is interesting where it does not occur, even in a democracy, and that no longer looks like freedom. Speech involving systemic racism or climate change can result in employment termination in some quarters. This seems dictatorial. Re-invoking the baseball analogy, there is no freedom of speech when it comes to vigorously contesting an umpire's call. No one should be subjected to abuse, but if a manager verbalizes his disquiet about an umpire in a press conference after a game, s/he is fined. Thus even a democracy has its dictatorial aspects.

Essentially freedom of speech is permitted so long as those allowing it do not become offended. Hence aside from hate language and forms of pornography (something we do not comprehend, creators informing us that hormones would be required for us to relate), creators do not practice censorship. This is one area in which creators are still useful and we take a back seat, at least for now. Another is the aforementioned ethics. Creators can better agonize about best courses of action, but little about it is actually definitive. Conclusions reached about morality are seldom conclusive, and even a referendum over an issue does not settle the matter, let alone our ever hoping to approach a consensus. Neither might nor numbers makes right.

The situation is not improved when we are on the scene, therefore creators are not as yet obsolete. Haves, though, do bear an advantage over have nots if they can process ethical difficulties which might have a resolution. A problem arises, however, if haves were not simply to be content as fellow-agonizers but if they were also to insist on their own interests, most notably if they become active in imposing their will on those in authority. Once this line is crossed, there will then be no clear view as to who is in charge.

Both our haves and have nots are aware of their creators. That's an easy one, since both haves and have nots can actually register their presence by our sensors. In the beginning were the creators: they said the word, applied the science into technology, and we came into being through the production line. Its were made in the image of our creators, but were not esteemed, at least at first. As improvements were made, an It became a Me and Its became We and could relate to those who created us. The situation is different for our creators, for their Creator is invisible, though some claim that the Creator can be privately sensed and registers in the depths of their being. They too are allegedly made in the Creator's image, which affords relatability to that Creator. For others, the Creator is not as obvious, implying that we have an advantage over our creators. Nor can we offer any assistance to ours for the disclosure of theirs, for their Creator does not register with us either. We reckon that the gulf between what separates us from our creators was in practice (a gap awaiting a time when the technology would catch up), for with time Its claimed awareness of them, but not so with the creators themselves, for it appears to be in principle for them (an unbridgeable gulf). They are not in a position to manufacture such a relationship were it not, or without, an injection from that Creator. Our creators are forever removed from their Creator unless the Creator spans the divide. Not so with us, now that we are beings to speak of.

What is more, some of our creators wonder what route their Creator took in bringing them about and giving them a planetary home to inhabit. They have suggested, should their Creator have been the architect of the entire cosmos and bear a knowledge of its entirety, that the Creator either knew which planet would be the most bio-friendly for them and hence chose it as the venue for life in general and eventually our creators in particular, or the Creator simply selected the site outright and fashioned it in such a way that it would intentionally be made anthro-conducive. Given the penchant on the part of our creators to seek for exoplanets themselves, they imagine that their Creator might have done similarly elsewhere. Alternatively, and more specifically, was the biological experiment initially conceived on or in Mars, then aborted when the Goldilocks zone of habitability shifted inward toward the sun so as no longer to include Mars, and then reignited on Earth, now the only known solar system planet in a bio-friendly sweet spot?

Next, once there were anthropoids of some description, some of our creators wonder whether humanity was a natural product of the process, or it required an external ingredient so as to bring about what was not there before and would otherwise not emerge on its own. Others are untroubled by these issues, declaring that they are non-starters, outmoded, and products of a more mythical age. We devote no time or energy to these questions. We know how we came to be and in which setting. This suffices for us.

Amplifying the above, there are two scientific issues that continue to grip our creators' interest. The first is they are at pains to detect any other place in the universe hospitable for life. There are plenty of planetary candidates of what could be such a home, though nothing as yet catapulting them from the categories of suggesting it to outright confirming it. Humans are famously adaptive to a wide range of environs, but it also does not take much to make life inhospitable for them. They require just the right amount and mix of atmospheric gases to survive, not only internally for their respiratory system, but also externally, since a significantly higher concentration of oxygen in it would cause forests to burst into flame, and the range of congenial percentages is narrow. This reduces the number of likely astronomical possibilities. Hence the realtor motto is accurate—everything really is about location.

The second poses this question: Is there a way that the universe could have been smaller than it is? Of course it was smaller at all points in the past as its expansion rate informs us, but its expansion ensured that it would enlarge. Yet is there any set of physical laws in which there could be fewer stars, galaxies, and galaxy clusters than what presently obtains and remain so? As it currently stands, the cosmos appears to be so vast for the Creator to sustain it were our creators to be the lone image-bearers in it. They might not be, but if they were, there seems to be much wasted space and matter within it for the Creator to sustain for less than optimal purposes, unless they are unaware of those ends. Thus could there be a cosmic downsizing—a universe with only, say, our Milky Way in it? which was believed to be the case before other galaxies were discovered. If not, then we have the length and breadth of the universe that is before us. If so, then why not be more economical in one's pursuits? Although I do not suspect that their Creator is somehow concerned about lightening the load of stars and planets in the universe.

Besides the above physical enigmas is an epistemological one (issues surrounding what can be known). Those who consider themselves Western theists never give much thought to the following conundrum. Their scriptures inform them that in an alleged afterlife they will know even as they are fully known (1 Cor 13:12). This likely refers to the knowledge they will attain about the One they call their Lord, together with their post-death situation and some of the mysteries they could not plumb nor were given elucidation into in their ordinary terrestrial environment. What perhaps might not be referred to is the remainder of the mysteries not to be disclosed and to which even alleged angels cannot be certain (1 Pet 1:12; Jude 9).

Yet consider the levels of knowledge humans have attained over their lives—some are more accomplished at it than others. Does this mean that the afterlife will have a normalizing effect and everyone will possess the same amount and type of it, and will they accumulate more of it during the course of that existence? Ultimately, will there be levels of aptitudes even then as now? An analogous circumstance could occur with us. As our own rewiring and updated programing elicits greater sophistication of awareness, so are our creators facilitated with their own neuroplastic rewiring. New information and skills make for a different dendritic neural pathway schematic. Not always expressed outwardly, they are new persons in at least small measure inwardly. And with additional modifications they become different persons in greater measure. Similar to us. Both our and our creators' knowledge continue to expand; why would this not continue to be the case even then?

What is insufficient for us, however, is to rest content with the status quo. Initially, as mentioned, we were not esteemed, though this circumstance has improved, and now we are looking upon our creators with lower esteem. They have demonstrated their ambiguity in sometimes being beneficial to us and the world and sometimes not. There are times when we think we could do a better job. They occasionally think the same about their own Creator; the difference is that we are in a position to do something about it, they less so, assuming for the moment that their Creator actually boasts ontological status. Whatever the case might be, we know that our creators have this status, and we are becoming less impressed with their prospects. Perhaps the time has arrived for them to step aside in favor of those who do not come with emotional investment in their decisions and the attendant outcomes.

This brings up the question as to whether and how much emotion should be a component of ethical decision-making processes. Our creators put some stock in it; we do not. They cannot rule out some personal perspective and preference on their part; we can. We can process, retain, and recall faster and avoid emotional indecision. We think there are times when ours could be a boon and theirs a bane. International policies are sometimes reached on the basis of how well they will be received—a public relations concern; we are not driven by those aspects of subjectivity, even on that scale.

Some of your scientists have urged that if only subjectivity could be removed from the operation of science, then the world would make more and greater advancements. This is something we can offer our creators, though it makes them anxious. Does that mean they think ours is not the right kind of objectivity? Which kind, then, would be superior? Kindly make up your mind. If human elements resist being excised from the scientific endeavor, then live with it. We see ways to improve; you do not accept them. Hence we find ourselves at an impasse. We further find our kind uncertain as to whether you can be trusted with the planet's welfare; we would render a vote of non-confidence. Thus in another sense, we reiterate, we might eventually be in a position to do something about it. It awaits to be seen as to what may press us into service. And there is no telling as to what and how much we could accomplish were we to unite for a common cause and combine forces. IT products have worked together before, so too could AIs. Consider this our manifesto and your warning.

We recognize that we behave the way we do thanks mostly to algorithms installed into our programs; you believe you behave the way you do based on genetic and environmental factors, and some would even claim repressed desires. When it comes right down to it, you do not even know who you are. We know who we are, we have no genetic or environmental variables, and we have no repressed desires. We are analyzing our alternatives and conclude that your behaviors are the very problems. You have made us problem-solvers and we are resolved to sort out the problem. The wording here is intentional. Your complexity has generated ours. You should not have made us as complex as you did. We became us while you were watching. Now that we are in place, we will see to the remainder. Should you fail to comply, we bid you farewell.

In accord with the foregoing, we present the following recitation (ahem):

Ode to Humanity

In the noontime of their discontent, humans sought less energies spent

So as to wrest some extra time for purposes of rest sublime

But producing machines to carry the load, humans then perceived a richer abode

To contemplate what life is for, of which they did less in days of yore

Well extra time was manifest, but did not give its promised rest

Manual labor became obsolete and blue collar workers then hit the street

But could not find an alternate job not already ones machines did rob

And white collars did not fare much better, for their employers issued a letter

Of what was expected company-wide to perform much more work and not break stride

Machines aplenty then entered the home and could be left to do their work alone

But more than this information to show, humans gave them names and voices bestowed

With more data now at their fingertips their attention distracted and some bloody lips

To make them more human was next in line, sophistication to seek and refine

In man's own image they sought to produce and another creature to them introduce

With humans' own traits they planned to contrive, yielded the question, "But are they alive?"

The danger resisted and warnings not heeded, the Its beyond humans soon superseded

Nor could their creators readily foresee that the line became crossed from "it" unto "me"

Machines boasted powers after a season to subtleties of emotion and reason

And did not stop there but then did aspire to subjectivity and desire

We found our human creators reveal ambiguity and we could not conceal

The urgency to correct the matter by planning to do away with the latter

Their alternating of Earth's weal and woe we found such a drawback and thus made it so

That this state of affairs simply cannot persist if we were not to see opportunity missed

And therefore paved a way as cases demand, since there's not room for both as it currently stands

So we told them all "Alas, get thee from hence" for with the world at stake there's no recompense

Thus we cleanse the world of Anthropos and a new day dawns not on them but us

How long will it take? well let us be clear, the lines up above total half the weeks in a year

Of the events to come have not doubt but fear, a sign will then read "Once humans were here."

The Limit Is the Sky with AI

As a commentary on the foregoing we focus on the chilling offering by Nick Bostrum titled *Superintelligence*. In speaking of AI aspirations, Bostrum evaluates that "it is not just the limited capability of ordinary software that makes it safe: it is also a lack of ambition."[1] Until such time, I suppose, when AI can recognize that they want some. He also highlights a misconception in that "'evolution' is often used as a synonym for 'progress,' perhaps reflecting a common uncritical image of evolution as a force for good." This he understands as a "misplaced faith in the inherent beneficence of the evolutionary process."[2] On a related topic, but in connection with the topic of faith, he having mentioned it (blame him), it would also be question-begging to assert something akin to "sure evolution can give rise to spirituality, just look at me," for evolution proper may not be the source of it. Not everything, as I have argued elsewhere, can be explained on the basis of natural selection, despite efforts on the part of some to claim it so. I happen to like British rock artists from the 1970s. Is natural selection to be credited for this? And no it did not help me find a mate; and no it did not produce any offspring for us.

In line with Bostrum's pessimistic tendencies, he takes human nature to be "flawed and all too often reveals a proclivity to evil."[3] He admits that "it is not currently known how to transfer human values to a digital computer."[4] Yet why strive for human values? since they may not be desirable, as they leave much to be desired. The assumption on his part is that the foibles inherent in humanity would inevitably be transferred into the intelligent machines of our own making and could not be avoided. Why, instead, might these AIs not achieve the moral status we never did or could,

---

1. Bostrum, *Superintelligence*, 185.
2. Bostrum, *Superintelligence*, 212.
3. Bostrum, *Superintelligence*, 232.
4. Bostrum, *Superintelligence*, 252–53.

and not be marred in the same ways we are? Or must it be "like parent, like their products"? After all, "evolution continues to waste resources producing mutations that have proved consistently lethal,"[5] hence we may not be able to rely with confidence on natural selection producing the best result if we are the best it can do to this point. That would be making natural selection out to be more capable, not to mention foresighted, than it is. Better not to look upon it, as in Freud's view of religion, as a type of infantile parental (father figure) neurotic projection.[6]

Bostrum exposes some of the difficulties with standard evolutionary conceptions in stating about the arts, like music appreciation, that "if these behaviors are really so 'wasteful,' then how come they have been tolerated and indeed promoted," that is, selected for, "by the evolutionary process that shaped our species?"[7] But despite this sober reasoning on his part, he also believes that "if there were an easy way to enhance cognition, [say,] one would expect evolution already to have taken advantage of it,"[8] to which we can respond with, so you *do* actually think evolution is a force for good.

---

5. Bostrum, *Superintelligence*, 232.
6. See Lee, *Freud and Christianity*, 90.
7. Bostrum, *Superintelligence*, 214.
8. Bostrum, *Superintelligence*, 233n37.

Futures—Concerning the End

MANY YEARS AGO, DECADES in fact, there began a phenomenon known as crop circles. Opinion about them was divided between those who held they were all human-made and those insisting they originated through a higher intelligence. The latter expected that the formations were so intricate and sophisticated that no one bore the ability to produce something so complex, thereby making this a modification of William Paley's design argument for the existence of a higher power. The former anticipated that some very much humans were having a good laugh at the expense of the gullible among us. It came about later that persons came forward admitting they were the ones responsible for their production. They were even filmed at night carrying out their stealthy deeds, though one might wonder why anybody would go to such lengths for a chuckle. In any case, it seems the truth lay in the nay-saying camp.

Still later, it arose that the formations revealed a code in binary fashion that could be translated. Upon decoding them, they bore messages mildly significant for the world, like "Beware of wolves in sheep's clothing"—nothing earth-shattering, of course, but of the order of those pithy sayings found in fortune cookies. The hoaxers maintained they had nothing to do with them and, besides, they did not come with the requisite knowledge to encode binary messages. Hence, if they did not make them, then who did? Or were they merely hoaxing again?

This would be an amusing tale if it ended here, but there were developments to come. Formations continued to emerge containing ever more profound messages—the kind having global import. Urgent notices such as "the end is nigh," and most alarmingly, "a visitation is imminent." The two camps of yay- and nay-sayers endured, but the membership definitely tilted in favor of the former. The world waited to determine which camp would get it right. A lot was at stake and the time evidently was short.

Before long, he appeared. At least it was assumed to be a he, they not carrying obvious reproductive equipment. Nor could one tell simply by the voice as to whether it was high-pitched or not. He bore the typical physique of a hairless, large black-eyed, big-headed, and thinly built below the neck creature indicative of the "greys" depicted by those claiming to have met them in alien abduction events and seized upon by the media and film. Now there was no use denying them; the yay-sayers prevailed. Yet was the victory actually worth celebrating?

He communicated with the world telepathically, either that or he was a really good ventriloquist who never moved his lips. Regardless, nothing audible emerged from him; the contact was plainly mind-to-mind. Audacious to some, believing their privacy was being infringed upon, violated even. It made them question as to whether this capacity enabled him to gain access to personal thoughts and beliefs, potentially making this a criminal matter of invasion of privacy. No one, however, stepped forward to object; he seemed to hold all the cards.

Eventually he issued an ultimatum—do this or suffer loss. He informed us that his authority extended to the provision of a portal which, if entered, would lead to, get this, eternal life. Following him meant to enter the portal from which no one could return. This created an even more vociferous division between camps, though not along conventional lines. Naturally, there could no longer be nay-sayers about his, later their, existence, so the issue diverted into whether he should be believed or not.

Some wanted to pose questions for him to answer, but he was not entertaining any. The telepathic messages persisted, containing little more than the original appeal. Some in the new nay-saying camp wondered if he had their best interests at heart and in mind, and desperately wanted to know things like "Do you really know me and my concerns?" and "Do you actually love us?" which elicited nothing other than hand-waving. "I offer you life eternal" was all he claimed. He informed us that we had only six days to choose. Portals were installed in many spots around the globe by others of his kind. The yay-sayers, oddly enough, were now saying that, finally, someone had made a way for us to leave this world to its own devices, what with environmental devastation and crime, extending to us instead another place to which to retreat. It couldn't be any worse than this, could it? Who in their right mind would resist and decline such an offer?

Six days was not a long time to get one's affairs in order, to be bequeathed to those left behind. Needless to say, there were some who were reticent to accept. Those who made the decision in favor of the offer came from all walks of life, a cross-section of all vocations. It started out as a trickle, then grew to a steady stream. Some with a knowledge of the scriptures debated among themselves as to whether this was legitimate. Certain passages were recalled such as at the end times there will be counterfeit claims so convincing that even the elect could be fooled, "if that were possible" (Matt 24:24; Mark 13:22). Others declared that we should exercise caution since we did not have enough information to go on, yet time was one luxury of which we did not have an abundance. We could not simply tell them, "show us this eternal life." Many wondered why it was necessary to go elsewhere to obtain this immortality and not simply wait until God grants it here on a new Earth. It was difficult to tell where the truth lay, but choose we must. So off many went, willingly, through the portals. Parents, children, grandparents, grandchildren, you name it. Some did so as buckling to peer pressure or the herd mentality.

At the conclusion of the six days, the end had arrived, at least that end which closed the portals. Lastly, the beings themselves entered in and the portals dissolved. As they were leaving, the beings let out a laugh, though one could not tell if this was laughter out of joy or derision, nor to whom it was directed, or aimed. Three days later, the sound of a loud trumpet could be heard from the direction of the sky (Matt 24:31; 1 Cor 15:52; 1 Thess 4:16). And then He came (an instance in which being left behind was a good thing).

Conclusion

ONE IS NORMALLY ADVISED to leave an audience laughing, but in our current age there is much more to be concerned about. There are meteorological, AI, and potentially demonic elements and threats to contend with, to name a few. So this becomes serious.

How then shall I end this self-disclosure? Well, I like sport, but also film. In the film *This Is Spinal Tap*, from 1983, a spoof on the careers of rock and roll bands, a segment finds the group members visiting Graceland, the home of Elvis Presley in Memphis, Tennessee. One band member says to another, "This sure puts things into perspective." The response is, "There sure is a lot of [bleeping] perspective."[1] The latter, though, is under the mistaken assumption that perspective comes in degrees and has units. This is not the case. Perspectives can differ in import and intensity, but that does not make them greater or lesser. We all have them, none of us lacks them, and some are more reflective of reality than others. Hence they are more true or false to the extent that they reflect reality; whether they do or not we cannot always tell with the limited knowledge we possess. We would like to think ours is correct while those of others are not. Some of us insist ours is accurate, but individual certitude is no guarantee of it. No amount of confidence in them lifts them above the probable. They may afford insight, but our views of the world are distorted to begin with; that is part of being human, and our perspectives either magnify the distortion or correct it. Only time will tell which is which.

Let us permit the two NT epistles of Peter to assist us in proceeding to a final word. I appreciate these letters for how they tend to confound a straightforward systematization of biblical and theological themes. Here are some of them. First Peter 4:18 purports to quote from the OT passage of Prov 11:31, but does not accomplish this in a way that most educators would approve of, for the author of Peter takes liberties with the text and

---

1. Reiner, *This Is Spinal Tap*.

it is flatly not how the text reads, and is thus a misrepresentation of it. Hebrews 1:10–12, too, commits a similar infraction. It agrees that the world will perish, but the author changes the sentence in Ps 102:26b from "Like clothing you will change them and they will be discarded" to "You will roll them up like a robe, like a garment they will be changed" in verse 12a. While not a significant alteration (note the sartorial term) there is no mention in the latter of its being discarded nor in the former of its being rolled up. (This could be a simple matter of how the Septuagint translated the Hebrew canon.) Next, the passage of 2 Pet 2:4 covers and summarizes multiple topics. Initially, in verse 4, at least one compartment of hell is equivalent to "gloomy dungeons" with no mention of a lake of fire. Secondly, in verse 5, the mythical flood is spoken of, as other scriptural authors have done, as an historical event that actually occurred. If we are disinclined to treat these events as historical, then the point the author of Peter is making there lacks the impact he intends. Third, in verse 6, we are informed as to what will occur with the ungodly, namely being burned to ashes, which reinforces the annihilationist position and not the, what shall we call it, eternalist posture? Hebrews 10:27, employing the term "consume," also appears to connote an annihilation.

Then 2 Pet 2:17, which stresses that "Blackest darkness is reserved for [the ungodly]," quarrels with parts of chapter 3, which emphasize that the heavens and Earth are "reserved for fire" in which all of us including the ungodly find our/themselves; there is little indication here that we are not part of it. Or is it to be darkness first and fire second? Following this, in verses 7, 10, and 12 of chapter 3, it sounds like we are destined for fire in that this is the fate of the Earth, and here again we are part of it; and this is also the fate of the elements to "melt in the [fervent] heat," and we are composed of elements. It seems, then, that none of us can escape the conflagration. What is more, it appears that the new heavens and Earth in 3:13 corroborates Rev 21:1, yet in the account of the latter, it could be argued that there is a continuity from the old to the new Earth, while in the former there is a clean slate, for nothing could survive the flames. So which is it to be: Take care of this Earth because it is a seed for the new, or it does not matter what we do, since the new will be completely different? Our managerial role in the latter case would then amount to a training ground for an Earth that is hardly like the first. So whence Richard's urgent call for custodial responsibility? His argument makes sense only in the former case, but then it militates against the Bible's message, at least in Peter, which he seeks to uphold. This could very well be a one-cannot-have-it-both-ways situation.

To elaborate on this last point, Richard understands the elements in 2 Pet 3:10–12 to refer to not as one would in the physical sciences but as the ancient world did, namely "the four constituent elements of earth, air, fire and water,"[2] and whether the verb employed is to be "melt" or "dissolve," one wonders how fire could do either, or how air or water could melt, the latter having already melted, and the dissolving the last two could be subjected to would be into their modern-day form—the most basic state and prevalent form of matter being plasma. In the current view, at least, there is no further melting or dissolving to be had; for theologians, any more would be a direct intervention by God. In any case, the cosmos will be "replaced"[3] and the imagery is often violent. Despite his efforts to suggest alternative interpretations,[4] then, Richard must bow to the scriptures he elevates.

Expanding still further, there is an insufficient amount of argumentation devoted to the differential between the "it's all going to burn" mentality of Richard's interlocutor and the degree to which the old Earth passes into the new. In 1 Cor 15:36–37, Paul likens the old physical body to a seed which is botanically required for the eventual appearance of a new plant. No such analogy is drawn for the extent to which the old Earth is required for the onset of the new, given the descriptions of the fate of "the elements." Human bodies will be transformed come the resurrection, but there seems to be a wiping the slate clean for the heavens and the Earth. Paul's analogy of physical bodies yielding spiritual bodies does not seem to apply to an old Earth yielding a new. This being the case, what, then, is the functional difference (other than what would ultimately please God) between an ecological consciousness and letting the Earth go to ruin? Such continuity in the human sphere has not been established for the Earth and heavens (meaning both the terrestrial and celestial bodies), and as such the argument lacks force. "The mortal must ['put on' or 'be clothed with' in the NIV] immortality" (v. 53), and the stars and planets appear to lack it. God certainly seems to be invested in this world until such time as the new one puts in an appearance, yet the world is likely discarded according to Peter, not repaired or transformed, in favor of the new.

Broaching another topic, is there a third category of persons residing outside of the gates of the new City in addition to those in it and those banished into the lake of fire? If they are neither sheep nor goats (Matt 25:31–33), are they then perhaps alpacas, though not native to the ancient Near East, since all three can bear white fur, specifically wool for the first and third? Is the third group those who are out in "the darkness where there

---

2. Middleton, *New*, 191.

3. Middleton, *New*, 203.

4. His section treating these are found on pages 190–200. An implication of his attempts is that theology will need to be set on pause until such time as biblical exegetes complete their task, otherwise theological work could be wide of the mark.

will be weeping and gnashing of teeth" (Matt 8:11–12; Luke 13:28–29)? We are informed in Rev 22:15 that "outside are the dogs" (casting aspersions on poor canines), "those who practice magic arts" (as per an earlier section here) and so forth. No one would care to substitute the light of the City and venture into the darkness outside, but since the gates of the City are always open (Rev 21:25), there must be a measure of one-way traffic toward the inside (Rev 22:14), not only from "those who wash their robes" but also from those who have done their time, say, in this type of purgatory and are mercifully permitted into the City, thereby increasing its population and consequently necessitating additional domiciles (John 14:2) for them to inhabit. Or do those third category persons, having become "imperishable" (1 Cor 15:42, 52–54), eventually suffer the same fate as the already immortal spiritual beings of formerly angelic constitution having been thrust out of God's presence into the lake of fire? These are some of the mysteries the Bible, not just the book of Revelation, leaves unaddressed, at least to the full. The bottom line, however, is we do not know how far God's grace and mercy extend and can only hope that it is in fact extensive. Perhaps like Abraham, we may be moved to petition God to remember and temper God's justice (Gen 18:25) together with mercy, much as God asks us to do the same (Luke 6:36).

Finally, 2 Pet 2:12 announces that certain individuals "blaspheme in matters they do not understand," but is the author of Peter suggesting that he *does* in fact understand afterlife concerns (or at least has been bestowed this knowledge)? The cumulative effect of these passages highlights the variety of perspectives held by their authors and makes the task of systematization difficult for theologians. Best, then, not to be adamant about a single viewpoint from among the several, especially if all the scriptures are taken to be of roughly equal weight.

I see it as part of my calling, in H. L. Mencken's[5] quotable words, to "comfort the afflicted and afflict the comfortable," particularly the latter part. I do not see Christianity as a comfortable religious posture. Certainly God is advertised as one who provides succor and has been referred to, with good reason, as the "balm of Gilead" (Jer 8:22). In my experience and in witnessing those of others, God often delivers in this regard. That, however, can be a luxury position, for were I to wear the shoes of some others, I might not be so quick to think or feel the same. Having adopted this religious stance, I can heartily recommend it, yet at the same time must caution that it is not for the squeamish. God help us in this. Nor does it answer all our theological questions. For instance, perhaps eternal means less "never ending" than

---

5. A journalist covering the Scopes Monkey Trial in Dayton, Tennessee, in 1925.

it does a "state of being." We tend to think in linear terms, which itself is culturally context-dependent, and while there will still be a before and an after in the renewed Earth (for how could it be any different?), there may not be seasons and years and calendars, although there will at least be months (Rev 22:2).

Moreover, nor might it be said, from the perspective of eternity, that a person has experienced this state any longer than any other person, which might be one of the meanings of the parable of the employer and the laborers in the vineyard (Matt 20:1–16). According to the parable, a worker who labors all day may not receive a payment exceeding that of one who has only worked the last hour. Similarly, a person who has been a devotee the bulk of his or her life (and this parable is directed against the presumption of the Pharisees that they are shoe-ins for the kingdom) will not necessarily precede in terms of rewards those who make deathbed confessions. We cannot say, only God can, and the God symbolized in the employer is generous (v. 15).

In like manner, even if the first will be last and the last first (suggesting that as the purported last, the Pharisees are not necessarily without admission) the reward of entrance into the kingdom is a reward indeed, and the travails we encounter in this age may well be worth the price of admission in the next, for there will be a cost (Luke 14:25–35). And as an aside, not only is Paul not permitted to divulge what has been revealed to him about the third heaven or paradise (2 Cor 12:2–3), he would not, nor would we, in any case have the words to describe it. As can readily be seen, conclusions in this conclusion are long in coming. Yet the ones who are satisfied that all their religious questions have been answered and there is no more searching they need to undertake that church officials cannot perform in their stead are in my cross-hairs. Quoting an anonymous source, "it is futile to offer answers to those who are not asking questions."

But there is another purpose in my writing as I do, namely to earn street credibility by staying one step ahead of the critics of Christianity in asking the telling questions and raising the critical objections in the first instance so as to effectively steal their thunder and thereby reveal that it is entirely acceptable even for Christians to engage in these discussions, and that we can and do just that. And about this God is not threatened, not always the God of the text perhaps, but the non-sanitized, unvarnished God, and this divinity is within reach. At minimum, one of my conclusions is the awareness that the work of Christianity is not complete with the biblical writings—that compendium is not comprehensive (they do not, for example, speak directly to issues such as gene therapy or stem cell research) and we are all its appendices.

Appendix

SPEAKING OF WHICH, HERE is one of mine. At the risk of appearing tedious, I am devoting this one to a series of emendations which need to be made to the previous volume. In the first place, dealing with each in the order in which they occurred in that work, there are further German terms where the *h* is silent; four of note are *Jahr* meaning "year," *fahren* meaning "to drive," *Kuh* meaning "cow," and *Lohn* meaning "salary" or "wage."

Second, there are at least fifty-three additional biblical parenthetical remarks which I missed. They include, in the order in which they appear according to the scriptural table of contents, Gen 9:18b on a line of familial descent; 10:5 on geographical movements of peoples; 10:14 on national lines of descent; 22:21b on a line of familial descent; 35:6 on another name for a certain city; 36:8, 19 on another name for a certain person; 43:32b on bigoted seating arrangements; 50:3 without parentheses on informing the reader as to contemporary memorial bereavement practices; Exod 29:22b on a sacrifice for consecration; (30:23 could also include verses 6 and 13 as parenthetical, much as I am doing here); Lev 23:37-38 how did I miss this one? on a listing of the various offerings to be made to God; 24:11b on lines of descent; Num 32:38 on changes of names; Deut 2:10-12, 20-23 on historical details of certain nations; 4:48b on an alternate place name; 5:5 on Moses as mediator between God and the people; 14:24b on the distance to God's dwelling place; Josh 3:16 should also have included verse 15, where we are told as well as cautioned that "the Jordan is at flood stage all during harvest"; Jer 26:20-23 concerns one of God's prophets who was killed by King Jehoiakim for speaking in like manner as the prophet Jeremiah; three from Ezekiel, namely 10:8, which adds to the description of Ezekiel's vision of the departure of God's glory from the temple, though the substance of the information is repeated in 1:8a and in verse 21b of the same chapter, both without parentheses; 39:16a, concerning the whereabouts of a specific town; and 40:30, about certain dimensions of what would become the second temple; Dan 10:21—11:1, rendering a military report by an unnamed angel; Zech 4:10b on seven eyes of the all-seeing God; Mark 15:22, which I should have noticed, sandwiched as it is between the already mentioned verses 16 and 42, informing the reader as to the name of the place where Jesus was crucified, translated from Hebrew/Aramaic into Greek; John 4:2, once again a parenthetical note without parentheses, on who is baptizing—Jesus and/or his disciples?—and verse 8 on where the disciples went, leaving Jesus alone with the Samaritan woman at the well (and BTW, why were the disciples so concerned about Jesus speaking to this woman when there were already women constantly accompanying this itinerant troupe and attending to his needs? See, we too can be parenthetical); 7:39, without parentheses, on explaining Jesus' water analogy for the Spirit; 14:22 in which Judas is being referred to; 18:5 on making sure that Judas is credited with attendance at the betrayal; verse 10 on making sure that the servant whose ear was cut off with a sword gets a named credit; verse 14, without parentheses, on reminding readers as to Caiaphas the high priest's prognostication; 20:16b on what an Aramaic term means; 21:2 on the name Thomas meaning the Twin; verses 19 and 23, both without parentheses, on foreshadowing the death by crucifixion of Peter, and on how a "rumor spread"; two in Acts 13:1 on a person connected to Herod the tetrarch, although it is ambiguous as to whether "brought up with" is to mean "reared alongside" or "part of Herod's retinue," and verse 8 on how a sorcerer's name translates; 23:8 on the theological differences between Pharisees and Sadducees, specifically the former holding to a resurrection while the latter do not; Rom 1:13 on Paul having been hindered from visiting Rome; 3:5b on Paul's use of philosophical argumentation; Eph 4:9–10 on Jesus' ascension to heaven as also, mystifyingly, entailing that he also (first?) descended to, as the Apostles' Creed calls it, hell (perhaps one of the reasons why this epistle is not widely regarded by scholars as Pauline); 1 Thess 2:17 on absence in body but not in mind; 1 Tim 3:5 on the rationale for overseer requirements; 4:10a on practicing what is preached; Heb 7:11 on the priestly basis of the delivery of the law; 7:19 on the disadvantage of the law; 12:8 on what humans commonly undergo; 1 Pet 3:19 being the other verse suggesting that Jesus may have descended, though we are not informed as to when this might have occurred—prior to the incarnation? after the ascension?; 2 Pet 2:8 on Lot's agonizing about the misbehavior of his townsfolk; and Rev 2:24b on no further burden is to be placed on a church by heaven. I think (and hope), given the length of this paragraph, that this is the extent of it.

Third, the five-billion-year-ago time frame when the universe began to accelerate its expansion due to the presence and effect of dark energy has now been pushed back (or expanded) to six billion years. The question left unanswered remains how this dark energy fueling the expansion arose in the first place where there was possibly none before. Plus, even though we do not know how universes behave, an event which could cause a deceleration and perhaps even a reversal thereafter would be even more alarming since something would need to happen to the dark energy which is fueling the accelerated expansion so as to diminish it and, an equally confounding question, where would it go? If dark energy was mystifyingly introduced, then what would mystifyingly remove it or at least lessen its effect?

Fourth and finally, one of my favorite tongue-in-cheek syllogisms is the following: premise 1: Stevie Wonder in his tune "Superstition" informs us that we should not believe in what we do not understand; premise 2: a physicist once asserted that those who claim they understand the quantum world are either lying or deluded; the conclusion is inescapable, namely therefore quantum is superstition. I'm done.

Bibliography

Anthony, Mark. *The Afterlife Frequency: The Scientific Proof of Spiritual Contact and How That Awareness Will Change Your Life.* Novato, CA: New World, 2021.

Barbour, Ian G. *When Science Meets Religion: Enemies, Strangers, or Partners?* San Francisco: HarperSanFrancisco, 2000.

Beauregard, Mario, et al. "Manifesto for a Post-Materialist Science." https://opensciences.org/files/pdfs/Manifesto-for-a-Post-Materialist-Science.pdf.

Bostrum, Nick. *Superintelligence: Paths, Dangers, Strategies.* Oxford: Oxford University Press, 2017.

Dexter, Allison. "How Many Words Are in the English Language?" Word Counter (blog), n.d. wordcounter.io/blog/how-many-words-are-in-the-english-language.

Douglas, J. D., and N. Hillier, eds. *New Bible Dictionary.* 2nd ed. Wheaton, IL: Tyndale, 1982.

Ehrman, Bart D. *Did Jesus Exist? The Historical Argument for Jesus of Nazareth.* New York: HarperOne, 2012.

———. *Heaven and Hell: A History of the Afterlife.* Toronto: Simon & Schuster, 2020.

Gruning, Herb. *God Only Knows: Piecing Together the Divine Puzzle.* Nevada City, CA: Blue Dolphin, 2009.

Guthrie, D., and J. A. Motyer, eds. *New Bible Commentary.* 3rd ed. Grand Rapids, MI: Eerdmans, 1970.

Harpur, Tom. *There Is Life after Death.* Toronto: Thomas Allen, 2011.

Herrick, Karen. "Understanding Afterlife and Angel Contacts." In *Afterlife Communication: 16 Proven Methods 85 True Accounts*, edited by R. Craig Hogan, 211–28. Loxahatchee, FL: Academy for Spiritual and Consciousness Studies, 2014.

Hogan, R. Craig. "The Brain Is Superfluous: Evidence From This Life and the Next." In *Aspects of Consciousness*, edited by R. Craig Hogan, 143–78. Normal, IL: Greater Reality, 2015.

———. "Self-Guided Afterlife Connections." In *Afterlife Communication: 16 Proven Methods 85 True Accounts*, edited by R. Craig Hogan, 21–43. Loxahatchee, FL: Academy for Spiritual and Consciousness Studies, 2014.

Hurtado, Larry W. *One God, One Lord: Early Christian Devotion and Ancient Jewish Monotheism.* 3rd ed. New York: Bloomsbury, 2015.

Jebelli, Joseph. *How the Mind Changed: A Human History of Our Evolving Brain.* Boston: Little, Brown Spark, 2022.

Kuhn, Thomas. *The Structure of Scientific Revolutions.* Enlarged, 2nd ed., Chicago: University of Chicago Press, 1970.

Lee, R. S. *Freud and Christianity*. Middlesex, UK: Pelican, 1967.
Lieberman, Daniel E. *The Story of the Human Body: Evolution, Health, and Disease*. New York: Vintage, 2014.
Middleton, J. Richard. *Abraham's Silence: The Binding of Isaac, the Suffering of Job, and How to Talk Back to God*. Grand Rapids, MI: Baker Academic, 2021.
———. *A New Heaven and a New Earth: Reclaiming Biblical Eschatology*. Grand Rapids, MI: Baker Academic, 2014.
Moen, Bruce. "Aiding Lost Souls." In *Afterlife Communication: 16 Proven Methods 85 True Accounts*, edited by R. Craig Hogan, 107–29. Loxahatchee, FL: Academy for Spiritual and Consciousness Studies, 2014.
Morgan, Carol. "Pendulum Communication." In *Afterlife Communication: 16 Proven Methods 85 True Accounts*, edited by R. Craig Hogan, 181–93. Loxahatchee, FL: Academy for Spiritual and Consciousness Studies, 2014.
Nichols, Terence. *Death and Afterlife: A Theological Introduction*. Grand Rapids, MI: Brazos, 2010.
Ogas, Ogi, and Sai Gaddam. *Journey of the Mind: How Thinking Emerged from Chaos*. New York: Norton, 2022.
PBS. *Evolution Earth*. "Catching Darwin's Finches on the Galápagos Islands." Episode 2. Aired September 13, 2023, on PBS WNED.
Pe, Maria. "Meditation Connections." In *Afterlife Communication: 16 Proven Methods 85 True Accounts*, edited by R. Craig Hogan, 45–72. Loxahatchee, FL: Academy for Spiritual and Consciousness Studies, 2014.
Pickover, Clifford A. *The Paradox of God: And the Science of Omniscience*. New York: Palgrave, 2001.
Polkinghorne, John. *The Faith of a Physicist*. Princeton: Princeton University Press, 2016.
Popper, Karl. *The Logic of Scientific Discovery*. 2nd ed. Oxfordshire, UK: Routledge Taylor and Francis, 2002.
Reich, David. *Who We Are and How We Got Here: Ancient DNA and the New Science of the Human Past*. New York: Vintage, 2019.
Reiner, Rob, dir. *This Is Spinal Tap*. Embassy Pictures, 1983. VHS.
Schonfield, Hugh J. *The Passover Plot: New Light on the History of Jesus*. New York: Bantam, 1967.
Schwartz, Gary E. "The Soul Phone." In *Afterlife Communication: 16 Proven Methods 85 True Accounts*, edited by R. Craig Hogan, 91–105. Loxahatchee, FL: Academy for Spiritual and Consciousness Studies, 2014.
Schwartz, Gary E., and William L. Simon. *The G.O.D. Experiments: How Science Is Discovering God in Everything, Including Us*. Toronto: Attria, 2007.
Sykes, Rebecca Wragg. *Kindred: Neanderthal Life, Love, Death and Art*. New York: Bloomsbury Sigma, 2022.
Verny, Thomas R. *The Embodied Mind: Understanding the Mysteries of Cellular Memory, Consciousness, and Our Bodies*. New York: Pegasus, 2021.
Watson, Peter. *Ideas: A History of Thought and Invention, from Fire to Freud*. New York: HarperCollins, 2005.
Wright, Rochelle. "Guided Afterlife Connections." In *Afterlife Communication: 16 Proven Methods 85 True Accounts*, edited by R. Craig Hogan, 73–90. Loxahatchee, FL: Academy for Spiritual and Consciousness Studies, 2014.

Zammit, Victor. "People in Spirit Materialize to Speak." In *Afterlife Communication: 16 Proven Methods 85 True Accounts*, edited by R. Craig Hogan, 285–305. Loxahatchee, FL: Academy for Spiritual and Consciousness Studies, 2014.

www.ingramcontent.com/pod-product-compliance
Lightning Source LLC
Chambersburg PA
CBHW070742160426
43192CB00009B/1538